Nathalie Milian

Relational Skills Development for Next Generation Leaders

Nathalie Milian

Relational Skills Development for Next Generation Leaders

A Business Insider's Perspective

DE GRUYTER

ISBN 978-3-11-133514-8
e-ISBN(PDF) 978-3-11-133533-9
e-ISBN(EPUB) 978-3-11-133534-6

Library of Congress Control Number: 2023946664

Bibliographic information published by the Deutsche Nationalbibliothek
The Deutsche Nationalbibliothek lists this publication in the Deutsche Nationalbibliografie;
detailed bibliographic data are available on the Internet at http://dnb.dnb.de.

© 2024 Walter de Gruyter GmbH, Berlin/Boston
Imagecredit: tomozina/iStock/Getty Images Plus
Typesetting: Integra Software Services Pvt. Ltd.
Printing and Binding: CPI books GmbH, Leck

www.degruyter.com

To B & JM

Acknowledgments

This book has come to fruition owing to the profound influence of numerous individuals and their unwavering support. I am profoundly grateful to the students who sparked the inception of this project. Their curiosity and interest in exploring soft skills not only as a lecture but as a comprehensive book served as the catalyst for its creation.

Throughout the journey of collecting ideas, theories, and experiences, the encouragement and unwavering support of my beloved husband, Colin, stood as the cornerstone. His dedication, insightful guidance, meticulous editing, and unyielding belief in this endeavor were invaluable.

The pivotal moment of sharing Chapter 1's first draft with Colin remains etched in my memory. His honesty and encouragement were the driving force behind my determination to persevere. His continuous support during discussions, whether over coffee on our serene Dolomites balcony or amidst an afternoon stroll through the woods, has been instrumental in refining this book.

Furthermore, I extend my heartfelt appreciation to Fabrice Holler, whose connection in the industry led to a fortuitous collaboration with one of Europe's most distinguished publishing houses, De Gruyter. Their belief in this unique approach – a perspective from a corporate insider, distinct from the traditional academic or seasoned CEO viewpoints – contributed significantly to the book's clarity and distinctiveness.

I am indebted to Sandra Martinez, Rita Valerio, Prof. Dilip Subramanian, and the anonymous reviewer provided by De Gruyter for fearlessly delving into the initial draft and offering invaluable feedback. Their insights and suggestions undoubtedly enhanced the book's value for its readers.

The exceptional team at De Gruyter deserves profound gratitude for their patience, unwavering support, and enthusiasm throughout this journey. Their professionalism and dedication played an instrumental role in bringing this book to fruition.

Finally, to you, the reader, I extend my heartfelt acknowledgment for embarking on this journey with me. This book was crafted with the intention to assist individuals in cultivating essential relational skills for the business landscape, and your presence in this journey is sincerely appreciated.

https://doi.org/10.1515/9783111335339-202

Contents

Author biography

Nathalie Milian is a distinguished figure in the luxury industry, serving as the Founder and Managing Director of Euphros Advisory. Her consultancy specializes in enabling companies to navigate the evolving landscape of premium and luxury brands, with a strong focus on enhancing client-centricity. Guided by the overarching philosophy, "Where Brand Love meets Customer Loyalty," Nathalie brings a wealth of experience and expertise to the forefront.

With an impressive career spanning two decades, Nathalie Milian has held influential roles in some of the world's most renowned luxury houses, including Louis Vuitton, Chanel, and Gucci. This extensive tenure has given her a profound insight into the ever-changing global marketplace, customer expectations, and the strategic assets necessary for success. Nathalie has successfully established enduring marketing capabilities across diverse geographies and contexts, leading to significant sales growth and enhanced brand equity.

Nathalie's unwavering commitment to leadership development has been a driving force throughout her career. She continually engages in self-reflection and the cultivation of new leadership skills while refining her existing ones. Her dedication extends beyond her personal growth, as she fosters a diverse mentoring community that spans from her former international teams to students in prestigious Master programs at institutions like ESADE and NEOMA Business School. In addition, she maintains a dedicated following on LinkedIn, providing valuable insights and guidance to her loyal audience.

https://doi.org/10.1515/9783111335339-204

Introduction

The reason for this book

It became clear that an unease I had felt long before ever exchanging with postgraduates in our workshops was a real and legitimate concern: they showed genuine interest in developing the necessary relational skills to succeed in business. The Q&A session in one class was not sufficiently long to field all the questions. Clearly, it showed a curiosity for more in-depth questioning. Then the interest in a book on these topics was suggested by many of these postgraduate students. It was no sooner said than done. That was the last push I needed; my motivation for a book already existed, but I needed the nudge. I started writing seriously for this endeavour in early 2022.

In addition to these students' high interest, I perceive a need to shed light on how these lessons are revealed within one's leadership journey. The mastering of intra- and interpersonal skills is rarely a priority in the business school curriculum. Not every company offers a leadership program; when they do, not every potential candidate may be enrolled. Not every boss may be a suitable role model, and not every person has the necessary self-awareness to understand on their own or the sensitivity to grasp specific mechanisms that exist inside the companies.

I believe that additional skills should be acknowledged for evolving leaders to develop observational skills of people's behaviours. Leadership revelations are not taught; they are observed. People watch others walking the talk – or not. This is why the most enriching lessons come from within organisations. Businesses are people, and people create and need relationships to perform.

My ambition with this book is to add another perspective to leadership learning. Mentoring can happen one to one, but what if you don't have that valuable mentor next to you when they are most needed? Mentoring knowledge may also be found through your own effort, reading and research. Not someone walking ahead and explaining how to achieve things, but rather alongside shining a light on possibilities to be unlocked. Instead of supposing you can uncover the lessons yourself, you may find guidance in this book to support you in this adventure.

The extremely high interest from young professionals can be explained by the shifting business environment post-pandemic

The pandemic has been a fundamental catalyst for getting the strategic digital transformation right and work-life balance in the form of much more flexible work times and locations. Flexibility is the ability to choose one's work schedule; it no longer means just working remotely. Working asynchronously requires employers to make a

https://doi.org/10.1515/9783111335339-001

cultural shift where work-life boundaries are respected. Executives are trusted to do their jobs outside a traditional 9–5 workday. Employers set guardrails where live synchronous work can occur.

We are also facing enormous pressure from unsolved crises that have unfolded after the pandemic: irregular economic recovery between regions, the rising cost of living, the energy transition impasse and uneven wealth distribution. An increased call for action on diversity and inclusion issues, highlighted in some geographies by an atmosphere resentful of privilege, geopolitical power alignment, democratic vs. autocratic leadership, etc.

On top of these societal shifts in the world, we also witness a generational "pass the baton" moment: from Boomer to Gen X and Millennial leadership exchange and Gen Z upcoming leadership. These generations have evolved through very diverse leadership styles and upheld different expectations from their leaders and themselves.

Most important is the need – in my opinion – for a book on these topics

What skills are needed for a future workplace where 1 billion jobs will be transformed by technology by 2030? Pearson's Skills Outlook report on 'Power Skills' analysed labour market trends in four major economies – US, UK, Australia and Canada – and found that, while technical skills remain highly valued, the top five most sought-after skills that employers are seeking today are all human: Communication, Customer Service, Leadership, Attention to Detail and Collaboration.

Looking ahead to 2026, the Pearson Skill Outlook identified three additional human skills: Personal Learning and Mastery, Achievement Focus and Cultural and Social Intelligence.

John Rogers, Vice President at Pearson, reinforces the need to focus on developing human skills in a future of increased digitalisation, "we are seeing the level of proficiency in human skills is important across all job roles, and they will be critical to one's future employability, and underpinning all of this is one's commitment to continuous learning [1]."

Business and HR leaders have always known that human skills are crucial, but now we're seeing a heightened demand for them as they become the "new hard skills." They rely on human connections and the ability to lead others and cannot be automated [2].

This coincides with the most recent World Economic Forum's 'Future of Job report'. There it is stated that the future workplace will be much more dynamic regarding skill set requirements and that we should place ourselves in a constant reskilling cycle. For a start, Digital and Data Literacy will be paramount. Beyond job-specific technical skills, every employer will be after the so-called soft skills. We can group them into three areas [3]:

A) Critical thinking and creativity for problem-solving
B) Curiosity, continuous learning, resilience and flexibility
C) Collaboration, leadership and social influence

Within the previous generational paradigm, the CEO ideal was seniority-driven authority, which led to a command-and-control leadership. The shift is from a model of telling people what to do and then sitting back and evaluating them to a model where leaders' main task is coaching fellow future leaders. Where authority can be acquired by accomplishing initiatives in serving others, this begs for a vital mastery of relational skills, which is the proposition of this book.

My approach to leadership skills development

I was touched by a statement from the late Javier Marías – one of Spain's most recognised writers these past decades – during a tribute given to him in Santillana del Mar in 2008. He confessed to "writing with a compass, not using a map". I believe this insightful metaphor deserves our attention for navigating life in general. With all life's uncertainties, our best strategy is to hold a compass close in our hand rather than navigate our path with routes specified and detailed on a map.

He continued, "If I would know beforehand the entire story that I am about to tell, if I would have it in its entirety in my head before I start writing, the most probable is that I would not even bother to write it."

He leaves us a message about the enigmatic power of discovery. In his case, it occurs through the evolution of stories in his head and then the writing for the final construction of his novels. In our case, it could be about our lives. Shall we set out to discover the opportunities in our lives, or instead set course and navigate towards a given destination?

This is the difference in mindset when navigating life or a professional career with a compass rather than a map. Some people know exactly where they are heading; they have a plan of precisely what and when they wish to accomplish particular ambitions. Some people walk through life with a checklist. It might work for certain people and under certain circumstances, but I believe these are exceptions.

As a leader, you must catalyse change rather than plan for it. Those who rely on traditional "linear and deterministic" strategic thinking will be less attuned to emergent factors to which they must respond. Therefore leaders need to think and act with an outside-in perspective, cultivating a 360-degree view of the dynamics within their organisations and those of the ecosystems in which they operate.

In a world of constant change and so much uncertainty, it may be more prudent to set out by building a strong and reliable compass around your belief system that will guide you in whatever life throws at you. So many circumstances in life are out of our control, which may cause us frustration and pain. It is better to become as least dependent as possible on those external factors and rely entirely on one's strengths and capabilities. Take the saying about the bird, for example: "A bird sitting on a tree is not afraid of the branch breaking because its trust is not on the branch but its wings".

The more you can trust your wings – your values, your resilience, your integrity – the better prepared you will be in life and for your professional trajectory.

My message is that people who have developed a solid moral compass and feel that sometimes it may get their way in the workplace: don't. We need leaders who follow the courageous actions of others and stand for doing the right thing – executives who are authentic, compassionate and driven by a sense of purpose.

The oldest playbook for the education of emotions in life is probably the Greek Seven Virtues. I find the analogy made by Cartier's CEO, Cyrille Vigneron, very inspiring.

He reminds us that prudence, justice, temperance, fortitude, faith, hope and charity apply to all groups, whether a sports team, a family or a company. More than ever, they are a true compass for modern leaders embarking on a transformation process.

The first four – the cardinal virtues – "are cornerstones keeping human groups together. There is no peaceful life together if these pillars are not strong enough".

"To be respected", he writes, "leaders must be strong and courageous, lead with prudence, stay calm and well-tempered, and enforce common rules with justice".

The final three – the theological virtues – "allow the community to move out of its comfort zone, reach new territories or ambitious goals, or simply face crises and uncertainties".

"Faith can be understood as convictions and values; hope as ambition and vision; charity as a blend of care, charm and charisma. People will follow leaders with a clear vision, live by strong shared values, care for others with empathy and have charisma".

As mentioned, the current moment is very interesting and challenging. Our societies are accelerating, and humanity has important topics to solve and master. Various coinciding crises unfold, and we must be prepared for continuous transformation.

Let's agree that business contributes to society's well-being and forms an integral part of its structure. It goes without saying that it will maintain a key role. Even with technology supporting more and more jobs, the essence remains: businesses are people. And for people to thrive in a new paradigm, we must collectively set the necessary conditions.

One of those conditions is great leadership. Therefore, my sincere intention is to contribute to next-generation leaders' development through my work, lectures and writing.

Being a leader is not about oneself but the people in your lead and how you help them become successful leaders. Moving away from the commanding model towards the coaching model, where a leader does not direct others but inspires them.

To a larger extent, it is necessary to influence corporate cultures for the better, to achieve conditions where more people benefit from a supporting, trusting and enjoyable work environment. This will only be possible with the ability to manage emotions – that is, emotional intelligence – at an individual and a collective level.

Embracing the necessary relational skills with authenticity and building bridges of collaboration and understanding within the business environment – would be the movement that would take us all forward in the best possible sense.

A unique experience in a lifelong journey

Albert Einstein was four or five years old when his father gave him a magnetic pocket compass to play with while he was sick in bed. The little boy was impressed by a wonder: the needle's northward swing – guided by an invisible force. The compass made a deep and lasting impression on him and convinced Einstein that "something deeply hidden had to be behind things".

A mysterious and unique object like a compass can catalyse a lifelong scientific curiosity. As an adult, curiosity for business psychology may be similarly sparked by encountering an unexpected animal. Here is the story . . .

It is a beautiful morning in June: warm and sunny; the birds are out singing – what a pleasure to discover the hinterland of the French Basque Coastline. This was years ago, during an off-site with my work colleagues. Part of the leadership development program this year is to discover the lessons from horse whispering for business.

I am very intrigued and guess everyone else is too. I am unsure what to expect and curious to discover what we will learn today. Overly grateful to even be able to have this experience. For the lessons to come, but also for the incredibly beautiful setting. Everyone is in a good mood – no wonder.

My personal relationship with horses has been relatively limited over the years. I had some riding lessons to make sure I had the basics, to get on and hopefully not fall off a horse – anticipating moments like being invited over a weekend at someone's house in the country where they have horses or any situation where I might be required to horseback ride: to be able to join the group and not being the weakest link that might hinder anyone's enjoyment. Would this prior experience be of any help today? I didn't know at the time but in retrospect, no, definitely no.

We arrive at the stables and start sensing the environment in which we will be immersed for the next couple of hours. First thing, we are split up into different groups. Not quite sure about the others, but in my group, we ended up with five people for four horses.

"No problem," the instructor said, "we will take turns". I was okay with this and volunteered to observe first and see how my colleagues managed, and I thought maybe this could be to my advantage.

Big mistake. When it came to my turn, it felt rushed, and I was given little time to build the necessary rapport with the horse compared to the others. With the instructor's help, they started to approach the horse, making sure not to frighten it, caressing it, placing themselves in the right spots, talking to the horse and trying different body postures. I observed and could appreciate the right moves. I realised later that the instructor didn't want four people standing around for long and began to move to the next exercise. Once handed the horse, I had little time to develop the rapport or practice the techniques. The first lesson learned: the time for connection is key.

My horse was responding as if he did not know me. "Who are you?" "Have you introduced yourself?" – he seemed to be saying. And "Why are you late to this exercise?". In my head, the answers were: "Hey, no. I am not late. I just had to wait for my turn". I felt like arriving late to his appointment. Lesson two: place yourself in the horse's shoes. I realised that instead of waiting for my turn, I could have participated in the bonding session with the horse with someone else and done the exercise together. "What if you view the world from the horse's eyes?"

Well, now, the situation is what it is. I am introducing myself and getting his confidence. I know I have to make some extra time for it. Lesson three: Trust takes time. There is no gain in rushing it. But I was not given that time by the instructor. We were moving on. "Damn, that's not fair" – silly but honest thoughts in my head.

Later in the day, I realised my lesson four: much more important than how much time you spend creating a bond with a horse is to find out how best to do it and approach connection efficiently.

These were the principal learnings from the day. It was not teaching given orally by instructors but by the horses themselves. They truly made us feel it. We all came away with a similar feeling: trust is earned, gained and maintained through our behaviour, gestures and movement.

Lesson number five: the stronger the trust built with the horse, the better he followed instructions. The aha moment came when I realised that the horse reacts to us as a mirror. He mimics our feelings and responds to them. In the beginning, I was not particularly at ease, I have to admit. Horses are huge animals, weighing half a ton, staring at you: I had to find out what to do. The first couple of tries: were not great. I was relaxed and did not make him fearful, at least. But he seemed bored or unclear on what to do, so he turned around and walked away from me. "Oh no, what did I do wrong?" The voices in my head were not being kind. I knew it was not the calming words I had been trying since the horse obviously could not understand me. Maybe not the words but the tone or the body language. My approach was passing him the wrong message. "What was it?"

When you try things out and start seeing different reactions, you realise the power of body language. After several attempts, it became easier. It amazed me the sense of achievement that just strolling around in circles with a horse at your shoulder can give you. It was a massive eye-opener for me. Only in a pure state of calmness, and with the correct gestures performed in a slow but apparent motion, can you quickly get your message across to the horse so that he can comfortably follow you in your venture.

The instructor pointed out that horses are incredibly eager to please – they want you, as their master, to be happy with them. The parallel in business with teams and their bosses or in sports with teams and their coaches is obvious. In general, people wish to do an excellent job for the boss or coach and contribute positively to the team's performance. It is your behaviour as the leader that helps facilitate outstanding performance. We all got a taste of what a horse whisperer might be: someone who knows how to connect with a horse effortlessly. A horse will naturally follow their lead without explaining why it would. It comes from shared vibrations of trust that cannot be seen and are accomplished in moments of harmony.

It is true to say that I had accumulated many learnings by the end of the day. My initial state was disappointment and frustration with not getting the exercise right, misconstruing the instructions and taking longer to achieve the desired result. By the end of the day, a most favourable outcome unfolded: many new lessons were integrated and ingrained into my leadership journey. Finding the horse whisperer within you is magic. What is so unique about such an experience is that it offers immediate feedback.

A horse whisperer knows that **trust** is the foundation of everything. That is why they observe, listen and figure out what the horse needs to feel safe. Safety is the horse's first priority. Horses are prey animals, so they naturally fear people who are predator animals. The horse's natural instinct is to protect itself from humans. A horse whisperer accepts that safety is the horse's primary criterion and knows that each action and nonverbal cue will either erode or build trust. Likewise, employees are free to be their best when leaders create an environment of trust where they are safe to flourish. As with horses, people gauge the trustworthiness of leaders by the consistency and congruence of their actions and communications.

A horse whisperer thinks from the horse's **perspective**. He understands the horse's point of view as he teaches the horse to cross streams, climb mountains and manoeuvre new or strange territories. The horse senses when you have its best interests and perspective in mind. It reads the intent of your viewpoint, just as people do with their leaders. Some of the best leaders are those who can think and communicate from multiple perspectives. They can pace the reality of their people so that they gain permission to be heard and lead their people to other realities. One of the central communication presuppositions is that once you accept the other person's reality, everything becomes more accessible. Once employees know you understand their reality, they are much more willing to follow your lead.

A horse's **nonverbal acuity** is amazingly exact. A horse whisperer knows the horse reads every microscopic movement to assess the threat level. "The horse is paying attention to everything you are projecting," says Jerilyn Caldwell – horse whisperer and leadership coach. "If you make a move that signals danger, they release adrenaline. If you make a move that signals safety, they relax, listen and follow your instructions," she adds. "In that relaxed zone, the horse is at his best and is very capable of doing amazing things." The horse senses if you are fearful or confident through your nonverbal cues. Likewise, people are constantly reading a leader's body language and gestures. Nonverbal communication accounts for more than 90% of the meaning of a leader's communication. Research shows that if a leader's nonverbal cues conflict with their words, people will believe the nonverbals over the verbal. The nonverbals tell people if a leader is congruent, confident and consistent.

Horse whispering is about leading with all of your senses. It is about clearing out your thinking and being a keen observer so that you can be a more effective leader and inspire your people to move toward a better future. The horse is a compelling teacher because the results do not lie. When you look into the horse's eyes, you will see yourself. You will see the leader that others see [4].

This exceptional experience is only a piece of a lifelong journey. In my opinion, one's leadership journey can be described as a path of essential revelations.

In my case, this path started, as many do, discovering as an adolescent that life is a series of choices and that those choices are our responsibility. I always felt comfortable with and even relished responsibility – as the older sibling and as a girl guide in charge of the welfare of others. Later on, managing retail teams needed constant attention to building motivation. I enjoyed that as much as inventing games and stories as a child. Next came the influence of all those leaders I have admired in my life, but particularly the reason why I admired them – the alignment of the values guiding our choices. I loved following their example and started working on the influence I wished to develop. I realised years later that the "fil rouge" in my career has been to build entirely new capabilities and teams in the roles I have been given. Very often, with significant obstacles to surpass, but always with great joy. I have always felt a caring love for my teams and developed them with the best intentions. I recently read that Satya Nadella – CEO at Microsoft – failed to answer well a question related to empathy at his entry interview for Microsoft. But he learned from the experience and made empathy a central foundation in his career. With all humility, I feel I learned and adjusted from the failures of my first horse whispering lessons. I have always given my absolute best to develop and move forward. I have found the sentiment of compassion more challenging to crack. Having been raised to "be strong" and "uncomplaining" and then experiencing toxic work environments where unhealthy competition sometimes overshadows collaboration, I know some behaviours take longer to master.

Other 'aha' moments in my journey have been discovering three interesting matrices to explain behaviour in business. They will be unveiled in the book, among other frameworks. The first one is by Adam Grant: the Givers vs Takers matrix. The second is by Cuddy, Fiske and Glick: the Warmth vs Competence matrix. The third is by Simon Sinek: the Navy Seals' Performance vs Trust matrix. Another key moment of revelation was when I embarked on a 360-degree colleague feedback assessment and discovered some unexpected perspectives on my leadership personality. This is when it becomes real; that perception is all that counts. Similarly, it took me some time to realise that *impact* is way more fulfilling in business than *power*.

What you can expect from this book

Established CEOs, academics and coaches have written much about leadership skills development, but what about someone from within the corporate world? What about someone who has had first-hand experience leading these upcoming new generations? What about a point of view that is not male and US based?

The drive of young people in life and business has evolved dramatically – where should they head for inspiration?

Actually, from a multitude of sources. As I realised when I started out on my journey. What is inspiring in one's leadership path is to listen and savour as many points of view as possible. Hopefully, this book allows for an additional one for its readers. One that comes from a place of collated reading, training, exchange, coaching and experience.

This book is a practical compilation of crucial relational skills to develop next-generation executives intending to succeed in the transition from manager to leader in the corporate world.

I write with an insider's view and from a 20+ years career in blue chip Fashion Luxury companies, leading teams and projects with a global transformational impact.

Hopefully, the format I have chosen is like that of a supportive mentor. As a mentee, you may find helpful insights and lessons to be applied daily to speed up your learning curve and potentially avoid mistakes. As a mentor yourself, you may find it interesting to gain an additional perspective on your knowledge for mentoring young professionals in their transition to leaders.

In this book, I explain – through a practical lens – how the most valuable leadership skills can be developed and why, as well as the underlying potential pitfalls, difficulties and priorities. Similar to the way a personal mentor might do for you – with understanding, patience and empathy.

This book is pragmatic. It will take you through situations from an insider perspective and guide you in the skills that need addressing, step by step.

Some fictitious narratives have been included throughout the book to allow for a practical glimpse into the corporate world. Any names, characters, businesses, places, events or incidents are fictitious. Any resemblance to actual persons or events is purely coincidental. The environment chosen for those narratives is mostly within the Industry of Personal Luxury, but not only. This industry is where the author has evolved professionally and might provide an appealing perspective for the readers. It offers accessible scenarios to allow for a clear understanding of the topic being addressed. However, the lessons revealed are universal and can be applied to any other workplace or industry. It is not Personal Luxury specific at all.

Plenty of business literature is out there based on extensive research and, with analysis, deduced outcomes. You will find them abundantly cited in this book. I have been collating much of this research and opinion because it is my passion and interest, filtering out those that I find most appropriate, realistic and helpful.

Existing current literature on leadership development is mainly US based. This book is more of a European take. Still, it is also influenced by American academic and business points of view that are globally adaptable and applicable. I believe it is essential that new generations of business leaders get access to a shared experience that does not only come from established long-time CEOs or C-level coaches who may not be so relatable for young professionals.

You will also read between the lines that I have had to change myself and my perspectives many times. This comes with a growth journey, especially if you are willing to step out of your comfort zone. Many people want everyone else to change, but it is vital to understand that making adaptations in yourself is often more effective. With the many crises we are experiencing in our world, one of the fundamentals of being an authentic leader is being adaptable to constant change.

Bibliography

[1]   Meister J. Top Ten HR Trends For The 2023 Workplace. Forbes. 2023.
[2]   Elkeiy G. Future-Proof Skills Can Help Balance Individual and Societal Progress: UN Chronicle; 2022.
[3]   Whiting K. These are the top 10 job skills of tomorrow – and how long it takes to learn them: Weforum.org; 2020.
[4]   Borden G. 3 Horse Whispering Leadership Lessons: Medium.com; 2019.

Chapter One
Enabling passion

Life is short. Break the Rules. Forgive quickly. Kiss slowly. Love truly.
Laugh uncontrollably and never regret anything that makes you smile.
Mark Twain

https://doi.org/10.1515/9783111335339-002

1.1 Emotions are luxury's business

It's early May waking up in Southern France near Grasse. The day reveals a blue and sunny sky ahead. The air is still fresh and cool; it's early morning. We take the cars to be on time at the fields. We are experiencing comparable levels of excitement and anticipation with our guests, whom we will accompany for this rendez-vous. Our group of chic ladies will have the privilege to enjoy the picking of the petals of the first "Rose de May" close to Grasse for the legendary Chanel Number 5 perfume.

"It's hard to tell what I enjoy more: living incredible moments myself or facilitating others to live them. What is true is that the more unimaginable the situation – when it is filled with happiness, joy and gratitude – the feeling of satisfaction is impossible to top".

Take the next scene: after having successfully picked a basket full of petals, following the precise instructions provided by the field women, our invited guests listened carefully to the explanations given by the farmers during the distillation process. The alchemy was happening: the steel tanks were being filled with the delicious pink rose petals while an amazing fragrance was infusing the air. Sometimes enjoyment just gives you wings, right? The wings to jump into a steel tank! This is precisely what happened. One lady started, made herself comfortable there, and of course, seconds later, another lady was in, and then another . . . Delighted faces, enjoying a Chanel Number 5 rose petal bath!

Similarly, this time in June, we are in Venice: witnessing the travels of Gabrielle Chanel a century ago. At the time, she was visiting her great friend Misia Sert. During lunch, she was introduced to Sergei Diaghilev – the renowned "Ballet Russes" impresario. Walking in the footsteps of Coco Chanel also brought us to visit beautiful Ottoman masterpieces in hidden chapels that so strongly inspired her style – a defining moment for the collaboration of Dance and Fashion.

Many of these brand occasions are unique and otherwise impossible to experience except by being part of the select club of 'best clients' of these Luxury Houses.

A similar immense privilege is to be invited to the Chanel Fashion Show in the Grand Palais in Paris during Fashion Week. It permanently closes the week on Tuesday morning. It is one of 'the' social events in Paris, and Parisians live it this way, as well as invited press, friends of the house and clients. Especially at the time of the late Karl Lagerfeld, shows were grandiloquent and marked an unquestionable highlight everyone expected to be magnificent.

These emotions that prestigious luxury brands skilfully bestow in so many different ways to their clients and devoted fans through various communication campaigns are vital for the business's success. These emotions nurture the luxury business to enhance the desirability of its products and the loyalty of its customer base.

Isabella stopped her story for a second and noticed Sara's expression: there was so much excitement in her eyes, and her smile just beamed with delight. One could picture how she had been painting the scenes in her mind while listening to Isabella. Both were sitting and having coffee after a business lunch in downtown Manhattan. Isabella is now in charge of Client Experience for a European Jewellery Brand in the Americas and recently recruited Sara to support her on several critical projects.

One might ask: Is there really a place for emotions in business? Some could argue that they should be excluded from the business inside and out. I believe the contrary; they are an integral part of life and so, therefore, of business.

Emotions must be understood, channelled and managed, of course, but not totally set aside.

I come from an industry that thrives on using emotion to sell products. Personal luxury items are primarily emotional drivers, as are hospitality offerings, selling holidays and the entertainment industry. Moments of joy. Long-lasting memories of vivid personal emotions. This is what the luxury industry is all about. Since this is the existential mission of the industry, I believe that successful executives working in this sphere need to master the indulgence of emotions.

Executives may not interact directly with customers, but those employees who do – Client Advisors or Fashion Advisors as they are known – really know how to influence those emotions. They feel them themselves and use them to lure their customers.

Once a luxury client advisor has sold their first top-of-the-range product – it might be a high-end handbag or a watch – they will likely develop a powerful emotional bond with their customer. A relationship so strong and with development potential that who knows where it can lead. It is not unheard of that they even attend a customer's wedding years later.

Most client advisors can tell you stories about their best customers; very often, the relationship was initially born out of disappointments or a bad service experience: but they made it happen to overcome the difficulties and then develop such a relationship that customers would not shop with the brand if it is not with that person.

This is one of the examples of Human Magic that this industry delivers to the happy few who can allow themselves such expensive products.

This is how Cyrille Vigneron – CEO of Cartier (2022) – describes this phenomena : « notre métier principal c'est de faire des produits tangibles pour des sentiments intangibles ». « Our main task, is to manufacture tangible products for intangible sentiments ».

Without overstating the obvious, customers and employees are people. And when dealing with people in the realm of personal luxury, we are dealing mainly with creatures of emotion, not creatures of logic. Customers pay a premium for the added value of powerfully charged positive emotions. Employees at all levels need to understand this and strive for the customer experience to be excellent and memorable. Those employees working closest to the final customer interaction must have the clearest understanding of handling these sentiments. Understanding and nurturing this concept within the organisation is prudent, starting with the Sales and Marketing teams. Usually, for any employee, the closer they are to the end customer, the better their understanding and sensitivity for these emotions and their ability to generate them. Listen to client advisors; they have their fingers on the pulse.

They are the ones who have a direct relationship with the customer and can help us understand their needs and desires the best.

By conceding that intimate knowledge of customer feelings are essential to selling our products successfully, we should probably recognise also – more crucially than in any other industry – that emotions exhibited by employees working in this industry must also be embraced in the daily working life and channelled appropriately. As with the other two sectors that sell emotions, as mentioned earlier, hospitality and entertainment, employees' feelings must be front and centre. As Richard Branson puts it: "Clients do not come first, employees come first." This is fundamental in an emotion-driven industry where customers pay a premium for excellence. If, in the execution of that service or product, you include a human touch element or not, employees still need to be driven by the positive emotion the completion of a purchase will be felt by the customer. And my point here is that successful executives in the industry will have a high level of both emotional intelligence and intellectual intelligence. By analysing the successful leaders in the luxury industry, we may provide insights that help develop successful leaders in many other sectors. Guided by the principle that emotions have a place in business because businesses are people, and people have feelings.

Friedrich Dürrenmatt – a 20th-century Swiss playwriter – stated the following: "Emotions have no place in business unless you do business with them." Well, yes, the luxury, entertainment and hospitality industries conduct business with emotions, so there is unequivocally a place for emotion in business, right? Dürrenmatt is known for being a moralist out of nihilism. This radical scepticism is what I would like to challenge. I am an optimist, as are all the successful leaders I have encountered in this industry. So this book will be on refuting Dürrenmatt's theory, also knowing that he has turned it in an interesting way which suits my purpose.

Friedrich Dürrenmatt is not our judge but perhaps our conscience. His universal negative insight comes from his belief that people cannot change. This is a statement with which I totally disagree. Life is a learning journey, so we need to, can and should evolve and change.

To share knowledge along the way, and to ease the path for younger generations, is another mission I gave myself for this book.

1.2 The importance of excelling in group dynamics

This learning – the importance of excelling in group dynamics – came as an early one in his career, in fact, as early as his student days. The only moments that François remembers learning relational skills for business during his student times were at a group dynamics workshop at business school, held by one eminent professor in the form of a small class, and similarly by some PhD students at an off-site seminar.

At both events, his early lesson had been not only to always speak up in a group dynamics situation but, more importantly, to speak up in the earliest possible stages of the interaction.

It may sometimes be intimidating to share our views and opinions, especially at the beginning of your professional career, when we do not feel that we have enough expertise. Well, it doesn't matter. Because people around us know that and do not expect wisdom from us, but they expect interest and interaction with the topic once we have been invited to the table. Otherwise, we may not be asked again, right? And maybe someone else may take our precious seat and opportunity.

"What is key," said François, "is to use your voice in any group interaction opportunity. And to raise your confidence, it is advised to use it early. Don't wait until everyone has already given their opinion, so you arrive last. You have to give yourself the push to show up for your opinions. I also heard it in a candid interview given by a newly named CEO when he learned this lesson also in the early years of his career. Isn't it frustrating when you have an interesting view and because you waited too long to speak up, someone else relates it first, or no one does for the matter, but it turns out to be a great idea that will only be uncovered later? Have you ever had this same feeling? So, let it happen once or twice, but no more. You learned the lesson; it will provide you more confidence to apply this principle from your early stages".

"This is also what I told one of my mentees. Some people struggle with speaking up early when they are already in a management position, and this should be avoided at all costs. At this point, overcoming these group dynamics and communication difficulties may be more difficult. Trust me, start practising as early as possible. Because this is something absolutely everyone needs to learn, some do quickly and early, which is what you must demand of yourself".

In a business environment, to excel in group dynamics, the key elements are confidence and assertiveness, in my opinion.

Assertive communication will enable you to be convincing and build confidence when interacting with others. It takes practice, of course, but it's a significant communication skill that can make you more self-confident and result in a more effective and fulfilling career.

Being assertive means having the ability to confidently communicate what you want or need while also respecting the needs of others. Assertiveness is an interpersonal skill that is direct yet non-confrontational. Assertiveness is the successful middle-ground between an aggressive style and a passive style.

The benefits of being assertive are many: It builds self-confidence since you develop the ability to stand up for yourself. The more you become comfortable being open and honest with those around you, the more your self-worth will improve. Assertiveness is an excellent leadership quality that will surprisingly fast-track you to a leadership role or status. The ability to say what you need lets others know where you stand on a particular issue. It is a strategy that builds open, honest relationships. It will help if you try not to resist facing your fears since they will create stress and ultimately affect your health and well-being. From my experience, it is best to handle matters as they arise since this frees up room in your mind.

Assertiveness is an interpersonal skill in which you demonstrate the healthy confidence to stand up for yourself while still respecting the rights of others. When you are assertive, you are neither passive nor aggressive but direct and honest. You should not expect other people to know what you want, so speak up to ask for what you need calmly and confidently.

Assertive behaviour includes being an active listener, behaviour which includes good eye contact, not interrupting when the other person is talking and reflecting on what was just said to confirm the information was heard correctly.

In terms of communication, it shows the ability to put forward one's displeasure appropriately and politically effectively. There are times when we need to speak up, and we don't. Or occasions where we are taken advantage of (and we feel like a pushover!), and we just accept it. Both will ultimately undermine our confidence and trajectory to leadership. People will respect you more if you speak up; more importantly, you won't be kicking yourself for letting the opportunity slip. Besides, you will avoid carrying all this resentment with you all the time.

From these arguments, you can tell that the benefits of assertiveness certainly include stress reduction. Assertiveness helps you vent your feelings, get your voice heard and resolve your problem while maintaining harmony.

What I found helps a lot in easing the understanding of assertiveness is the following:

You are not assertive when you are either passive or aggressive.

With passive behaviour, your feelings and needs matter and not mine.
With aggressive behaviour, my feelings and needs matter and not yours.
With assertive behaviour, both my feelings and needs matter and yours too.

Assertive communication is what we should strive to achieve if we wish to ease relationships in corporate and better realise our goals. It has the significant benefit of making us feel good and, more importantly, not dismissed or ignored. This behaviour develops mutual respect. The most valuable advantage, however, is that it works brilliantly even if we disagree since we are not nullifying someone else's opinion. And for you, it will increase your self-esteem, help you achieve your goals, minimise hurting and alienating other people and reduces potential or existing anxiety.

Summarising assertive communication in a simple phrase from an unknown author: "Say what you mean and mean what you say, but don't say it mean".

What is it, then, that I need to be practising to develop my assertive communication skills?

Here is what "masterclass.com" recommends to start developing positive assertive habits [1]:

1. **Believe in yourself.** Being assertive is a clear sign of self-respect. Worrying about the opinion of others can stand in the way of being honest with yourself and others. There may be a situation where all people doubt you, but you can still "trust yourself while making allowance for their doubting too", as Rudyard Kipling wrote.

2. **Learn how to say no**. If you already have much on your plate and cannot take on more, simply say no. It's an empowering feeling; you can offer help at a time that works for you. Setting boundaries will allow you to know when you need to say yes and when you want to say no. Boundaries are the rules and limits you create that help you decide what you will and won't allow. You don't want people to walk all over you, but you don't want people to think you are disobliging. A smart option would be to make yourself the scapegoat. Let's say, "I have a policy . . ." and if you respect your boundaries, others respect them too.

3. **Practice what you are going to say**. Try roleplaying with a partner or friend or rehearse your actual pitch. A good option is to record yourself and listen to it back, noticing how it makes you feel. Be attentive to the words you use. I find it very powerful to develop the use of questions. When you exchange with someone, your position or idea won't come across in an aggressive tone if you phrase it as a question – especially when you have opposite views. While building your argument, ensuring you don't disqualify yourself by minimising your thoughts and feelings is vital.

4. **Be simple, direct and concise**. State what you know to be true for you, be specific about your problem and don't leave room for misinterpretation. Avoid beating about the bush or talking about trivial matters. When asserting yourself, remember that less is more. Keep your requests free of meandering or long-winded explanations. Talk about the most important or critical issues first. Tell the other person how you're feeling using the pronoun "I" – as in "I feel" or "I think". Say it with conviction; since it's

your stuff, own it. This is a confident approach. Beginning with "you", you presume to know what the other side is feeling and comes across as being a little arrogant and hostile. Make it a habit to say things like "I think . . ." or "I feel . . ." Never use aggressive language or phrases like "You never . . ." or "You always . . ." These statements trigger other people, leaving them frustrated, and they shut down the conversation. "I" statements allow you to be confident and assertive without alienating and eliminating other people. Remember that an assertive person is not an author of confusion. Do not attack people personally or suggest that they are biased or treated differently or unfairly. Instead, explain how an unfortunate decision or allegation undermines your rights or privileges. Persuade them to believe that you think they made a regrettable mistake rather than a deliberate attempt to undermine you. Remember: attack the issue, not the people.

5. **Leave negative emotions out of it**. You might be navigating a problematic situation and harbouring negative feelings towards the opposing party, but leave all those emotions out of your message. Even if the other person becomes reactive, stay calm. Getting angry or defensive can lead to an aggressive rather than an assertive response. You need to keep on track, which will help mitigate a bad situation. When practising assertiveness, speaking in a way that doesn't imply accusations or make the other person feel guilty is essential. Speaking your truth with candour shouldn't mean making others feel wrong. It might make you feel excited, but excitement can sometimes come across as aggression. Learn to stay cool and calm when expressing yourself. Be present with each other. Calm mind, calm speech, calm action – it gives you confidence and allows the other person to remain composed.

6. **Remember your body language**. Your words are only one part of how you're communicating with others. Your body language, tone of voice and facial expressions contribute to your message. Never expect people to read your mind; if you want something, say so, and if something bothers you, speak up. Look confident when making a request or stating a preference. Stand tall and straight, smile or keep a neutral facial expression and look the person in the eye. Practice in front of a mirror if you need to.

7. **Understand the other point of view**. A key ingredient of assertiveness is the ability to say what you need while also recognising the wishes of others. Assertive people are influential because they possess empathy and respect other opinions and ideas when negotiating. On the other hand, aggressive people demand that their needs be met with no regard for anyone else. Respecting the person you are communicating with often leads to a collaborative solution and a win-win scenario, with both sides getting what they are after. In this process, try not to let your differences upset or make you angry. Remember that differences don't necessarily mean you are right and the other person is wrong. Listen respectfully, don't interrupt when they are speaking and try to understand their point of view and signal flexibility by providing options. Assertive people are willing to compromise with others rather than always wanting their way.

8. **Keep it positive**. No one likes difficult conversations, so things go unresolved, leading to stress and complicated relationships. One way to stop procrastinating and deal with situations that require you to be assertive is to approach them with positive emotions. If you communicate with an upbeat tone, the other person will often let down their guard and respond accordingly.

9. **Stand your ground**. Don't give up if you don't get what you want the first time you ask. In assertiveness training, this technique is called a broken record. The person might not respond as you hoped the first time, but they might need time to process what you want. Go back and repeat what it is you need until you get it. Use the broken record technique.

10. **Start small**. Begin to practice daily rituals of putting yourself first. Assertiveness is like any other skill – it takes practice and time to get it right. Keep working through these techniques; very soon, you will begin to feel more confident. I find it helpful to be attentive to moments when you have been assertive and build on your successes. As a leader, it is also vital to help your team members recognise and appreciate small wins to build assertiveness and give them immediate feedback after a meeting, for example. Assertive communication is a human skill that will help you in every aspect of your life. Ask yourself, how can I find ways to transfer assertiveness skills from some areas of my life to others? Consider that you are likely to have a go-to behaviour: you may become either angry or anxious. Maybe you are more of an aggressive / fight person than a passive / flee person. You might be a combination where you become passive-aggressive – not an attractive demeanour. Start acknowledging that in some situations, your brain might be falling back on default behaviour, take a deep breath and then react assertively, telling yourself: "There is something to check out here".

Let me note, at this point, that you should never leave a meeting or interaction where you regret not making your point clearly and decisively. This is especially important.

To be prepared for those moments, you can watch a video you know you disagree with the speaker and then record yourself giving a solid response. Exercise yourself until you find the correct arguments and delivery.

Dr Paul Jenkins – a clinical psychologist specialising in the science and practice of positivity – incites us to practice another exercise, to train for two specific situations that need assertive communication [2].

The first is when you have been offended by someone. In this case, what you need to do is to react with three steps: identify, verify, accept. Repeat the affront that has been made and then explain how that made you feel, without blame, judgement or further accusation in a succinct manner. Then ask about the intentions behind that behaviour. Very often, the offender will back peddle or claim misinterpretation on your side. The best to do next is to accept and say "okay". By doing so, you have stood your ground, put that person on notice assertively, and such aggressive behaviour will probably not repeat itself.

There is a second type of situation that requires assertive communication. This is a case where you really feel the need to get your way. The first step is to start with an assumption of gratitude and benevolence. We are requesting something from somebody, who happens to be a person, so we need to put a lot of humanity into it. The person on the other side has feelings, history, narrative, etc. We need to treat them how we want to be treated, with empathy and kindness. There is no reason to exploit people to get our way but to use a positive, constructive relationship to get what we want and, at the same time, help them to get what they want. Approach the person with appreciation, a positive attitude and an assumption of goodwill that this person wants a good outcome for you. Whether they do or not is irrelevant. For you to start with that assumption will set the tone and energy of the interaction and how you show up. After that, you articulate the status quo by acknowledging what it is. The next step would be to express what you want or – in other words – the desired consequence. You wish to create the same picture in the other person's mind. You have stated where you are and also where you want to be. The last step would be to determine what the appropriate request would be. As a question, type "Would you be open to . . . ?" or "Would you consider . . . ?" and you deliver it straight on.

1.3 Why empathy is so important

The importance of assertiveness, and one of its key aspects, empathy, shows us how putting ourselves in the other person's shoes avoids aggressive but also passive communication and behaviour.

In a business context, empathy helps achieve collaboration. Trying to understand the other person's perspective can facilitate a compromise between two points of view.

Nevertheless, putting ourselves in someone else's shoes may not be enough; we should try to understand how the person ended up in those shoes, where those shoes come from and how it feels to walk in them. Going the extra mile will genuinely move us into an empathetic perspective.

In the words of Belinda Parmar in *Harvard Business Review*: "Empathy should be embedded into the entire organisation. There is nothing soft about it. It is a hard skill that should be required from the boardroom to the shop floor [3]."

This is also Satya Nadella's belief. The CEO of Microsoft answers the following when asked what empathy has to do with business: "I believe it has everything to do with work. If you say innovation is all about meeting unmet unarticulated needs of customers, where is that source of your ability to get in touch with that unmet unarticulated need going to come from? It's going to come from your ability – in some sense – to be able to listen between the lines, to be able to extrapolate. And that's to me, the deep sense of empathy." He continues with this outcome for empathy: "people talk about design thinking. I think design thinking is empathy. Empathy is the source to success in any innovative agenda you have."

You may ask yourself: why is empathy considered so important in business? You will develop a greater awareness and presence in your leadership role by better understanding others. Juggling responsibilities can be difficult and distracting, so demonstrating empathy increases your attentiveness and improves your patience and tolerance. If you can show empathy, people will feel safe talking to you.

Empathy is one of the most crucial skills for a great leader to develop.

Funnily enough, in one *Forbes* article I read recently, Aliza Knox – its author – proposed that the new meaning of CEO should be Chief Empathy Officer. And why not? If it needs to trickle down to every leader in the organisation, that could be an excellent way to start. And not leaving it with the title, of course, but actively working on it [4].

It is also important to note that you don't need to choose between empathy and accountability. This may have been the case in the past and not what enlightened organisations need in the present day. The best leaders combine both. A drive for results and empathy are not mutually exclusive.

As Phillip Kane, CEO and Managing Partner of Grace Ocean, put it in an *Inc.* article that appeared in February 2022: "Caring leaders know that it is possible to behave with empathy while holding others accountable to deliver results. They know that empathy is not always about being nice to people. It's about being aware of, understanding, and respecting the viewpoints of others. One of the biggest differences between an empathetic leader and a narcissistic leader can be observed when the business falls on rocky or difficult times. A narcissistic leader will most likely blame everyone but themselves and engage in insults, accusations and other possible attacks. Meanwhile, the more empathetic leader will put the situation behind them, learn from failures, set new goals, and talk in a way that does not detract from the dignity of the person they are addressing" [5].

If we are still asking ourselves, "Are empathy and accountability not mutually exclusive?" it is because, unfortunately, empathetic leaders were not the norm in historic HR models. Empathy has become a sought-after skill for C-level leaders in the corporate environment. Empathetic leaders have more innovative, productive teams and are more likely to retain good employees. About 90% of GenZ employees are more likely to stay with an empathetic employer.

These empathetic leaders know that results matter. They know that business is a game where their results are constantly scrutinised. They are deadly serious about achieving the objectives for which they are responsible. But they likewise know that results are more likely to be achieved through consideration than ruthlessness and by making all stakeholders party to successes (or even failures) rather than by making it just about themselves. They would include those they lead in decision-making and place value on what they have to say. They recognise and reward the achievement of others. They believe that the mental health of those who follow them is not something to be poked fun at but something to be cared about and cared for. They deliver results by caring for others. And they know better than to destroy trust over a short-term triviality like a missed objective.

So, how might one develop empathy?

I think it is essential to acknowledge that some people are born empathetic. We have probably met several in our lives. But for most, we sit somewhere on a grey scale between black and white – a narcissist or an empath. Our goal should be to assess where we sit on the scale first and then begin a journey of self-improvement.

Possibly the best starting point is active listening by paying attention to the other person, not using one's phone or looking at one's watch during the exchange, and listening carefully to words, observing facial expressions, body language and overall behaviour.

By talking to people, asking them about their interests, paying attention to what they are doing and praising them for what they are doing well, and encouraging them to speak up with their own ideas.

There is a well-known adage among landscape designers about determining where to lay a concrete path. Instead of thinking hard about where people ought to walk, observe where they do walk. Don't pour concrete yet. Lay down the lawn, wait for a path in the grass to get worn and then pave it.

The lesson here is not to pour your energies into upfront analysis but to create the conditions for observing peoples' actual behaviour. To achieve such conditions, there are two things you must have: data and patience. It goes without saying that any data collected must come from something observable, ideally a trend or pattern. As with the worn path in the lawn, it can take time – and patience – for patterns to emerge. But once you observe those patterns, you'll have a reliable signal that's priceless. It is far more valuable than what you think they do or what they say they do. Both are easier to come by, but both can be misleading.

From whom could we learn empathy best? What about great coaches? How do they ask and listen?

I especially like how Ed Batista describes it in his *Harvard Business Review* article appeared in 2015: "Coaching is about connecting with people, inspiring them to do their best, and helping them to grow. It's also about challenging people to come up with the answers they require on their own".

At this point, it is worth pointing out the difference between coaching and training. While a trainer will provide instructions to transfer their knowledge to us, a coach will provide an education that enhances our knowledge. A coach will build a relationship to guide us with a long-term plan, whilst a trainer tells us what to do in a much more formal way to achieve a short-term plan.

Coaching is far from an exact science, and all leaders have to develop their style, but we can break down the process into practices that any manager will need to explore and understand. Here are the three most important ones identified by Ed Batista [6]:

ASK: In coaching conversations, it is crucial to spend as much time as needed in the initial stages and resist the urge to jump ahead. The more time spent in a pure inquiry asking open-ended questions, the more likely the conversation will challenge your employee to develop their creative solutions. The unique knowledge gained from their proximity to the problem will surface. A coach will get the person to arrive at their best solution by asking the right questions.

LISTEN: Hearing is a cognitive process that happens internally – we absorb, interpret and sometimes understand sound. But listening is a whole-body process between two people that makes the other person feel heard. Listening in a coaching context requires significant eye contact. This ensures you capture as much data about the other person as possible – facial expressions, gestures, tics – and conveys a strong sense of interest and engagement. Effective listening requires focused attention. Coaching is fundamentally incompatible with multitasking. It is critical to eliminate distractions. Turn off your phone, close your laptop and find a dedicated space without interruption. This will be the only possible context to make the other person feel heard.

EMPATHISE: When you empathise, you comprehend another person's point of view and vicariously experience their emotions. I especially like how Brené Brown, a research professor at the University of Houston, puts it. Her work focuses on the topics of vulnerability, courage, worthiness and shame. Empathy, Brown notes, is "the antidote to shame". When employees need your help, they are likely experiencing some form of shame, even if it's just mild embarrassment – and the more serious the problem, the deeper the shame. Brown defines shame as "the intensely painful feeling or experience of believing that we are flawed and therefore unworthy of love and belonging." Feeling and expressing empathy is critical to helping the other person defuse their embarrassment and begin thinking creatively about solutions [7].

You may think that if empathy is not very present in corporate and has not been part of leaders' essential skills until recently, it is likely because it was not an essential requirement – no need for empathy where there is no shame. There is no shame where there is no feeling of unworthy belonging. This was not part of the reality in nepotistic and narcissistic organisations since reality was built differently. There is no way to dismiss empathy in modern and inclusive organisations.

You don't need to be the expert when you coach as a leader. You don't need to be the smartest or most experienced person in the room. And you don't need to have all the solutions. But you need to connect with people, inspire them to do their best, help them search inside and discover their answers.

Besides coaching, you can demonstrate empathy as a leader at every possible interaction with people. Make sure everyone in your organisation feels included, especially in these days of remote or hybrid working environments. Sometimes it is even advised to over-communicate updates to ensure transparency. Be flexible and allow for flexibility in your organisations. You will inevitably develop trust within your teams. Take the time to ensure that emails you send aren't misinterpreted as rude or abrasive – for rudeness is highly contagious. Mitigate interruptions in video calls, and monitor meetings to ensure that the speakers up last don't get cut off. Encourage managers to avoid sending so many emails that it feels like harassment, to not cancel Zoom sessions at the last minute and to try their hardest not to snap or be abrasive. Also, it is imperative to be curious about employees' lives, at least to the degree that helps you connect and empathise with their experiences and within the bounds of courtesy. Another effective way to acknowledge the human factor and generate loyalty is by accommodating other people's needs before they even ask – they will be surprised and impressed. This shows genuine empathy.

1.4 Being able to shift your perspective

"My leadership transition from a manager position was in Retail", said François. "In the leading company in the industry. When I was merely 30 years old and with the guidance of a great manager and the CEO, both were already charismatic leaders in the industry and knew me well and helped me enormously in this transition". François was having a chat with his mentee. They usually exchanged every second month or so. François is French and has evolved inside brands belonging to one of the French Luxury Groups these past years. Just recently, his dream has come true: to be transferred to Japan. But the most amazing of this new adventure is that he had made it to the General Manager position for one of these leading French luxury fashion brands.

"The key word that has guided me as a young leader in Retail is motivation – the daily motivation of my team. A Client Advisor in a luxury boutique does not have a rigid agenda but needs to be prepared for the unexpected and always provide excellent service. This is why motivation is the key driver to achieving this. Leading by example, developing trust, the team to know they always have your back, giving them clear and attainable objectives, plus a strong sense of belonging, all those aspects helped me develop the motivation of my first teams. It is clear that it was my responsibility to create the most favourable atmosphere for this trust and commitment to flourish. While I always took time to show them the way and gave them the necessary training and resources, I also allowed for favourable downtime for employees to relax, ideally together, as a team. I seldom came with them in my newly acquired position and additional responsibility. The team spirit was achieved through a healthy competition towards other teams and brands to make our objectives, while whining about others within the team was not tolerated".

François knew that he would need to adapt some motivational levers he used back in the day to his new reality in Japanese culture. But this challenge was something he was looking forward to. Getting out of his comfort zone would allow him to grow. He may fall flat on his face at some time, but he felt safe and confident that he would recover from those pitfalls.

"Luxury is an industry where the direct-to-consumer model prevails, either off- or online. Why is that? And does it mean that this industry understands its customers best, as we would expect?"

"Hmmm", François found his mentee's question quite interesting. In fact, during their exchange sessions, he always appreciated the reverse-mentoring possibilities, very often through candid questions.

"Well, since quite early stages – let's say in the late '90s and early 2000s – it was quite clear that to ensure great customer service within the established standards of the brand, the best option would be the owned retail network. By controlling the sales chan-

nel, customer satisfaction could be ensured. Don't forget customers pay a high premium and deserve the best quality in their product during the purchase moment. At those times, customer satisfaction through best-in-class service was the guiding principle. Later came the acknowledgement that loyalty and repeat purchases could be achieved by anticipating and surpassing customer expectations. How? Through customer knowledge and data. And how would you get to these best? Again, through directly operated stores! Double bonus. Bingo. There are some other benefits in terms of profitability, but this is another story. So, back to your question: absolutely yes: the Luxury Industry and its prevailing direct-to-consumer model – even years before eCommerce – should lead the way in knowing and understanding its customers best".

In the previous section, we discussed the importance of empathy in modern and inclusive organisations and the fact that it is a crucial skill for leaders to succeed in the current business context. In this section, we will go a step further, analysing the importance of compassion in business and how this – in contrast to toughness – can lead to improved results, especially in creative and innovative industries.

Generally, leaders with unhealthy temperaments will negatively impact a company's culture and its organisation. Leaders who exhibit negative emotions and unkind behaviours will affect the air that is the breath inside the organisation. As we have stated previously, rudeness is contagious.

An angry response by a leader will erode loyalty and trust. As Stanford University neurosurgeon Dr James Doty states in an article written by Emma Seppälä – PhD and faculty member at the Yale School of Management – and published by *Harvard Business Review*: "Creating an environment where there is fear, anxiety and lack of trust makes people shut down. If people have fear and anxiety, we know from neuroscience that their threat response is engaged, their cognitive control is impacted. As a consequence, their productivity and creativity diminish" [8].

On the contrary, brain imaging studies show that our brain's stress response is lower when we feel safe with lower stress and higher creative potential.

In the same article, Adam Grant, professor at the Wharton Business School and bestselling author of "Give & Take", points out: "When you respond in a frustrated, furious manner, the employee becomes less likely to take risks in the future because she/he worries about the negative consequences of making mistakes. In other words, you kill the culture of experimentation that is critical to learning and innovation." Grant refers to research by Fiona Lee at the University of Michigan that shows promoting a culture of safety, rather than fear of negative consequences, helps encourage the spirit of experimentation so critical for creativity [9].

This leads us to question how we can respond with more compassion the next time an employee makes an error. What is shared by Emma Seppälä is to forgive. She explains a whole journey to achieve that, but ultimately, forgiveness should be the goal.

The first thing would be to take a moment. Get a handle on your own emotions – anger, frustration or whatever the case may be. You must take a step back and control your emotional response first because if you act with an emotional knee-jerk, you will not be considerate and rational about your response to the problem. By stepping back and taking time to reflect, you enter a mental state allowing a more thoughtful, reasonable and discerned response. Practising meditation has been shown to help improve your self-awareness and emotional control.

Then, it is crucial to engage with empathy. Put yourself in your employee's shoes. The ability to perspective-take is a very valuable one. Studies have shown that it helps you see aspects of the situation you may not have noticed, leading to better results in interactions and negotiations. And because positions of power tend to reduce our natural inclinations for empathy, it is imperative that managers have the self-awareness to make sure they practice seeing situations from their employee's points of view.

Finally, forgive. Forgiveness not only strengthens your relationship with your employee by promoting loyalty, but it turns out it is also good for you. It lowers your blood pressure and that of the person you're forgiving. When trust, loyalty and creativity are high, and stress is low, employees are happier and more productive, and turnover is lower. Positive interactions even make employees healthier and require fewer sick days. Other studies have shown how compassionate management improves customer service, client outcomes and satisfaction.

At this point, I would like to include some valuable tips from a coach who helps leaders imagine what is possible and make their boldest visions real. Her name is Carrie-Ann Barrow. What she suggests to transition into a leadership position is the following [10]:

The first and most important topic is to shift your perspective. Start by celebrating the journey that has gotten you to this point. Think about what you did in your previous position and what you are charged with in your new role. How will your perspective change? Don't fall into the trap of trying to do both your old and new jobs. Then, decide before doing. Pause, evaluate and make informed decisions before you do anything. Create a new habit: instead of immediately doing an assigned task, use your new high-level leadership perspective and decide about that task. What are different ways you could approach this? What is the best way for you to use your resources? Do you delegate or possibly hire a temp? A common challenge for new leaders is learning to communicate with subordinates who used to be peers, mainly when some were competing for the same position. In these situations, it helps to disarm people with empathy and candour and then lead. It is also very critical to pay attention to the needs of both your leadership and your team. Listen actively: What are their goals and priorities? What is getting in their way? How can you help while still holding each member accountable? Finally, you will find your leadership approach with time and practice. You will either be leading from the front (a visionary leader), from within (a purpose-led leader), from beside (a collaborative leader), from behind (a servant leader) or from the field (an intuitive leader). Challenge yourself to think about how you can incorporate all of these styles. Do you naturally gravitate toward one approach? How does it serve you? What other leadership approaches could be effective in different scenarios?

As you start a new chapter in your career, you have an opportunity to create your brand as a leader. Don't be afraid to show others who you are and what you bring to the table, and don't let perfectionism hold you back. Too many leaders think that they have to be perfect to be successful. This is simply not true. Leaders make mistakes and fail every day. Never stop asking questions, and never stop learning, and you will keep growing as a leader.

1.5 Business is all about people and relationships

"Tell me, Peter, what has caught your attention the most in your new role and our corporate culture after these first 100 days? Is there anything that you wish to exchange with me?"

Peter was glad this question came up; otherwise, he would have put it forward. After grasping his thoughts, he continued, "Well, yes, in fact, I wanted to discuss a couple of topics with you".

"First of all, I really appreciated our President mentioning – during the welcome days for newcomers within this past year – that people and their enthusiasm make Companies". I fully agree with this statement and appreciate corporate environments where positive energy gets fuelled. It is such a driver for engagement and motivation. When the opposite happens, I feel it drains everyone's morale, things don't get done, and anxiety does not allow for open discussions. I like Albert Einstein's quote: "Stay away from negative people; they have a problem for every solution".

"Oh, that's so true, Peter; I agree. Positive energy fuels enthusiasm, and I am always looking forward to ways of increasing it".

"There is another topic I wish to ask you: how would you rate consensus to build loyalty? Do you think it is always necessary? As you know, I have evolved mainly in big organisations, where consensus was essentially the go-to way of working. This does not mean that dissent was not welcomed; it's just that most of the time, compromise solutions were privileged by the leadership team. How is it here?"

"Look, Peter, this is a fascinating question, which includes an aspect of corporate values and cultural preferences in society. I believe compromise solutions are not always the best; it depends on the topic's criticality. Also, if you believe that consensus is wrong, you have an obligation to disagree and state your point of view. I will totally recommend acting this way. And in regards to loyalty, it definitely does not require conformity".

"Thanks so much, Lucy; this open conversation means a lot to me".

Handling emotions correctly in business can make all the difference in your trajectory from manager to leader. A good leader will promote the idea of mastering emotions and not letting them get in the way.

What would the absence of emotions in business look like? Probably a very apathetic and tedious environment where it would be difficult to thrive and succeed. Likewise, an environment filled with toxic emotions would be unhealthy and unsustainable. We would wish for an environment where people in business master emotions for the benefit of everyone.

Research shows that, for better or worse, emotions influence employees' commitment, creativity, decision-making, work quality and the likelihood of sticking around. Ultimately you will see the effects on the bottom line. It becomes crucial to monitor and manage people's feelings as deliberately as you do their mindset.

Positive affect in business – such as cheerfulness, pride, enthusiasm, energy and joy – reflects present safety, satisfaction and achievement.

Here is the next topic to focus on: how to become a genuinely likeable person.

An excellent first impression is crucial: smile, make eye contact and be engaging. Most people may be able to handle this, but being genuinely likeable over the long haul is tougher.

The best way to view this achievement would be to remind ourselves of what Maya Angelou – civil rights activist and poet – described once: "I've learned that people will forget what you said, people will forget what you did, but people will never forget how you made them feel."

Building and maintaining excellent relationships, consistently influencing others in a good way and making people feel better about themselves are things relatively few people can do.

Jeff Haden provides an excellent overview of the most essential 11 topics to focus on. I transcribe them as they are in his article since I fully embrace all of them [11]:

1. **Give before you receive**, knowing you might never receive.
Never think about what you can get. Focus on what you can provide. Giving is the only way to establish a real connection and relationship.

2. **Shift the spotlight to other people**.
No one receives enough praise. You will make them feel more accomplished and a lot more important, and they will love you for making them feel that way.

3. **Listen three times more than you talk**.
Ask questions, maintain eye contact, smile, frown, nod and respond verbally and non-verbally. Don't offer advice unless you are asked. Speak only if you have something important to say – and always define important as what matters to the other person, not to you.

4. **Never practice selective hearing**.
Charismatic people listen closely to everyone, making all of us, regardless of our position, feel like we have something in common with them. Because we do, we are all human.

5. **Be thoughtful simply because you can.**
Instead of turning idle time into "me time", likeable people use their free time to do something nice – not because they are expected to, but just because they can.

6. **Put your stuff away**.
Don't check your phone, don't glance at your monitor and don't focus on anything else, even for a moment. You can never connect with others if you are busy connecting with your stuff. Give the gift of your full attention.

7. **Never act self-important**.
The only people impressed by your stuffy, pretentious, self-important self are other stuffy, pretentious, self-important people. The rest aren't impressed. They are irritated, put off and uncomfortable.

8. . . . ..**Because other people are always more important.**
You already know what you know. That stuff isn't important because it's already yours; you can't learn anything from yourself. But you don't know what other people know, and everyone, no matter who they are, knows things you don't know. That makes other people more important to you than you – because you can learn from them.

9. **Choose your words wisely.**
The words you use impact the attitude of others. Always frame your narrative with a positive angle. We all want to associate with happy, enthusiastic, fulfilled people. The words you choose can help others feel better about themselves – and make you feel better about yourself.

10. **Never talk about the failings of other people**.
We do not respect people who dish the dirt on others. It's not a desirable characteristic to laugh at other people's expense. If you do, people will wonder if you sometimes laugh at them. Similarly, if you are asked about potential weaknesses in a process, never identify people or names, but rather systems, functions or departments, and never make it personal.

11. . . . ..**But readily admit your own failings.**
You don't have to be incredibly successful to be remarkably charismatic. But you do have to be very genuine to be particularly charismatic. Be humble. Share your screwups. Admit your mistakes and laugh at yourself. People won't laugh at you. People will laugh with you. They'll like you better for it and want to be around you much more.

This makes me think about a remarkable Ted Talk in which two Stanford Business School teachers – Jennifer Aaker and Naomi Bagdonas – reflect on the power of humour in leadership [12].

They speak of moments of levity versus moments of gravity. It seems that leaders with a sense of humour are seen as 27% more motivating. Their teams are more bonded and creative. When we laugh, our brains release a cocktail of hormones: endorphins (like a runner's high), we lower our cortisol, making us feel calmer, and we release dopamine, the same hormone released during sex, making us feel more bonded. They say that, as far as our brains are concerned, laughing is like exercising, meditating and having sex at the same time. But logistically more accessible and efficient.

How to look for humour in our lives? Jennifer and Naomi mention that we should not look for what's funny but just notice what's true – looking at the world differently.

A psychological principle called the "priming effect" says that our brains are wired to see what we have been set up to expect. In essence, we find what we choose to look for. We must shift how we interact with the world and how it interacts back. It's all about being human, from transactional to human. Humour is a choice, and the balance between gravity and levity gives power to both. We can do profound things without taking ourselves so seriously. Start by practising but not thinking, "Will this make me sound funny?"; instead ask, "How will this make other people feel?" Start with what's true and start small.

This makes me think of the late Javier Marías – one of Spain's most celebrated novelists, sometimes referred to as "the Proust of our times" – once opined on telling something true: "The only way to tell something true is under the elegant and reserved disguise of an invention, precisely because the one who invents or fables – if he does it well and with consideration – will never yield to rude and bizarre impositions of reality". He read this in his speech in Santillana del Mar at a tribute organised in 2008 by his publishing house. I would agree with this observation and add that humour allows for invention and exaggeration to make your point more relevant [13].

1.6 How to normalise emotions in business

It was already late. Isabella was still at her computer in her office. She knew she needed to leave soon. Staying this long always seemed ludicrous to her. But she is also a person with a strong work ethic coupled with an ardent capacity to focus, and she was, at this moment, analysing a recent problem that she would like to solve sooner than later.

During a recent off-site leadership program, she learned about the NVC process, in other words: "The non-violent communication process". Since then, she has thought of possible techniques to help her get around some extremely difficult people in her organisation.

Since hearing some of Angela Ahrendt's or Pol Polman's podcasts, Isabella concluded that this could transition her into a "servant" leadership style that she had wanted to develop anyway. She has thought that evolving her communication skills using such a technique might also influence her leadership style.

On the other hand, she could also evolve towards a more collaborative leadership style in some aspects. In fact, this is what she has set herself as a goal for tomorrow at the feedback meeting with her team members after a key milestone gathering of one of her most critical current projects.

She would keep the servant leadership style for the one-on-one feedback sessions with her team. That was it – she had decided and could finally pack up and head home.

Isabella switched off the computer, closed the door and hurried to the lift.

Feelings have a tainted reputation in business. I would suggest that this bias needs to be challenged. In business, we are conditioned to believe emotions are less legitimate than thoughts. We all know the saying, "It's not personal; it's just business." This statement implies that rational logic supersedes subjective feelings. Yet, feelings are part of human experience, and leaving them out of decision-making, judgment and interaction is impossible and imprudent.

What I find helpful in any circumstance is to remind myself of the old adage of "cool head, firm hand and warm heart". Feelings need to be acknowledged and canalised. A warm heart is definitely part of the equation.

So, what tools do we have to handle emotions in a corporate situation? How might we normalise their usage of them? What would be my suggestion?

When I first came across non-violent communication techniques during a leadership retreat, I learned that there is one overriding strategy: practice. It is a whole process with four steps to master, and to master, we need to practice.

The entire process is about observation, feelings, needs and requests. In a way, it resonates as an additional step to mastering assertiveness [14].

But before we go further into the NVC process, I would like to give this process a contextual framework. In other words, to agree first that the mind is dually processing thought and emotion, determining if the situation is positive or negative and then resolving how to act. Here are two big takeaways from neuroscience research as it pertains to business:

– Cognition and emotion are not handled separately by the brain
– The resulting intentions have huge implications on employee goal pursuits and organisational outcomes

Cognition, emotion and motivation are inextricably linked and combined as they drive how people perceive and respond. Pretending that feelings don't matter in business sabotages interpersonal effectiveness, sustainable results, employee commitment and job satisfaction. No matter your position in the organisation, your responsibility is to 1) acknowledge the emotion; 2) modulate the highs and lows and 3) integrate emotions so that you can act with more positive intent, motivation and awareness of the whole situation.

To start normalising emotion, accept feeling as feeling. Don't react to it or judge it. This goes for both your own emotions and those of others. Accept the emotion as natural and neutral, not right or wrong. Doing this lessens the likelihood that shame enters the equation. Tell yourself that all feelings are permissible; it's just that certain behaviours are not – violence, insults, outbursts, etc.

Unpleasant emotions can cease to be unpleasant by not overly identifying with them. Getting some distance from the feeling helps us know it's not us; it's information. Writing is often a great way to externalise and observe emotions.

After that, study your emotion. Get curious. Sometimes everything appears logical, but you still don't feel right about a situation. Seek the learning available in the emotion. You will probably be approaching your "gut feeling" or intuition. It takes some practice and experience over your logical apprenticeship, also in business.

One great leader in business who speaks openly about instincts is Angela Ahrendts, former CEO of Burberry and EVP Retail for Apple. She states that using your instinct is the only way to know if you trust someone. Use it while slowing down. Take the necessary time, don't talk too much, but rather listen. Let your feelings emerge and observe. Ask yourself, for example: Do I believe this person? Do I like this person? Would I travel around the world with this person? Is there a nice and easy flow established with this person?

Without trust, it is difficult to build respect; without trust comes judgementalism; this results in a lack of unity, and if people are not united, they will never make an impact.

It is crucial to realise sooner than later that teams succeed or fail, not individuals; everyone has to work together for a common goal as a collective and collaborative effort.

This is why Angela Ahrendts believes that trust is probably the ultimate value, together with integrity and respect. Because once you trust, you can be open and non-judgmental. In this context, you will allow yourself to be vulnerable, which others find reassuring since you will be appreciated as authentic. Don't forget that everyone is insecure in one way or another and that you can't make everyone like you. This is why it is so important to focus on impact and understanding why we are doing what we are doing. Once you create this positive energy consciously, a self-fulfilling spin will begin to act, as Angela says in her podcast "Lessons from a CEO". The closer you are to your teams and colleagues, and the better your relationships, the more your team members will wish to give and not let you down as a boss or their colleagues [15].

Let's get back now to the NVC Process. The required outcome is the same: finding an intelligent way to handle and canalise emotions for good. That is, to build trust.

If you are at the centre of the process, you should initiate by clearly expressing how you feel without blaming or criticising. Then you move to the concerns of the person whose feelings you are trying to address.

Then you state what you **observe** that does or does not contribute to your well-being.

Next, you explain how you **feel** in relation to what you observe.

Then, you clearly state your **need** that causes those feelings.

And finally, you **request** the concrete actions you would like taken, which would enrich your life without demanding.

The phrase could be something like: "When I see, hear . . . (what is an observed situation free from my evaluations) . . . I feel . . . (this and that emotion, rather than thought) because I need/value . . . (this and that)." The following and decisive phrase should be: "Would you be willing to . . . ."

If, on the contrary, you are setting the other person in the centre of the process – it is their feelings you are trying to address – then you should instead initiate receiving empathically how you are, without hearing blame or criticism.

Then you state what the other person **observes** that does or does not contribute to their well-being.

Next, you explain how this makes them feel about what they observe.

Then, you clearly state the **need** that causes those feelings.

And finally, you clearly **request** the concrete actions they would like to be taken by you. This empathetically means receiving that which would enrich their life without hearing any demand.

In this case, the phrase could be something like: "When you see/hear . . . (an observed situation without your evaluations) . . . you feel . . . (this and that emotion or sensation, rather than a thought) . . . because you need/value . . . (this and that)." The next and decisive phrase should be: "Would you like me to . . . ."

I would suggest that you start practising this technique to normalise emotions in an effective way in business. Nevertheless, what I have observed is that it requires that you are not only perceived as a relatively assertive person but also that your empathy for that person is perceived as authentic. First, you may need to work on those two aspects to achieve higher success rates. And very important: if the person you are addressing has a strong inclination for not trusting others, this process will not be easy, like pushing water uphill. Those are the most complex characters for the NVC Process.

1.7 Technical versus relational skills

Hard skills refer to employees' job-related knowledge and abilities to perform their duties effectively. On the other hand, soft skills are the personality traits that help employees thrive in the workplace.

To differentiate both sets of skills, I instead prefer to use the terms "technical" and "relational" skills. Those terms are more self-explanatory and do not denote a sense of power. The term "soft" may transmit a particular judgement and bias and indicate a specific weakness for some people.

It also shows that "soft" skills transcend the workplace since they are developed and needed for life. "Hard" or "Technical" skills are related to our ability to get a specific job done, whilst "Soft" or "Relational" skills allow us to better navigate our lives, not just our jobs.

It won't be new for you to read about the dilemma of hiring for expertise versus hiring for attitude. Which one is best, in your own opinion? Or in which circumstances is one or the other preferable?

As Seth Godin argues in one of his latest papers, the reality of the millions of online job listings is overwhelming: "From the title to the requirements, companies hire for expertise" [16].

If the organisation needs people with expertise in the top decile, they will have to pay more and go to extraordinary lengths to find and retain that sort of skill. So most companies don't try. They create jobs that can be done pretty well by people with average expertise. That means that the actual differentiator in almost every job is attitude. From plumbers to carpenters to radiologists to pharmacists, someone with extraordinary human skills (honesty, commitment, compassion, resilience, enrolment in the journey, empathy, willingness to be coached – the actual skills we care about) will be the one to outperform the average.

If this is so obviously true, why don't organisations hire for character and personality and train for knowledge?

In my opinion, this would be because the attitude and human skills still don't have the value they deserve in the corporate world or because they are difficult to both measure and be used as a benchmark for employees' potential. Human skills end up being the "icing on the cake" when they should be the fundamental columns of corporate culture and should be predominant in the hiring and promoting processes.

If we look at "The Triangle of Success", attitude stands at 1/3 of success factors, human skills at another 1/3 and knowledge as the final 1/3. The reality shows, however, a very different picture and the weightings used in hiring processes.

The aim would be to develop more space for attitude and skills.

Why? Because it is what one does that changes the world, not what one knows. And one does not need to start doing great things but rather start small in this journey. The best way I have come across to illustrate this is by watching, arguably, one of the best motivational speeches ever made. It was delivered in 2014 by Admiral McRaven when he gave a commencement address at the University of Texas in Austin – "If you want to change the world, start off by making your bed". It would be worth your while to check it out on YouTube – the attitudes to master to be able to change the world [17].

How to measure respect and humility? How do people treat others? Especially when no one is watching? Have you found someone that has helped you through life?

How can I tell if this person in front of me is courageous? Do they take risks? Do they step up when times are tough? Do they face down the bullies? Have I seen them lift up the downtrodden?

And what about their resilience levels? Do they move forward quickly when life has not treated them fairly? Are they not afraid to fail often? Do they give up? Never?

Are these questions not possible to answer? How do we instinctively judge our leaders? Be it in corporate, politics, communities, etc. Is it not through these types of attitude and personality ratings?

1.8 How to embrace key relational skills in business

Isabella took a break. She had been practising her speech for over an hour at this point. She is finding ways to memorise key topics, explaining them with ease, without interruptions and with good body language. She has already watched five moments of her speech that she has recorded on her phone. Thanks to the small table tripod, she finds this practice accessible and helpful. She immediately adjusts and records only crucial moments, not the whole speech.

Before, she studied her voice modulation, tone, and breaks and recorded only her voice. To improve her public speaking skills, she finds it much more interesting to do it now with the camera, rather than just the voice recorder.

She feels she has improved dramatically over this past year just with this simple technique. Some people seem just to cream it, not her; she needs practice, practice and more practice.

Like Isabella, legendary investor Warren Buffett grew up terrified of public speaking. What changed his life was taking a Dale Carnegie public speaking course. Remember: what you do changes the world, not what you know! Today, the only thing you'll see hanging from his office wall is the certification from Carnegie's course.

These are three simple tips he shares that have worked for him [18]:

1. **Be a storyteller**. The reason is that stories build trust with your audience or the person sitting in a one-on-one meeting. In Richard Branson's words: "What moves people is someone credible." We all see that very clearly in the example of social media engagement. If you did not watch the captivating presentation of the iPhone in 2007 by Steve Jobs, please do. A simple story that inspired millions of people.

2. **Watch other speakers**. Quite simply, observe other people who excel in this human skill. One of my favourites (along with W. Buffet) is Simon Sinek. We need to focus on how to master the three moments of a speech. The introduction: grabbing your audience's attention with an engaging first sentence, possibly including a personal story. The main message: enabling emotional connections with an easy structure to follow. The conclusion: a strong (clear and concise) takeaway contributing to a compelling call to action.

3. **Watch yourself**. As mentioned before, to develop your assertiveness skills, here also, recording and watching yourself for a few minutes is very helpful. It will take a few days of practice until you get comfortable with how you're presenting yourself.

Having shared how one of the greatest investors overcame his biggest weakness leads me to the next major weakness lurking in corporate organisations: ineffective communication amongst their members.

In my opinion, focusing on efficient communication within the organisation can help immensely to achieve higher performance. We may probably not need *The Economists*' Intelligence Unit to point out the obvious in a report ("Communication Barriers in the modern workplace"), where they found that poor communication results in low morale, delayed projects, obstacles to innovation, and worse – lost sales and lost clients. I believe we can all relate to that. And I have sometimes thought that life would be much easier with clear and fluent communication within the workplace and a more rapid go-to-market for many projects. Slow processes may get in the way; this is where small teams and start-up organisations tend to be better equipped for these scenarios. But in current times of high uncertainty, where organisations need to be agile and execute at speed, not everything should rely on simplifying processes and reducing ambiguity [19].

Further on in the report, an interesting fact is highlighted: in an organisation – no matter the size – different workplace communication styles will cohabit. And navigating efficiently within these various styles will be fundamental to better performance. Understanding that professionals fall into one of four categories is paramount to communicating effectively. By this means, we can identify them and adapt accordingly.

The four workplace communication styles stated are: personal, intuitive, functional or analytical.

What was an eye-opener to me in this report is that style is not determined by how empathetic someone is whilst communicating or how casual, straight to the point, concise, long-winded, comical or stoic as it may be. These attributes highlight an approach but not a style. A communication style is how you share information with others, that is, what kind of information you prioritise and value in workplace conversations. And the same applies to how you like information to be shared with you.

Once we can recognise our own and our colleagues' communication style, we may become more effective in our communication because we can speak to different people in "their language". This will allow us to know what information to emphasise so the listener can more clearly and immediately understand the value of your idea, recommendation, instruction or call to action. Be aware that professionals with different communication styles emphasise and convey different information when speaking.

The overview and implications of all four styles are provided by Lawrese Brown – founder at C-track Training – in an *Inc.* article titled, "How to overcome the top cause of poor communication in the workplace":

1. **Personal Communication Style**. These professionals emphasise how other stakeholders feel. They prioritise details related to shared interests and values when sharing and listening for information. They need to know how your idea, recommendation, instruction or call to action will influence the stakeholder's attitude or point of view.

2. **Functional Communication Style**. These professionals emphasise the order of operations. When sharing and listening for information, they prioritise tasks and timelines. They need to know how your idea, recommendation, instruction or call to action impacts their day-to-day or department plan.

3. **Intuitive Communication Style**. These professionals emphasise the big picture. They prioritise the desired result and overarching story when sharing and listening for information. They need to know how your idea, recommendation, instruction or call to action helps them achieve an important goal in the near future.

4. **Analytical Communication Style**. These professionals emphasise accuracy and mathematical reasoning. When sharing and listening for information, they prioritise data and facts. They need to know how your idea, recommendation, instruction or call to action provides an explicit path to a performance indicator or established outcome.

Mastering the awareness of your individual communication style and the information style of your colleagues will help you effectively share ideas, seek buy-in, deliver instructions, articulate visions and share recommendations.

To find out what your audience's preferred information style is, address the topic directly with a question: "What information would most help you understand the value of this idea/project/initiative? Is it stakeholder impact, analysis and evidence, day-to-day implementation or a broad overview of achieving the bottom line?"

With these minor adjustments in the short term, we will reduce stress and reduce wasted time and, in the long run, allow for a more significant impact.

At this point, I would also like to emphasise developing some essential relational skills to become the leader others wish to work for. I believe this to be the ultimate goal of a leader. To have the necessary magnetism for others to relish being part of your team, to accomplish great things together and to learn from you.

Once you're consistently achieving results, your promotion prospects will come down to dependable relationships. If it's clear to management that you attract followership among your colleagues and achieve results through others, they're likely to bet on you the next time a promotion opens up.

If you wish to become a kind of "magnet leader", so to speak, you need to develop a great employee experience. People within your sphere of influence will have become aware and value very positively how you do the following:

1. Provide freedom for your team members and support them in their personal development.
2. Show recognition of their accomplishments and compassion in their moments of failure.

As the great Jack Welch said: "Before you are a leader, success is all about growing yourself. When you become a leader, success is all about growing others [20]."

Developing a sense of trust and belonging is vital to creating a space where freedom prevails instead of controlling management and giving the team a purpose and a way of doing things that allows them to be confident and effective and not take themselves too seriously. Allowing for moments to relax and laugh is imperative. It also means checking in frequently with employees, listening to how they are doing and how they feel about their energy levels and giving obstacles new perspectives – like a bird's eye view of current projects and developments. For the employee to know that the door is always open for a catch-up, or the phone for a quick chat, will mean a lot to them. When people feel safe, included, supported and not alone, they will innovate, cooperate and show up as their complete selves at work. To be able to take risks without fear of negative consequences. It is vital to give frequent feedback to your team members and support and help them navigate constructive conflict within and outside the department. If these initiatives are in place, they will provide the best possible scenario to give employees the freedom and courage to make their own decisions. The team should be able to decide, participate, create opportunities and determine how tasks are best accomplished. Employees who feel their ideas and suggestions matter enjoy a positive employee experience. Within this intrapreneurial backdrop, they will feel invested in the company and perform at a higher level. Ultimately, suppose the employee feels supported to become the best version of themselves and be helped to prepare for their next job. In that case, they will feel that the leader prioritises their personal development over just being part of a value chain. This shows if a company cares and why training every leader as a coach is of utmost importance to help facilitate and guide employees to achieve their personal goals.

The second aspect is how to express recognition or compassion depending on the outcome of a completed mission. A leader can create and develop a great employee experience by judicious use of recognition or understanding. Recognition and appreciation is an innate and necessary human need. It is part of being human to appreciate being acknowledged for excellence at work. Leaders will need to tap into this need effectively. Most satisfied employees are those who are rewarded through a recognition program and for exhibiting organisational core values.

To become a leader others wish to work for within an organisation is undoubtedly a laudable goal, but this will not be enough to gain influence and power. Establishing good results and relationships with your team is fundamental for first-level leadership positions. Nevertheless, for leadership positions in higher echelons, you will need to excel at a different level regarding results and relationships: with your peers and the contemporaries of your boss.

This is it; once you have acquired the skills to lead a team, you must lead your peers and bosses. We will look into this in more detail in the following chapters. For the time being, what we can focus on, to begin with, are the next six points. Be warned – they require loads of dedication and practice, though:

1. Assume your ambitions, make them known and communicate your successes
2. Form alliances, do not seek to progress alone
3. Cultivate humour as a way to bounce back
4. Be able to say "no" firmly and explain why
5. Active listening that commands respect
6. Constantly adjusting between prudence and audacity

To finalise this chapter, called "Enabling Passion", I cannot feel it is complete without mentioning the difficulties I have encountered with people that either find it challenging to "find" their passion or to "show" their passion. Passion unquestionably hinges on things you love doing.

Regarding showing your passion – an example might be the net promoter scores of Client Advisors in the Luxury Retail Business. In a nutshell, it means how they express their expertise. It is about how expertise is demonstrated to others.

If you ask yourself, "What does passion look like?" Have you experienced it yourself on occasion? Alternatively, observe people when they are describing their passion. The facts are always the same: their eyes light up and widen, they use an abundance of hand gestures, they chatter, and with a slightly higher pitch of voice tone, they lean in as if telling a secret . . . . Since the person listening actually feels the same – passion is contagious.

If you express your expertise in business with passion, with your whole self and a warm heart, the receiver will be positively inclined to tune in and listen attentively, and you may start changing the world.

Simon Sinek – author of five books on leadership practices and inspirational speaker – says it differently: "Change the narrative, interpret your body as excitement instead of nervousness. It works brilliantly well." He gives an excellent example of how every journalist at the London Olympics in 2012 asked the athletes before or after their run if they were nervous. Not a single one answered "yes" to this answer. On the contrary, they all said they were excited about it. And, of course, these elite athletes had learned to interpret body stimuli – like the heartbeat rising, getting clammy hands and visualising the future – as signs of excitement rather than nervousness [21].

This technique of re-interpreting emotions for your benefit can be done in any other situation where you may become nervous: before a big audience presentation, some turbulences during a plane trip, etc. Just try it out.

Enjoy and relish the excitement and passion of what you are doing or communicating in the present moment.

Bibliography

[1]   Masterclass staff. "How to Be Assertive: 10 Tips for Becoming More Assertive".

[2]   Jenkins P. "Develop Assertiveness": @LiveOnPurposeTV, YouTube; 2018.

[3]   Permar B. "Corporate empathy is not an oxymoron". Harvard Business Review. 2015 January.

[4]   Knox A. "The new meaning of CEO: Chief Empathy Officer – 4 reasons leaders need empathy now": forbes.com; 2021.

[5]   Kane P. "You don't need to choose between empathy and accountability": Inc.; 2022.

[6]   Batista E. "How great coaches ask, listen and empathize": hbr.org; 2015.

[7]   Brown B. "Listen to shame": YouTube; 2012.

[8]   Seppälä E. "Why compassion is a better managerial tactic than toughness": hbr.org; 2015.

[9]   Grant A. "Give and take": Penguin Books; 2014.

[10]   Barrow CA. "Five strategies for transitioning into a leadership role": Forbes.com; 2021.

[11]   Haden J. "11 Habits of genuinely likable people": Inc.com; 2017.

[12]   Aaker, Bagdonas. "Why great leaders take humor seriously": ted.com; 2022.

[13]   Marías J. "la única manera de contar algo verdadero es bajo el disfraz de una invención": @Epcultura, Youtube; 2008.

[14]   Marshall, Rosenberg. "NVC Process": Center for Non-Violent Communication.

[15]   Ahrendts A. "Lessons From a CEO: The Power of Authenticity, Human Energy & Uniting As A Team": @Makingmovespodcast, YouTube; 2022.

[16]   Godin S. "Expertise Vs Attitude": https://www.Seths.Blog; 2022.

[17]   McRaven AWH. "University of Texas at Austin 2014 Commencement Address": Texas Exes, YouTube; 2014.

[18]   Schwantes M. "Warren Buffet says: All the brainpower in the world won't matter unless you have this skill": Inc.com; 2020.

[19]   Brown L. "How to overcome the top cause of poor communication in the workplace": Inc.com; 2022.

[20]   Welsh J. "Winning: The Ultimate Business How-To Book": Harperbusiness; 2005.

[21]   SimonSinek. "Nervous vs. Excited": @SimonSinek, YouTube; 2018.

Chapter Two
Fostering curiosity

Imagination is more important than knowledge.
For knowledge is limited to all we now know and understand,
while imagination embraces the entire world and
all there ever will be to know and understand.
Albert Einstein

https://doi.org/10.1515/9783111335339-003

2.1 A beginner's mind

Carla was sitting at her desk, letting her mind wander. She was trying to understand what was behind a behaviour pattern that seemed to elevate particular behaviour amongst her working entourage. What was it this time?

Carla has been VP for International Communications of this American Technology Firm for two years. She took on her role just before the pandemic and is relieved that normality has returned. She felt confident and accomplished in her job organising all the complexities of a trade show in London. The first step is orchestrating the wishes of all the invited companies and the production agency. Then ensuring all invited guests experience the desired emotions she and her teams promote on all the new technology showcased. These events fulfil her with a strong sense of responsibility and pride.

Carla realised that Monica, her new boss – who only arrived a week ago – would impact the journey with a new and unique imprint. She wishes everybody to be as innovative and creative as possible. Every meeting amongst the team should start with a game. Why is that? Carla asked. Monica explains that play is something kids do and are encouraged to do all day. Why? It helps to provide the brain with nerve connections that develop imagination and curiosity. By suggesting a game to play to start the meeting in a rotative manner, we find ourselves in a "play mode", kids mode, or said, in a different way, "safe mode". We develop a sense of trust in each other through some genuine laughs. I think it's a great idea, Carla thought to herself.

In her previous job, she experienced the most amazing off-site meetings: 3 days in the Camargue (including horse riding), wine tasting in Bordeaux, sleeping in the most amazing French chateaux and team-building activities that had long-lasting memories for her and all her colleagues. When she left her previous job, she realised that her most decisive fulfilment and bond with the brand came through the relations with her colleagues developed during those yearly off-site experience days.

Carla continued wondering about those surprisingly euphoric moments with her colleagues; the ambience achieved was that of a happy and trusting family, a little like a reunion, like a modest holiday. The achieved vibe helped blossom some true friendships within the team.

Just recently, Carla had been invited by a friend to celebrate her 30th birthday in Tuscany over a weekend. A beautiful villa in the countryside, where a group of friends enjoyed themselves playing padel tennis, sipping Aperol spritz at the pool, laughing at jokes, competing on best-tasting pasta dishes, listening to their favourite music and dancing through the night in the garden. A three-day break with the rare luxury of zero worries or responsibilities and a complete charge of happiness and energy.

It seemed amazing to Carla that an experience in a corporate environment could generate some sincere trust and come that close to friendship.

What do the worlds of Harry Potter and Peter Pan have in common? They both capture and bring out our inner child. Here is where we experience joy, laughter, friendship and freedom.

Imagination can offer us a momentary escape, allowing us to join hands with creativity. This harmonious friendship enables us to change how we perceive the world, shaping our beliefs, sparking ideas and innovation and bringing concepts yet to be sensorially experienced to our lives.

Our imaginations allow us, as humans, to experience empathy – allowing us to understand how others feel without ever having to be 'in their shoes'. Collective empathy is a robust intangible bond that unites us. Empathy is an igniting emotion; it breeds understanding, sparks passion and fuels change.

I want to introduce the concept of "Shoshin" in this Section. It is a word from Zen Buddhism and has a very valuable meaning for one's attitude to remain young in body and soul and keep a curious learning mindset. This word refers to having an attitude of openness, eagerness and lack of preconceptions when studying a subject; even at an advanced level, we should learn just as a beginner would. Particularly remarkable is the phrase used by Shunryu Suzuki – a Zen teacher. He outlines the framework behind "Shoshin", noting, "In the beginner's mind there are many possibilities; in the expert's mind there are few" [1].

He means that for new possibilities and creative choices to flourish, we need to immerse ourselves into this beginner's mindset and disregard our knowledge and expertise since it will only serve as a hindrance. So, what needs to be done? How do we achieve this state of mind?

The beginner's mindset is an orientation we must bring to the present moment. Focusing on the present moment and remaining mindful will allow us to see things as if for the first time.

It is something to bring to any moment; it has the virtue of the clarity of innocence. Sometimes we are so expert that our minds are full of our expertise. Still, it leaves us without any realm for novelty or new possibilities. In the expert's mind, they say there are very few possibilities, but in the beginner's mind, there are infinite possibilities because we come to it fresh.

When we approach challenges or learning with this freshness, it reveals tremendous, transformative possibilities we can tap into. And when you introduce it into a group dynamic, and you are open and spacious with them, the playing field is levelled; everyone's history and expertise are nullified, and they feel seen and recognised and regarded in a way they might not typically experience.

This clearly demonstrates that such a mindset is indispensable for innovation to take place. If innovation is the ultimate goal for businesses to stay competitive, companies should ignite their employees' natural curiosity and develop a culture favourable for curiosity to flourish.

Curiosity fuels imagination, and that potential fantasy 'creates the magic'. We can see the magic happening in industries like Retail, Luxury, Fashion and Technology.

Pablo Picasso, one of the most admired creative geniuses, stated: "It takes a long time to become young".

2.2 Lateral thinking

A company that is capable of completely changing the narrative in an obdurate Fashion Industry, reinventing its brand and hitting the sense of relevance for a new generation of consumers is what Gucci has accomplished with creative director Alessandro Michele at its helm. The brand understood the full meaning of inclusivity and self-expression in an industry that had a predominant "directional" narrative. That such a radical move would have such a great business success was far from predictable. If one brand in the Fashion sphere has been pushing the envelope of change, it has clearly been Gucci.

More recently, in the wake of Gucci's success, other brands have seen similar shifts. Another example of defying the odds has been Bottega Veneta. Who would dare to close down their own Instagram account and finish off all social media content from one day to another? It seems courageous and risky, yet that is precisely what they did.

Thinking of those courageous business decisions made Carla smile.

She had just left her office and was walking back home along San Francisco Bay Trail when she decided to sit on one of the terraces this sunny afternoon. There she started reading some Fast Company articles she had bookmarked for when she would have some spare time. This was when she came across a piece on these disruptive moves that have marked the Luxury Fashion Industry. She reflected upon the disruptions happening in every industry, not just tech corporations in California but also the possible similarities in how things happen inside these companies.

"How often have I deliberated new ways of doing things with peers? With peers who seem particularly averse to change, feel more than comfortable maintaining the status quo and see themselves as the guardians rather than innovators of a brand? The ones who preserve the holy grail of equilibrium in business and are nervous of and reject all ideas and alternatives that might threaten that permanence? How much time have I dedicated to those people and situations and wasted my energy with no result?" Carla relished change and innovation, but she was well aware that she had to pick her battles carefully, that sometimes she may be wrong and that things might be better left alone in some contexts.

Lateral thinking means taking a creative approach to a problem or challenge. It's a great skill to have at work. It requires the creativity we have discussed in the previous Section. And creativity requires curiosity.

What is lateral thinking?

It means being able to use your imagination to look at a problem in a fresh way and come up with a new solution.

Usually, logical thinking is used to solve problems directly and straightforwardly (also known as vertical thinking). Lateral thinking, however, looks at things from a sideways perspective (also known as horizontal thinking) to find answers that aren't immediately apparent.

Lateral thinking comes more naturally to some people than others. This is why improving these skills can be challenging.

Carla remembers a Kienbaum self-assessment workshop she did some time ago for a recruiting process. Even if those assessments are pretty time-consuming, she found it worthwhile since there is nearly always some learning from these behavioural assessments, for example, your behaviour, attitudes and connection with others. And what is more enriching in life than learning about yourself and being on a path of continuous self-improvement? The evaluators mentioned to Carla that she presented a mind that worked in a multidirectional manner and that this offered interesting ways of problem-solving. Besides the apparent advantage of navigating more complex business environments, lateral thinking may have some complications. Carla had been told, on occasion, that it can be challenging for other people – maybe more linear-thinking people – to follow her thoughts. This is crucial to bear in mind: lateral thinking is generally a very positive quality and should be developed, but communicating lateral ideas cohesively and understandably is essential when working with groups of people. You still need to be understood clearly by all you are communicating with.

At this point, an anecdote comes to Carla's mind: the first time she tried to introduce mind mapping to her team. It took her ages! She couldn't believe it. Why? While she was ready for a new communication method, her team just wasn't. They liked, understood and supported it but never really implemented it in the long run. Mind maps can be a great way to solve problems when logical thinking doesn't help. Because mind maps are visual aids, they require your brain to adjust its thought processes, which can often help you find answers unexpectedly. Mind maps allow you to put all your ideas down on paper and then step back to gather and arrange your thoughts logically and cohesively.

Despite the barriers to overcoming change, Carla used a mind-mapping application on a project that needed complex approval processes and required the involvement of many stakeholders.

We all have five senses – sight, touch, hearing, smell and taste – yet we rarely use them all to solve problems. Typically, we use our visual senses to make sense of complexities, but using our other senses can sometimes have valuable results. For example, when faced with a problem, why not speak your thoughts aloud and record them on your mobile phone? You may find something you would have missed otherwise when you listen back. Listening to my recordings was a great way to address the problem of getting feedback on my communication skills. It was instrumental in adjusting my communication voice and tone when preparing for job interviews.

Reverse rationale – or **reverse reasoning** – involves analysing what people might generally do when approaching a problem and then doing the exact opposite. If you find yourself only getting so far into a problem and then getting stuck, you might want to start at the end and work backwards. For example, identify the problem and then describe your ideal solution. From there, you can begin working backwards to find the starting point for your answer.

"What would Bruce Lee do?" might not be the most conventional start to a conversation about strategy, but it might help you shake up your thinking. A **transitional object** is someone or something embodying specific characteristics or qualities you can use to inspire new ideas. (Whether or not the person or thing concerned actually does embody those qualities in real life is irrelevant. Perception is reality.) Transitional objects can be people or things that you respect or admire – or the opposite. The point here is that they embody a set of qualities that do not exist in your organisation (or life) today. To return to the above example, Bruce Lee taught the importance of working with – rather than against – your attacker's energy.

"What's the one thing we **absolutely should not do** in this situation?" is an irreverent question that can challenge conventional thinking about an advisable course of action.

In the 2011 Black Friday edition of *The New York Times*, Patagonia published an audacious full-page ad telling viewers not to buy their jackets. Below the jacket's image was a message detailing why customers shouldn't buy the product. Among the listed factors are the 36 gallons of water required to produce the jacket (enough to fill the daily needs of 45 people), the 20 pounds of carbon dioxide emitted (24 times the weight of the jacket) and the amount of waste produced (two-thirds of its weight in waste) [2].

The message was intended to encourage people to consider the effect of consumerism on the environment and purchase only what they need. It raised awareness of an increasingly pressing problem and helped establish a strong community of people who appreciate the brand's values and products. Sales rose 30% following the campaign. European marketing director Jonathan Petty said: "Our customers expect very high quality, and that's why they always come back to us. At the same time, we help consumers change their behaviour for the better by encouraging them to make more considered purchases [3]."

Another example was when Louis Vuitton did the Olafur Eliasson art project Christmas windows "Eye See You" in 2006, making a presentation that challenged the typical commercial luxury goods display. Starting on November 9th, one "Eye see you" lamp was on view in each store window at every Louis Vuitton location worldwide. Resembling the pupil of an eye, the sculpture comprised a low-pressure sodium lamp, which consumes an insignificant amount of energy yet produces a strong monochromatic yellow light. Vibrant and illuminating, the piece creates a dialogue and connection between the store's interior and the exterior spectator, flooding the street with light as the evening darkens and transgressing the physical and psychological boundary represented by a commercial window display. Seen by millions of pedestrians, "Eye see you" became part of the urban streetscape in Paris, New York and elsewhere for the duration of its installation, combining the typical notion of window shopping with the intellectual and visually stimulating experience of looking at art [4].

At the time, I was the Head of the Louis Vuitton Madrid flagship. It was very daring for the brand not to showcase any product during the Festive Season in none of their windows worldwide. We saw it as a great pioneering step to take the opposite direction of any other competitor. It marked a sensational moment in Luxury Retail and also here grabbed the attention of the Louis Vuitton community. The intention was to continue positioning the brand in a strategic collaborative space with contemporary art and let the audience sense an artistic message. This has been followed through until today and has contributed to placing the brand entirely within the cultural space.

Bear in mind that, when innovating, it is sometimes easier and more productive to go way out there and rewind, rather than try solving problems by iterating from a conservative starting point. Even if the answer to a counterintuitive question is, in reality, altogether the wrong thing to do, it can pave the way to new thinking about what's right.

As Phil Lewis puts it in his *Forbes* article, published in 2020 [5]: Most strategies and tactics are additive – they often involve doing more things in ever-shorter timescales, diluting impact and burning people out. Asking, "What would happen **if we stopped doing** – or asked others to stop doing – the following?" can stimulate new thinking about your customer experience, employee experience or overall strategy. Doing so will also challenge your organisation's perceived wisdom about resource deployment, which can be valuable when trading is tough. Take Twitter (now X), for example – a business that can stake a reasonable claim to have changed the world – was invented not by adding but subtracting. In this example, the element taken away was the ability to use more than 140 characters when posting.

According to the author Christopher Booker, **all narratives orient around a minimal number of primary, archetypal plots** that human beings are pre-programmed to understand: Quest, Voyage and Return, Rebirth, Comedy, Tragedy, Overcoming the monster, Rags to riches. This is not just a prototype for fiction writers. Consider which plot currently underpins your business or project. Now pick another one – and rewrite the future. For example, are you running a plucky scale-up that is "overcoming the monster" in your category? What would happen if you attempted to "rebirth" your marketplace or customer offering instead? Might that change, for example, your appetite for finance? In times of crisis, the plot many leaders unconsciously follow is "tragedy". Try reframing your struggles as "voyage and return," You might be surprised at both the emotional and strategic shifts this particular exercise in lateral thinking helps you achieve.

To finalise this section on lateral thinking and its power for innovative brands and people, it is important to underline that with new methods of invention, there may be projects that struggle or even fail. Failures must be tolerated in a pioneering organisation, provided we use them as essential learning experiences and recover rapidly.

An example would be the "Not Your Mother's Tiffany" advertising campaign. It had some backlash online since it was controversial, and some customers felt alienated by the content. This does have the risk of happening at a rebranding moment, and this campaign was the most literal statement against the brands' past following the LVMH takeover. A turnaround transition must be fast to be effective and allow the customer to evolve rapidly. As Alexandre Arnault – in charge of Tiffany's Brand Communication – puts it, when reflecting on the campaign in a Wall Street Journal interview in February 2022: "The brand is looked at with binoculars and sniper guns, and people are really waiting to see what we're doing. It's quite fascinating to see the level of engagement we have." He says he stands by the campaign since it allowed new audiences to be included in the brand [6].

In the same interview, Alexandre Arnault also speaks about one of the most iconic and innovative figures in the cultural landscape, who entered the luxury sphere by direct invitation from LVMH. I am talking about Virgil Abloh. Arnault admired Abloh's 'never-be-scared mentality'. "His creativity was endless, and he constantly pushed boundaries in everything he was doing."

A culture of trust and support is required for lateral thinking to thrive. Innovation is difficult to achieve in a toxic corporate culture of threat and control. As Albert Einstein said, "A person who never made a mistake never tried anything new."

An important question might be, what exactly do we aspire for in an organisation? What behaviour do we want to promote? Should we only celebrate those who always succeed and never make mistakes? Is it best to encourage an attitude of safety and remain inside 'the good old wheels', or do we dare to motivate people to try new things? That would be the question and the framework to assess as an employee of that organisation. Every organisation is different, and there is no one-size-fits-all. Some organisations are daring, innovative and courageous; others are at their best as guardians of a legacy – some may succeed as a hybrid of the two approaches.

Whether the organisation is innovative or conservative, there is no reason why the inner spirit or culture needs to lack creativity. We should remain open for lateral thinking during strategy and objective meetings. Here is how Adam Grant – professor at Wharton and best-selling author – puts it: "The goal of a great discussion isn't to land on the same page. It's to explore different views. Nods and smiles stroke your ego and close your mind. Thoughtful questions stoke your curiosity and stretch your thinking. Consensus makes you comfortable. Dissent makes you smarter" [7].

2.3 How to foster a culture of curiosity

Carla is having lunch at their great canteen: natural light, high ceilings, small tables in different shapes, a chatty atmosphere, great menus and variety to choose from. In her last meeting before the lunch break, she had been introduced to a new colleague who had just arrived, tasked with a compelling mission for one of their most important business partners: change the mindset of the thousands of Sales Executives World Wide to become more proactive salespeople within their digital journey.

Transforming the Retail salesforce from being mainly transactional to becoming more proactive by using data and technology to be more effective will be a tough ask. The challenge seemed alluring to Carla. But she was more interested in understanding the reason her new colleague would join this company in the first place. Carla wanted to know more and suggested having lunch together.

Immediately after the first bite, Carla asked her new colleague the question, with almost no hesitation; she answered: "Oh, this is an easy one! Since it appears to me as the ultimate Yes company!"

"What do you mean?" Carla seemed confused.

"Well, as I said, it seems that the working culture here provides a framework for everything being possible, a kind of Alice in Wonderland culture and environment . . . this is the impression I get and the compelling reason for me to join. Kind of, where the first answer to initiatives would be, 'Why not?' Rather than the constant need to explain 'But why?' Or worse, to systematically become a 'No' as an answer. Due to the engrained reluctance to change and innovation. Am I right? Is that the way it works here?"

"Oh, absolutely", was Carla's answer with a grin.

I'm sure some of you may never have heard of the 'Friday attire' – it sounds ridiculous these days when the evolution has already gone into what type of hybrid work scheme a company is ok with. Have you ever thought about the possibility of corporate culture spilling over into the unwritten clothing code inside a company? I do not mean a scenario where a rather serious and traditional working environment like an investment bank has allowed a Friday dress code, meaning it's ok going 'tie-free' or 'sneakers-allowed'. Ties have almost wholly disappeared (it became very obvious at the G7 summit in the Bavarian Alps in June 2022), and sneakers at work do not surprise anyone anymore. More the contrary: it seems like a robust rebellious sign these days to wear high heels at work.

So, what is my point here exactly? In the world of Luxury Fashion, I have indeed observed a more subtle but very revealing connection. On my arrival at Chanel, it struck me in the first couple of days and weeks how much more elegant my colleagues appeared to me than in my previous working environments. I asked myself why this would be. It certainly was my overall visual impression. The offices were all very tidy, arranged in symmetry and coded in black and white. All reminiscent of the style of the founder, Gabrielle Chanel. The employees moved slowly within the premises; there was never a bright spotlight, and people wore primarily black and white attire. What specifically gave me a clue: the sensation of an elegant environment came from these strong but subtle signals. One day I realised my dress code was somewhat out of sync with everyone else's silent monochromatic demeanour. It did not take long before I got it. In the first exchange with my new boss, the message came solid and clear: "You should see my wardrobe", she said, "it's full of black dresses and trousers, it makes it so much faster and easier to dress every morning". "Clear, I got you", I thought.

You might be aware of the resolute corporate culture Chanel has developed. This is constantly reinforced and is a crucial element to the business's success. I wish to underline here that if you are aware and look closely, you will find ways to decode the corporate culture easily, including often visual cues. Decoding corporate culture rapidly will reap huge benefits on your career journey. This is valid for your own company culture or even that of your competitors or business partners.

Sometime later in my professional journey, I was eager to be exposed to a very different corporate culture – a more exuberant and joyful one. It was eye-opening to arrive at the Gucci Head office, where colour was everywhere, with people with pink hair and tattoos. I would rate my boss there as one of the most elegant executives I have known, with no dark suits, ties or checkers combined with flowers. He found his own perfectly aligned style, so he totally conveyed the corporate culture without, I guess, spending endless time every morning. Talking of office attire, one of the fantastic perks of working for Luxury Fashion brands is the clothing allowance. Wearing the brand you represent is pretty much obligatory. I am sure you can imagine the thrill of the first session, having to get through a very respectable clothing allowance in the Chanel Cambon and Gucci Montenapoleone flagship boutiques, respectively, but this is a story for another day.

It is for everyone to read on the Gucci website: "We believe that the best place to work is an environment in which employees are happy; this is why we are constantly investing in developing a strong corporate culture". How did Gucci convey a culture of happiness in the workplace? It is described on the website by some choice words: "We are daring, we are responsible, we are inclusive, we are trustworthy, we are respectful, we are changemakers". I believe that the sense of pride and joy as a corporate culture objective can be achieved if people can embrace the company's values in their daily work lives. Maybe not all of them all the time, but if there are enough, then at least some can be leveraged. Joy is highly contagious, so if you make moments of joy compellingly visible, sharable and engaging physically in person and on internal media platforms, part of the job is done.

What about a culture of curiosity?

This is where I would concentrate my focus – it is a fundamental element for success. In my opinion, a curious mind has such a high achievement potential; it can learn much but, likewise, unlearn – a necessary skill in this fast-moving world. Openness and flexibility come to the fore with the power of curiosity. Just recently, I came across a *BBC* article that highlighted precisely this. The subtitle was "Exploring your curiosity can be incredibly good for your mind, with benefits for learning, creativity and even job enjoyment". Here are the main lessons stated, supported by scientific research [8]:

– Curiosity is a memory booster, therefore, supports you in a continuous learning process
– Curiosity links ideas together, therefore supports you in developing your creativity
– Curiosity develops engagement and well-being, both essential qualities regarding job satisfaction.

"When we feel curious about a subject, the fact that we are studying, the points of interest become more deeply encoded, and more accessible when they are later needed". We most likely all had these sensations at school, university or any learning environment. Even children with attention deficit difficulties can benefit from generating and encouraging curiosity. How curious are they really about the topic they are trying to learn?

Serendipity as a curiosity booster? In the article, there is evidence from studies of creative problem solving, with signs that curiosity helps people build more exciting and original ideas. There is some indication that "FOMO", the fear of missing out, which often has negative connotations, might drive curiosity and the benefits it can deliver. I might add that engaging in online searches generally drives interest.

Some research conducted by Todd Kashdan, professor of psychology at George Mason University in Fairfax, Virginia, found that "greater curiosity can also make people more open to hearing others' opinions, even if they differ from their own. That's essential if we want to have constructive disagreements and avoid issues like confirmation bias and groupthink". I couldn't agree more from my own real-life experiences. I firmly believe that showing an open mind and empathy and going out of one's comfort zone leads to better relationships and less friction and anxiety [9].

The final question would be understanding how a company that wishes to develop a corporate culture of curiosity moves forward with it. Some ideas to cultivate curiosity stated by researchers and scientists are:

– Encourage managers to give employees more autonomy.
– Encourage managers to look beyond the 'staying in your lane' approach.

- Encourage employees to focus on the big picture in moments of confusion or frustration.
- Encourage employees to find holes in their knowledge by compiling a list of questions that need solving.

The article ends with this great sentence: "And with the proven benefits for your learning, creativity and general well-being, you may be pleasantly surprised where this new-found curiosity eventually leads you".

Similarly, I invite you to listen to Julia Dhar's theory in one of her Ted Talks. She proposes that there is a great way to reduce hostility during discussions in the workplace by suggesting a new angle to explore: curiosity. In her opinion, a curious mind and an attitude toward progress – rather than victory – will allow us to build constructive conversations and move them forward as world-class persuaders do.

Julia Dhar, managing director and partner at Boston Consulting Group, leads the Global Behavioural Science Lab.

She explains how those constructive conversations have three essential features that move the dialogue forward [10]:

1. Choosing Curiosity over Clash
The objective is to focus on understanding the other person's perspective and preventing people from shutting down. They tend to become curious about you by showing curiosity for others rather than being closed to dialogue. She offers helpful guiding phrases, like "I never thought about it exactly in that way before . . . . What can you share that would help me see what you see?" In my view, questions are rarely perceived as aggressive.

2. View a discussion as a climbing wall, not a cage fight.
If you go into an encounter expecting everyone to walk out with the same point of view that you walked in with, there's really no chance for progress. Instead, we need to think about conversations like facing a climbing wall, where we adapt and re-explain when an idea is attacked – very much like in a formal debate or successful high-stakes negotiations. The objective is that your vision is refined and improves through challenge and criticism.

3. Anchor everything in common purpose.
Make sure the purpose of the discussion is clear. Start with the big picture, the global ambition, not personalities, politics or strategies. Once this is achieved, you can move on to discuss principles. Another option is to paint an ideal situation in the future and invite people to inhabit this future possibility. This opens up the chance for a conversation with a purpose.

What kind of environment would a culture of curiosity require?

My answer to this question would be to make joy a priority at work. In organizations where there may be too much admin to get things done, teams working in silos, and people afraid of leaving their comfort zones and/or resistant to new ways of connecting and working, spreading curiosity may be highly difficult. Joy can be part of the solution to this problem, for two reasons:

- People intrinsically seek joy
- Joy connects people more powerfully than almost any other human experience

The connective power of joy is clearly visible in sports. When a team performs at its awe-inspiring best, overcoming its limitations and challenges, every player experiences a brimming ecstasy that lifts the team even further. Success sparks joy. Joy fuels further success. Everyone is caught up in the moment.

Can the joy that is so apparent in team sports be replicated in business? Absolutely. In any team environment, joy arises from a combination of harmony, impact and acknowledgement – all of which business leaders can engender in their organizations.

Crafting business cultures that more consistently engender such experiences can create a much stronger sense of personal interconnection, shared purpose and heartfelt pride across the organization [11].

2.4 Always staying ahead of expectations

Carla sits in the beautiful Swans Bar at Maison Assouline in London's Piccadilly. It is her favourite place in town for a shopping break or to meet friends that are foreigners to the city. Two of her best friends from business school are also in town, and they had planned an entire Fashion immersion weekend.

One of her friends, an investment banker in New York, eyes the Luxury and Fashion industry from the sidelines with admiration for its glamour and financial success. Carla – from her tech industry point of view – is very aware of the disruptive moves some successful Luxury Houses have accomplished. Her other friend – Anna – has evolved within European Luxury Fashion Brands for more than 15 years.

After their first sip of 'Mariage Frères Marco Polo', Anna tells her friends that the Luxury Industry has been at the forefront of innovation and continuous transformation. This comes from the heritage and DNA of this industry: it is an industry of Creativity and Artist Talent.

This statement comes somehow as a shock to the investment banker. It doesn't seem easy to believe with the impressive Regent Street Apple Store Flagship only a few streets away. Seeing her friend's expression of mild scepticism, Anna comes up with some examples.

"When Louis Vuitton pivoted from a Leathergoods' to a Fashion House, when Chanel pivoted from regulated Paris Fashion Week fashion shows to include also owned travelling fashion shows, and when Gucci pivoted from imposing fashion trends to self-expression, identity and community building. These were all transformational milestones in this industry that marked a change forever and impacted and forced a re-think by most of the other players".

Anna wanted to be very clear with her friends on one aspect: "Incremental moves keep you in the game, but it takes iconic moves to stay ahead of expectations", she said. And these three examples are the types of iconic and rule-breaking moves.

"Staying ahead of expectations is precisely what needs to be achieved daily in the Luxury Fashion Industry. It is a business that does not cater to consumers' needs – no one needs another LV bag or Chanel jacket – but everyone is delighted to be surprised by a new set of innovative assortments by these brands".

"Yes, I get it. You are completely correct, Anna. When we think about innovative companies, we tend to think of Tech or maybe sportswear like Nike. Still, substantial innovations in the Marketing, Manufacturing and Retail business areas come from the Luxury / Fashion industries".

Anna smiled at her friend: "Would you like another cup of tea?"

For this continuous transformation to occur, risks must be taken; there is hardly an alternative.

Here are some thoughts of Christian Klein, CEO of SAP (42 years old): "In these times, you need speed and agility, and you need leaders with courage and a willingness to take risks". With new ways of doing things and innovation comes learning. He says the following on this topic: "It's always good when you can say in a meeting: I learned something here, and because of that, we are going to course-correct some of our decisions. My approach is always to ask, how do we solve it? What kind of people do we need to bring together? What outcome are we working toward? People who can think creatively and solve problems are in very high demand".

As mentioned, the Luxury Fashion Industry – guided by creativity and innovation – must always stay ahead of expectations, much like the tech industry. Both industries do nurture each other. Tech offers the Luxury Fashion Industry ways to innovate with customer and product data, manufacturing, logistics and Omni retail processes. The Luxury Fashion Industry offers Tech a 'tastemaker' touch through creative design while pushing cultural boundaries forward. Both industries thrive when their brands become changemakers.

For that reason, I would recommend keeping an eye on both. They have loads to offer. And yes, you may tell yourself: "Watching a fashion show online? Me? Why?"

If you analyse it deeply, the impact of Fashion goes beyond what you may believe. Even German car manufacturers would agree, I think.

It goes without saying that an imperative characteristic to succeed in Marketing or business, in general, is knowing your market and customers and staying ahead of their expectations.

"Let Chanel surprise you!" – this is one of the brand's guiding principles. You must stay ahead of expectations to surprise highly discerning customers with access to the most extraordinary experiences, products and services. Meeting their expectations would not be enough, but constantly surpassing and surprising ever more demanding clients is no easy task.

So, how is this achieved? You need to be curious or at least develop this quality. Only with curiosity will you be able to expound your level of knowledge of your market and customers. And this has been important for executives working in Marketing and Sales in the past and present and will only upturn in the future. The development of machine learning and AI is a significant reality today. Knowing your market and customer well and anticipating purchase behaviours will remain a defining competitive business advantage. This is why I believe every executive should show interest in market trends and customer purchasing behaviour. It impacts the top and bottom lines. In some business models and industries, more in one or the other direction, but its impact is undeniable.

This phrase from Maya Angelou comes to mind: "You can't use up curiosity. The more you use, the more you have" [12].

Reading customer study reports on trends, behavioural changes and differences among generations, cultures, communities, etc., is fascinating and fundamental to truly understanding your customers. It is a muscle that needs exercising and should therefore be used frequently. Start on your own, discuss them with trusted colleagues, exchange for a different point of view, compare with internal corporate data and compare against other studies you will see; the more you start investigating, the more you will want to know. And you will always nourish your curiosity and the people around you.

Another necessary behaviour you can refine is your power of observation, to be constantly out there on the urban landscape and have your eyes wide open.

An attitude and action that could best showcase this are what Akio Morita of Sony and Steve Jobs of Apple did. They were both famous for never commissioning market research. "Instead, they'd just walk around the world watching what people did. They'd put themselves in their customer's shoes", writes James Allworth in *Harvard Business Review* [13].

Steve Jobs famously declared, "Get so close [to your customer] that you tell them what they need well before they realise it themselves". Getting close comes not from hearing what customers say they do but from observing what they actually do.

You will also develop a particular sensitivity and keep an open eye to changes. Have you noticed the sudden reappearance of the cool vintage Coca-Cola bottles on terraces, bars and restaurants during summer 2022, at least in Southern Europe? With rampant inflation and consumers feeling their purchasing power shrink, what has the brand that stands for joyful moments decided to do for its consumers during their summer holiday break? The brand looked at ways to reduce costs by implementing recycling measures, not stopping their consumption but encouraging them to reach for their favourite drink. Clever? Well, it was pretty easy, just transferring what's already (or shall I say, still?) the norm in less favourable markets in Africa. The very agile way this was achieved is what surprised me the most. Some say that Coke even tastes better out of a bottle! Additionally, when a war occurs in a geographically adjacent region, a sense of nostalgia for a bottled rather than a canned drink may comfort our souls.

In the Luxury Industry, customers pay a high premium for unique designs, constant innovation and best-in-class quality. They love to be surprised by their favourite artistic directors with their creativity. They can feel let down due to a lack of service in their discovery or purchasing journey. This is why here, the challenge is never to fail to meet expectations but at least match or preferably surpass them.

It is essential to understand where the expectation bar needs to be set. Whatever industry you are involved in, you should understand where this service expectation bar sits. Customer Satisfaction surveys, NPS scores, CRM data, focus groups, behavioural science analysis, customer analysis surveys, etc. There are many reports and ad-hoc analyses that will help and will nourish your curiosity to know more. Often there may be occasions to discover unknown realities and unlock potential opportunities. Developing curiosity and all it signifies will help you progress in your initiatives and career.

To develop your innovative mindset, develop an interest in other industries, markets and business models. Read a lot, attend conferences, exchange with your network and expand your network.

You may ask yourself all manner of questions, but don't hesitate to 'go wild':

- What is the driver for a Lego customer? For a child, for an adult?
- How is the Barbie brand evolving along the #metoo movement?
- Why is TikTok such a success?
- How did Nike pivot to a "direct-to-consumer model"?
- How did SAP pivot to become a Cloud based company?
- What are my sons' expectations of the latest video game I purchased for him?
- Aren't Nike fans happy despite Serena Williams's decision to depart from professional tennis?
- What might they have thought about Allyson Felix?
- What's the next big thing with Apple? Disney? Netflix?
- Which brand will be the first to crack a more immersive online shopping experience?

Innovators are problem solvers. Unsolved questions move the world forward. This means progress.

The ultimate goal of any company nowadays is to stay in the game through innovation.

2.5 Courage and competitiveness in sports

Liam leaned back on his armchair. He was sitting in one of those vintage leather arm-chairs by the fireplace in an 18ᵗʰ-century French château. It was the first night of a three-day off-site team-building event with his colleagues. The question he just had been asked was not new to him but had never been asked of him in a professional context. He had to reflect for a couple of seconds if his answer should be any different. No, he thought.

"Daniel, I have often been asked about my experience in the England National Junior Rugby team. Though never by a work colleague. I appreciate your interest. I fondly re-member those years of training, and weekend matches were wonderful. Especially those relating to the deep camaraderie that developed naturally over time, through wins but also in defeat. That sense of belonging, of giving it all for the match, your sport, your team and your coach, is totally unique. It is difficult to experience elsewhere".

"Why do you say that, Liam? You are a super team player at work!"

"Well, I certainly hope so. It's just that in team sports, this sense of 'all together' is the only way forward; nothing else matters. I am not sure; this is always the case in the corporate world".

"What do you mean, Liam?"

"Well, it's quite easy. For team sports like rugby, sailing or hockey, we all train and play for a common goal; what counts is to give the best of ourselves, nothing else. No personal egos, disruptive behaviour, or acts of individual glory, only the willingness to perform at your best, all for the greater good – for the team. Never mind if we win or lose, both are part of the game and happen; what is required is the endeavour, the total effort. And guess for whom? Not for ourselves, not even for the team, but mostly for the coach! We do as best we can for them, that's it. And this is probably the single biggest difference between team and individual sports, like tennis, e.g., where an athlete tends to perform primarily for themselves. The coach is the one who nurtures the team, who is responsible for team selection, defines the strategy and sets the best training and skills development for each of its players. We owe our successes to the coach. We are accountable to the coach. This is very clear in everyone's mind. And if you adopt this working methodology, people don't fight over decisions, ego issues or priority setting; this is where I see a marked difference with the corporate world. Corporate manage-ment could and should learn from the management of team sports. Teams should work in first place for their coach/manager and less for their personal agenda. Athletes from all sports are naturally competitive, but in team sports, the primary object of the com-petition is against the other competing teams, not towards other members of their own team". Having said that, the journey to make it onto the team is enormously competi-

tive and is all about the individual, their skills and character – this can be equated to a challenging interview process in the corporate environment.

Maybe this is the moment to introduce the importance of courage and competitiveness in sports. Let's also explore the possibility that courage and competitive drive might become a potential risk factor when exhibited in excess.

Sportsmen and women, particularly in team sports, develop a deep trust with the other team members. Still, at the same time, their competitive streak is heightened, and they have a compulsive drive to win. Sportsmen and sportswomen are averse to losing. It is pretty binary: win over lose. Much against the Olympic philosophy, "The importance is to participate".

This drive exhibited in competitive sports can also be harnessed in a business environment. I would suggest that this competitive winner's drive should be nurtured and directed towards industry fellows – i.e. 'the competition' rather than encouraging highly competitive environments within the company between individuals, teams and departments. This is when the similarities with sports are highlighted: on a playing field, we collectively wish to beat our competitors. Even if an uneven playing field has little consequence, we will all enjoy the competition.

A great example is the America's Cup sailing race – the world's oldest international sporting trophy. America's Cup class yachts, designed to sail windward/leeward courses around marks, are now hitting speeds that, just over a decade ago, were the preserve of specialist record attempts. The current boats – the AC75s – are unlike anything seen before and showcase to the world what is possible under sail power alone. Some yachts manage 40 knots of boat speed upwind in around 17 knots of wind. That is unheard of in performance terms and almost unimaginable just three years ago. The AC75 crews might be sailing in only 18 knots of breeze – what would feel like a decent summer breeze on any other boat – but they experience winds of around 50 knots. To put that into context, that is a storm force ten on the Beaufort scale!

How is this performance even possible? Like any sport, it is about always surpassing oneself and an ongoing quest for ever-increasing speed performance. A whole new level of technology and data has come into play to achieve that the development process is genuinely getting closer to motorsports Formula 1.

The most radical development of the AC75s has been removing the keel altogether. By doing so, the design is now like nothing we have ever seen, particularly regarding how dynamic the power transition is between foiling and not foiling. This is impossible to explain in this book; if you are interested, check it out on YouTube for a better and more entertaining explanation and illustration.

Furthermore, a new America's Cup boat is an enormously complex kit. Each team has powerful Computational Fluid Dynamics software packages and simulators to try to understand the various gains and losses. Each unit has been getting as much data as possible to make these simulators and computer projections as accurate as possible over their three-year development cycle. INEOS Team UK has been able to work alongside the all-powerful Mercedes F1 team (both backed by INEOS) and has been open about how much this has helped their development process. "It's really similar to F1," explains Mercedes Applied Science Principal Engineer Thomas Batch, who has 11 F1 titles to his name and is with INEOS in Auckland. "That level of data analysis and feedback with the sailors is similar to working with an F1 driver." Please look online at how this works on the race course; it is unique.

This incursion into the F1 of sailing is to explain how competition paired with high-tech can have an extraordinary impact on innovation and team performance in a legendary sport.

How is this relatable to business? Continuous innovation and a healthy team spirit will allow ever-evolving products, industries, business models, etc. And the competition and outcome will be relished by each participant.

In a sailing race like the America's Cup, the objective is to accumulate points during match races – one yacht against another – to establish the winner. It is like every other game – like chess: the players are known, the rules are fixed and the endpoint is clear. The winners and losers are easily identified. These are generally regarded as finite games.

Playing the infinite and finite game is the difference between being focused on the journey and vision versus your immediate competition. In an infinite game, the situation is quite different: there are known and unknown players, the rules are changeable and the objective is not to win – the objective is to keep playing, to stay in the game, to perpetuate the game. Simon Sinek – the book's author, published in 2019 – also described the critical difference between finite and infinite players: one is playing to win, and one is playing to continue the game. While infinite players act according to their vision, finite players act in favour of their interests [14].

We've learned from Sinek that most companies are playing the finite game. So, is your company a finite player or a participant in the infinite game? Here are a few signs that your firm is one of them:

1. You are driven by the need to 'beat' other competitor brands and groups in the industry.
2. You view attorneys and industry players as 'winners' or 'losers'.
3. You focus on day-to-day short-term wins rather than the 'long game'.
4. You aren't sure or don't have a clear sense of what game you are in.

5. Your company or individuals within the company cannot articulate a higher purpose for the work that you do.
6. Decisions are made by considering interests first and values second.

The strategy may have been too short-sighted when a company becomes a finite
player and sees itself as a battlefield with winners and losers. The comparison with a
sports competition is taken too literally.

Where are the limits then to competition within a company?

It might be argued that competition needs to be prevented within an organisation
since it tends to be divisive and inefficient. Constructive collaboration should be the
norm. A damaging policy would be to encourage teams or individuals to openly compete against each other and then apply a winners-and-losers game. A healthy internal
team or inter-departmental competition is acceptable but not on an individual level.

I read somewhere this statement by Canadian poet Stacie Martin: "We should be lifting
each other up and cheering each other on, not trying to outshine one another – the sky
would be awfully dark with just one star", and I would totally agree and fully promote
this sentiment. Nevertheless, I am convinced that this has a generous sprinkling of
wishful thinking and reflects the reality of what actually happens in the corporate
world. To best support the leaders for the immediate future in current corporations, I
believe it is much more credible to find a pragmatic approach to the possible scenarios
in business. I was excited to have come across an insightful study prepared by Prof.
Randall S. Peterson and Prof. Kristin J. Behfar from London Business School [15].

They argue that all workplace relationships fall into one of five categories. Depending
on the degree to which the two people's personal interests clash or are aligned, relationships range from negative to neutral to very positive. Managing each type has risks and
requires careful thought in doing so. The trick is to step back and dispassionately analyse your relationship type: conflict, competition, independence, cooperation or collaboration. Where on this spectrum you and your colleague's connection resides will be
determined by the degree to which your interests align – or clash. The more in sync
your interests are, the more positive a relationship is. Each type calls for a different set
of tactics; over time, the nature of a relationship might change as self-interests shift.

Professors Peterson and Behfar suggest that we should acknowledge an uncomfortable
truth about workplaces: The people who thrive in them know how to collaborate and
compete with their colleagues. They clearly understand how work relationships affect
their interests and the organisation's; they carefully consider the risks and trade-offs
and dispassionately decide how much to invest in each coworker and when to walk
away – you might call it the art of corporate politics.

There are risks in all workplace relationships – not just those in which conflict or
competition is pronounced but also ones where you're readily collaborating with

someone or able to work largely independently of each other. That's because the parties involved often have differing agendas, which will never be 100% aligned and may diverge even more over time. Always keep this in mind.

The starting point is to manage these relationships skilfully. To do so, you must first understand where you and your colleagues fit on the conflict-collaboration spectrum. Professors Peterson and Behfar use the following wording, which I find pertinent: 'co-operative rivalries'.

Relationships are negative when interests are opposed and the parties are either in competition or outright conflict over goals. Bosses sometimes put colleagues into these challenging situations to test whether they can rise above personal feelings (or rivalries between teams or business units) to do what's right for the organisation. But most of us approach them warily, tending to focus on the harm that our counterparts may have done in the past or could inflict in the future.

Relationships are positive when people share interests and cooperate to achieve selective goals or collaborate when their goals are entirely unified. This always feels great, but if you assume that your colleague has a purely positive intent and is totally aligned with you, you might be mistaken, and in doing so, you've exposed and put yourself at risk.

In between are relationships in which two people predominantly work independently. But these can be hard to maintain and carry their own risks.

Once you've figured out the type of relationship you and your colleague have, you can use various tactics to manage it. That requires you to step back from the existing emotional and behavioural dynamics and carefully analyse your situation. Consider how your disparate and mutual interests align with your organisation's goals. Ask yourself what is in it for you and what is in it for the other person. How do their interests create risk for you? What can you tolerate, and what must you prevent? And how can you ensure that the benefits of working together are realised?

In an outright **conflict**, your counterpart is trying to take something you want or need or attempting to sabotage your efforts. A zero-sum relationship ends when one party wins and the other loses the sought-after reward, such as a promotion or a coveted assignment. In a conflicted relationship, given each circumstance, you must be clear about the facets you must protect and those you cannot or are willing to compromise. Confrontation is necessary and costly, so work closely with allies and do not engage your rival alone.

The **competition** type of rivalry is widespread in workplaces where pay and opportunities are routinely allocated by assessing and comparing the performance of employees. Unlike an outright win-or-lose conflict, competitive situations offer flexibility because the value can still be found in other, albeit less attractive, options. You and your colleague want the same things, but the supply is limited. The right move in cases like this one is to recognise where your goals and your rivals are compatible and where they're not and work from there to improve the odds of good outcomes while minimising unwanted ones. By recognising what drives a rivalry, those involved can find a way to reduce competition.

In the middle of the spectrum is **independence**, which means deliberately reducing your reliance on others as much as possible – evading the problem rather than trying to fix it. One challenge with this approach is that it is difficult to maintain over the long term. Given those dangers, this method is not recommended. Instead, people in this situation should consider treating the relationship as a conflict or a competition.

In a **cooperation** relationship, you and your counterpart share critical interests and their separate ones, so you choose to work together on specific issues where your interests align and not compete where they don't. That doesn't require you to like or make any material or long-term investments in each other. It's just a mutually beneficial transaction in which each party brings something to the table. The risks here are much lower than in relationships where partners are in conflict or competition. The principal danger stems from the fact that, at any moment, things can change.

Collaboration happens when two parties have many fundamental mutual interests and would both benefit from investing in the relationship to help each other. While such relationships feel psychologically safe and promise the most mutual gain, they are the hardest to disengage from if interests change because the parties' resources are intermingled.

We all navigate a range of cooperative rivalries at work. Understanding and figuring out how to optimise each of them is crucial. The solution is to find positive relationships and avoid negative ones. It would help if you recognised that conflict and competition inevitably arise among interdependent coworkers but can still be managed in ways that reap the rewards. Career success depends on relationship management as much as any other skill. Get it right, and both you and your organisation will benefit.

Every relationship – spouses, parents, siblings, coworkers, friends – is marked by a fundamental tension between cooperation and competition. It always exists. Our success in life depends on finding the right balance between those two forces.

The key question would be then, "How to find that right balance?" Adam Galinsky and Maurice Schweitzer stated in their book and talks [16], that it can be achieved through 'perspective-taking'. In their research, it boils down to understanding other peoples' perspective. Quite similarly to how Julia Dhar advises starting constructive conversations with curiosity (Section 3 in this Chapter).

Returning to the subject of courage and competitiveness in sports, integrity is another value we can transfer from that arena into a business environment. Competition between employees may be an inescapable part of many people's work lives, but when managed skilfully, it can lead to improved performance by all stakeholders. When fostered, it can lead to trust, honesty and transparency. But suppose leaders want to ensure that competition unleashes creativity, not unsavoury behaviour. In that case, they must resist the temptation to lead through fear. This statement is given in an article published by *Harvard Business Review* in 2017 on the pros and cons of employee competition, which I agree with [17].

Lastly, having the courage to ask for help and support when needed can also be gleaned from sportsmanship as a best practice. One of the most widely recognised rugby union coaches ever comes to mind: Eddie Jones. He is an Australian Rugby Union coach and was head coach of the England national team from 2015 to 2022 [18].

After winning the Six Nations Tournament End October 2020, he needed incremental growth for his team. He did not hesitate to ask for support in another unexpected direction: American basketball. As he describes in his book, he felt their Monday Training sessions were ineffective. "I wanted to find a new way to start the week for our squad. Curiosity and openness to new ideas helped change the old pattern", he writes. "I also benefited from a willingness, as a leader, to work with my rivals. I am old friends with another coach who is also eager to improve, so we often speak about our work. When I told him about my concerns about our Monday Sessions, we had a constructive conversation, and he mentioned the Gonzaga Bulldogs, a college basketball team in the US".

This relatively small basketball team made it year after year to the NCAA finals – their consistency shifted perceptions. Eddie Jones explains in his book that this basketball team with excellent performance results had faced the same issue he was facing and decided, at the time, to improve their Monday Sessions by giving the Bulldog Players more responsibility. They made that moment a growth day for the players. It felt as if they owned the Mondays. It was clear to them that off-court growth leads to on-court leadership and performance. On Mondays, the coaching staff kept their distance, and the players took control of their sessions, having been encouraged by the coach to be more curious. Their coach stressed that this special space helped the players become more connected, especially in a surreal year like 2020. Another learning from this exercise was that when the coach asked his players to list the three issues in their life that were the most significant barrier to success, there appeared to be dozens of human issues but no sports issues. This revelation underlined that the coaching staff must constantly pay attention to improving the player's environment. Their Monday meetings were short and sharp. They would be around 15 minutes in length, but the meaning and mood of them pulled the players out of the typical Monday low and set the tone for the rest of the week.

I want to finish this section with a scene from the epic film 'Chariots of Fire', in which Sir John Gielgud, Master of Trinity College, addresses leadership and sports. He speaks

about comradeship and uses the great phrase 'esprit de corps' to complete an English-
man's education. Without it, you are not accomplished, in his view – embodying the
guardianship of the conduct of the English elite [19].

Here is the transcript:

Master of Trinity:	My dear boy, your approach has been, if I may say so, a little too plebeian. You are the elite – and are therefore expected to behave as such.
Master of Trinity:	Here in Cambridge, we've always been proud of our athletic prowess. We believe we've always believed that our games are indispensable in helping to complete the education of an Englishman. They create character; they foster courage, honesty and leadership. But most of all, an unassailable spirit of loyalty, comradeship, and mutual responsibility. Would you agree?
Harold M. Abrahams:	Yes, sir. I would.
Master of Trinity:	Abrahams, there is a growing suspicion in the bosom of this university, and I tell you this without in any way decrying your achievements in which we all rejoice, that in your enthusiasm for success, you have perhaps lost sight of some of these ideals.
Master of Trinity:	For the past year, you've concentrated wholly on developing your own technique in the headlong pursuit, may I suggest, of individual glory. Not a policy very conducive to the fostering of esprit de corps.
Harold M. Abrahams:	I am a Cambridge man, first and last. I am an Englishman, first and last. What I have achieved, what I intend to achieve, is for my family, my university and my country. And I bitterly resent your suggesting otherwise.
Master of Caius:	Your aim is to win at all costs, is it not?
Harold M. Abrahams:	At all costs, no. But I do aim to win within the rules.
Master of Trinity:	Life slips by, Abrahams, life slips by!

2.6 Innovation and job to be done

Liam is sitting at the Soho House Barcelona restaurant, chatting with one of his team members.

"Years ago, during a worldwide leadership training, I was introduced to the concept of 'Job to be done' regarding innovation. It was put forward by the late Harvard Business School professor Clayton Christensen, and it strongly resonated with me. He is famous for his work on innovation and disruption. He states that it's important to figure out the 'job' people are 'hiring' a product to do. And that job may be very different from the product's function. Function Vs Job shifts perspective from the company to the customer."

"Looking at the market from the function of a product really originates from your competitors or your own employees deciding what you need", Christensen says. "Whereas the jobs-to-be-done point of view causes you to crawl into the skin of your customer and go with her as she goes about her day, always asking the question as she does something: Why did she do it that way?".

With this perspective, Disney provides warm, safe, fantasy vacations for families and OnStar insurance offers peace of mind.

Clayton M. Christensen, widely regarded as one of the world's top experts on innovation and growth and author of the theory of disruptive innovation, says executives often fail because they study the wrong product and customer data, which leads them to unwittingly design innovation processes that 'churn out mediocrity'.

"For years, I'd been focused on understanding why great companies fail, but I realised I had never really thought about the reverse problem: How do successful companies know how to grow?" writes Christensen, the late Kim B. Clark Professor of Business Administration at Harvard Business School [20].

The secret to winning the innovation game lies in understanding what causes customers to make choices that help them progress on something they are struggling with. To get the correct answers, Christensen says, executives should ask: "What job would consumers want to hire a product to do?"

"For me, this is a neat idea", Christensen writes of the Theory of Jobs to Be Done. "When we buy a product, we essentially 'hire' something to get a job done. If it does the job well, we hire that same product again when confronted with the same job. And if the product does a crummy job, we 'fire' it and look around for something else we might hire to solve the problem".

Some years ago, McDonald's was trying to increase the sales of their milkshakes. So, they would interview milkshake customers and explain that they were trying to improve the milkshakes to increase sales. They would ask if they would like bigger milkshakes, new flavours (like root beer or orange), chocolatier or thicker milkshakes. However, after improving the milkshakes as a consequence of the interview results, they found that customers didn't buy more milkshakes.

Christensen was hired as a consultant to help McDonald's to nail this problem, and he applied his brand new 'Jobs Theory' to solve it. To understand which job arose in some customers' lives that sometimes caused them to hire a milkshake, Christensen studied a McDonald's restaurant for 18 hours one day. It turned out that about half of the milkshakes were sold before 8:30 in the morning. It was the only thing the customer bought; they were alone and always got in the car and drove off with it.

To figure out what that job was, Christensen returned the following day and positioned himself outside the restaurant to confront these milkshake customers as they came out. He asked them: "What job are you trying to get done that causes you to come to McDonald's to hire a milkshake at 6:30 in the morning?"

It turned out that they all had the same job to do. That is, they had a long and tedious drive to work. And they just needed something to have while driving to stay engaged with life and not fall asleep. The customer wasn't hungry yet, but they knew they'd be hungry an hour later. So they needed something they could hold with their right hand while driving and keep for the whole commute.

This analysis showed that McDonald's milkshakes were not competing against Burger King's. They were competing against bananas, snickers, doughnuts or even bagels to do the same job. However, milkshakes were much more convenient than their competitors since they were easier to consume, only one hand was needed, and they were so dense that it would take the whole commute to finish them up with that thin straw.

Customers didn't care about the ingredients. All they cared about was to be still full at 10 am and have something to entertain them throughout their trip.

Unveiling what the job was put McDonald's on a very different trajectory. It explained the reason why there were no results after improving the milkshake on dimensions of performance that was irrelevant to the job-to-be-done [21].

To improve the milkshake for the morning JTBD, McDonald's moved the milkshake from behind the counter to the front. To help them not be late for work, they also gave people a prepaid swipe card so they could dash in, gas up and go without being caught behind a line. They also made milkshakes thicker to take longer to suck them up, and so on.

Once McDonald's had understood that they were competing against bananas, the sales of the milkshakes increased by 7x [22].

The lesson provided here is that our perspective needs to shift somewhat to understand profoundly what the customer is looking for. Not so much about a product variation or evolution, but more often, the physiological and emotional need to be addressed.

This reminds me of an iconic Chanel product and the distinction between its intrinsic value, the job it does, and the function it provides to the customer, much more than the design or category itself. The Chanel product that pops to mind immediately is the Chanel jacket. Again, it is less about the physical piece itself, even if it is an amazing product, but more about what it stands for. There is nothing, but absolutely nothing like it.

A Chanel jacket is a legend: a piece of unique fabric, stitched in a forever traditional and forever evolving way, with four pockets – not more, not less – great and uniquely sourced buttons, internally lined or not (depending on the season) and a small metallic chain all along the interior bottom couture, to make sure it falls adequately off the wearer's shoulders.

Beyond the physical achievement itself, around the evolution of this iconic garment, the crucial aspect is the emotions it delivers to the wearer. The Chanel jacket has been copied an innumerable number of times. But those copies will never deliver what the authentic one can achieve. Or, more importantly, what the wearer feels when she pulls it over her shoulders. At that instant, the Chanel jacket becomes an armour. Literally. An armour of strength and plenitude.

This is what this garment embodies – nothing less.

And herein lies the interest in purchasing or having one: it provides a metamorphosis. One that changes your appearance from the outside and exudes emotion on the inside. As for the jacket itself, that needs to look as good from the inside as from the outside – ask any seamstress or Fashion Advisor in a Chanel boutique.

If your product already provides this, how are you meant to innovate? Quite a challenge, right?

The key is to identify your domain, not just placing the jacket within a luxury RTW collection, but rather in the 'armour and strength' providing business. But in a metaphoric sense, not the literal sense. Perhaps this is why no competitor producing jackets can contest in this arena. The business is also protected by other products of the same brand, like one of their exclusive fragrances – the same story.

In the Luxury Fashion language, another example providing a similar 'armour' feeling might be the latest Gucci jumper from the runway to a non-binary person . . . in let's say . . . Brazil.

My message here is the perspective required when approaching innovation: what exactly is the emotion you wish to achieve for your clients? What is the real job to be done here?

So, when did I have a similar requirement for innovation? I recall once sitting in the Gucci showroom debating how to merchandise a specific collection item. One to pick out, set the focus, tell a unique story and develop a particular orchestration plan.

Regardless of the product or collection, the main driver was to achieve intense desirability throughout the customer journey and at every brand touchpoint.

The main attraction for customers is generated from the desire to possess and cherish some of these items because they stand for something very specific. By wearing them, the values the products represent through their branding carry over to the wearer. The undoubted benefit to those who desire and wear these luxury items is the feeling of desire for those brands and products, and then the chase, the process of 'hunting' them down and finally acquiring and possessing them. The level of desire and happiness will vary and depend on the timeframe. The desire and sense of accomplishment are coupled with the duration of the journey.

2.7 How to be innovative

"Sounds fascinating, Liam; being nurtured by people outside our industry and applying lessons to small incremental innovations at our company seems like a great opportunity. I want to ask you, well, how do I do to come up with truly innovative ideas? Is there any tip or hint you could share with me? What advice would you give me?"

Liam replied, "Look, at my previous job, I was asked to contribute to a pitch for a key marketing campaign for an important headset launch for that brand. In that previous company, the junior team members had difficulty speaking up and being heard. It was clear to me that with that assignment, I had an excellent opportunity to involve more voices across departments and seniority levels. I wanted to involve the younger members as much as possible, so I expressed it to my boss. She supported me without hesitation, and I knew I could experiment in new ways. More important than the ideas themselves, the real challenge was finding a new way to create an environment to let creativity thrive. Creating the right environment for creativity to flourish is vital. I mean here that it is less about the project itself nor its outcome, but how it is designed makes it attractive for the younger team members.

What we did was inspired by tech companies and proceeded as follows: the game-changer was that everything happened outside the office locations in amazingly inspiring places.

We mixed team members from different departments, had several sessions to share ideas, were able to laugh and relax, and created an environment of trust and security for any option to be listened to – and to my astonishment, we accomplished the set goals and ticked all the boxes".

"Also, it was not a one-shot moment but an iteration of several moments within a timeline. Each of these iterations happened with a different set of briefs and locations. I did not know the details of the Agile methodology back then; this was a gut feeling about what needed to be done. And the final cherry on the cake was a presentation to senior leaders in a truly innovative fashion, to ensure ultimate decision-makers would listen (not always easy), be convinced and inspired by the project".

"That is amazing, Liam; what you are telling me is to feel free to reach out to other people I think may be interested in brainstorming ideas and finding solutions together. Will I not be infringing on their time? What is there in it for them?"

The world's most successful creative minds and entrepreneurs all have one thing in common: they benefit from innovative thinking. Larry Alton describes it in his article on *Inc.*: "You can't force innovative ideas, but you can create the right environment for them" [23].

What does it take then to develop a truly innovative idea, and is it possible to optimise your environment to help you generate more innovation?

Do you have a growth mentality? In other words, can you turn on a dime and make significant changes for ideas worth pursuing? Does your organisation embrace it?

In this section, we will look into new ways that help unlock innovation. Creative people practice habits regularly to allow for their original ideas to flourish.

At the personal level, innovative people can develop ideas to improve their lives and change their environment. For an innovative organisation to emerge, it needs the power of creative individuals combined with internal mechanisms that allow those individuals and their ideas to thrive. In other words, creating environments that stimulate creativity and allow 'outside-the-box thinking' is critical.

The first habit I would like to put forward is to allow yourself and your teams to unfocus. To get away from daily business graft. It is commonly accepted that people often tend to come up with their best ideas in the shower, right? Yes, it is vital to allow for more downtime for your teams.

But why is this the case? Science suggests it is because we are bored. When our minds aren't occupied with anything, particularly interesting or important, they wander, and entirely novel ideas can strike. It is similar to the process of daydreaming. It is tough to daydream when our minds are preoccupied with problems or to-do lists.

Personally, it happens to me that I have my best ideas during holidays, weekends or sometimes just during a walk that I gift myself to break up an afternoon. It does work; great ideas strike when you decelerate for a while and let your mind relax, recharge and clean up, so to speak.

No question that downtime allows for ideas to flourish. Dining out on a beautiful terrace in Rome on the weekend, I devised a breakthrough concept for Chanel. Watching flamingos and pelicans flying during a Christmas safari trip to Kenya, I came up with a logo for a Gucci project.

You must be careful not to contaminate your precious downtime with business topics; this is not the idea. You keep a note of whatever is most accessible to you at the moment (your smartphone notebook, most probably) and then come back to it at the right time.

I also find it inspiring to do forest walks and invite you to try it out when possible. You may have heard about the way the Japanese cultivate this activity. "Shinrin-yoku" – or forest bathing – benefits are gleaned from the healing effects of contact with nature. It is the practice of immersing yourself in nature in a mindful way, using your senses to derive a range of benefits for your physical, mental, emotional and social health. It developed in Japan during the 1980s in response to a health crisis caused by mass urbanisation and a culture of extreme stress.

From my practice, it is not necessary to be alone to get its benefits; you can easily share the experience and even chat with someone to feel the appeasement to body and mind. But it is pretty much a requirement that your mobile phone is on silent.

Here I'd like to share some of the thoughts conveyed by my teams at Chanel that some of the most unforgettable moments in our time together (and for what I would be remembered most by my teams) were the off-site days we had every year, where relaxing, un-learning, un-focusing and then re-focusing were the main goals.

Consider also that people think in different ways. **Exposing yourself to intellectually diverse groups** encourages you to think in new ways. The more people you talk to, and the more ideas and perspectives you see, the more creatively you'll come to think. There is great merit in the concept of collective intelligence.

Never take for granted the worth of an idea by exchanging it with the people you consider the experts in the subject. You will be surprised how much value you can unearth in people you did not consider before but allowed for an open and transparent conversation. Of course, it demands some degree of nerve, humbleness and opening up. Remember we touched upon how we should walk away from the 'stay in your lane attitude' and that all new points of view should always be embraced? Well, when other people wish to help with their opinions and expertise, let them in. We are all better off collectively.

These networking practices can be held internally within your company or with people you trust from your external business network, including friends or mentors.

In a broader sense, without any specific topic in mind, creative inspiration can strike you anywhere, anytime, from any impulse. So, **get stimulated**: Movies, TV shows, books, podcasts, works of art and even nature can accelerate inspiration, so find something that interests you and piques your creative thinking.

What I remember as particularly inspiring was Fast Company's European Innovation Festival, organised at the Gucci Hub in July 2019. Including the participation of Yuval Noah Harari. Amazing.

It is essential to **keep learning from other innovative thinkers**. In this respect, I am very much motivated by like-minded professionals and business influencers in my industry and in touch with similar topics. Someone who immediately pops into my mind is Ana Andjelic. Ana is currently Chief Brand Officer at Esprit in New York. She has a successful career in Fashion Branding, is an author and public speaker and I follow her newsletter with great interest. I was delighted when she reached out to me, and we had an extended exchange about various topics.

I make sure I follow conferences every year: VivaTech, Business of Fashion and Hub-Spot. Also, specific newsletters, podcasts and novelties from innovative brands and organizations like Apple, Salesforce, Fast Company, Nike, The Future Laboratory, Highsnobiety, and Hypebeast. Another inspiration area can be concept stores like Merci, WOW, Colette (at the time), Dover Street Market, Antonia Milano, e-tailers like Moda Operandi, Farfetch, MatchesFashion, stylish and cool places that I visit in my travels – art galleries, bars, restaurants, etc.

You must find genuinely innovative minds to inspire you and determine what drives their passion and innovation. Ask them. They may have certain habits or approaches to learning that help them think in dynamic new ways; try these techniques for yourself to see if they work for you just as well.

All people and all levels. Giving everyone a chance to speak up and embrace ideas regardless of origin is essential. You may have heard about the 'shadow board' of younger employees created by Nespresso. Its success resided in tackling two apparently unrelated problems simultaneously: disengaged younger workers and a weak response to changing market conditions. The purpose here was to leverage the younger groups' insights and to diversify the perspectives that executives are exposed to.

2.8 Agile at scale

Agility in a decentralised and empowered organisation is paramount. Give department leaders and geographical markets the autonomy to make their own decisions
and realise changes as they see fit rather than trying to force them to submit every
idea to a bureaucratic review process.

Focus should be on ways of working, empowerment of the markets and simplified
processes. The most innovative organisations have wholly embraced this way of
working for years. Even by giant behemoths, since business size should not be an
impediment.

Darrel Rigby – partner in the Boston office of Bain & Company and heads the firm's
global Innovation Practice – describes how these new ways of working can work in
any organisation [24].

In a world of rapidly changing market conditions and customer needs and expectations, it becomes even more apparent to facilitate a flexible approach to help develop
innovative initiatives. Because what counts is not only to be the fastest in terms of go-
to-market abilities but also to re-orient inevitable mistakes or failures. As Mr Rigby
says, "to be quick is part of the performance equation".

By now, most business leaders are familiar with agile innovation teams. These small,
entrepreneurial groups are designed to stay close to customers and adapt quickly to
changing conditions. When implemented correctly, they almost always result in
higher team productivity and morale, faster time to market, better quality and lower
risk than traditional approaches can achieve.

For anyone who isn't familiar with Agile, here's a short review given by Mr Rigby:

Agile teams are best suited to innovation – the profitable application of creativity to
improve products and services, processes or business models. They are small and
multidisciplinary. Confronted with a significant, complex problem, they break it into
modules, develop solutions to each component through rapid prototyping and tight
feedback loops and integrate them into a coherent whole. They value adapting to
change more than sticking to a plan. They hold themselves accountable for outcomes
(such as growth, profitability and customer loyalty), not outputs (such as lines of code
or the number of new products).

Agile teams work differently from chain-of-command bureaucracies. They are primarily self-governing: Senior leaders tell team members where to innovate but not how.
And the teams work closely with customers, both external and internal. Ideally, this
puts responsibility for innovation in the hands of those closest to customers. It reduces layers of control and approval, speeding up work and increasing the teams' motivation. It also frees up senior leaders to do what they can: create and communicate

long-term visions, set and sequence strategic priorities and build the organisational capabilities to achieve those goals [25].

Even the most advanced agile enterprises – Amazon, Spotify, Google, Netflix, Bosch, Saab, SAP, Salesforce, Riot Games, Tesla and SpaceX, to name a few – operate with a mix of agile teams and traditional structures. The most successful companies focus on vital customer experiences that cause the most significant frustrations among functional silos. Equally important is how those teams interact with the rest of the organisation.

For example, Amazon can deploy software hundreds of times daily because its IT architecture was designed to help developers make fast, frequent releases without jeopardising the firm's complex systems. But many large companies, no matter how quickly they can code programs, can deploy software only a few times a day or a week; that's how their architecture works.

Companies that successfully scale up Agile see significant changes in their business. Scaling up shifts the mix of work so that the business is doing more innovation relative to routine operations. The business can better read and react to changing conditions and priorities, develop adaptive solutions and avoid the constant crises that frequently hit traditional hierarchies. Disruptive innovations will feel less disruptive and more like adaptive business as usual. The scaling up also brings Agile values and principles to business operations and support functions, even if many routine activities remain. It increases efficiency and productivity in some of the business's big cost centres. It improves operating architectures and organisational models to enhance coordination between Agile teams and routine operations. Changes come online faster and are more responsive to customer needs. Finally, the business delivers measurable improvements in outcomes – not only better financial results but also more significant customer and employee loyalty and engagement.

To summarise, Agile in practice has big ambitions and step-by-step progress. It shows the way to proceed even when the future is uncertain.

What would be the best way to enable agile in practice? In the view of Joerg Esser, PhD and partner at consulting firm Roland Berger, it would be an adaptable organisation. He describes a 'less is more' approach to adaptability, where management loosens its hold and gives the organisation the freedom to work effectively. The idea is that management should define *what* they want to achieve and let the organisation focus on *how* to achieve it [26].

Inspired by the scientific concept of 'emergence', Esser suggests four design principles to help leaders write adaptability into their organisation's DNA.

–   **Address purpose.** Define the purpose of the transformation right at the outset. Specify goals, priorities, rules and boundaries. Steer changes in advance as much as possible. Back this up by providing continuous feedback on whether individual actions contribute to the common goal.

- **Nominate owners.** Choose 'pilots' and 'co-pilots' who take end-to-end ownership of their topics. Employees must be able to group and regroup seamlessly in response to new tasks. Make teams flexible, diverse and cross-functional to avoid organisational silos.
- **Test, don't guess.** Run actual experiments rather than relying on so-called expert opinions. Use the results of these experiments as the basis for designing measurable solutions.
- **Spark collisions.** Enable direct interactions, planned and random, between individuals within the organisation. Encourage people to exchange ideas and experiences. Dynamic networking is an excellent basis for decision-making and achieving a common purpose.

These principles can help business leaders build an organisation that can learn from the bottom, using local knowledge and expertise. Like a colony of ants, the organisation derives its strength and adaptability from the power of emergence.

In traditional organisations, the person at the top focuses on making operational decisions, especially the big ones. In adaptable organisations, the leader focuses on facilitating the right environment.

Another critical element for Agile practice to succeed is that it requires humility from leaders. This sort of humility accelerates learning and bolsters the confidence of every team member. Humble people recognise the futility of predicting the unpredictable and instead build rapid feedback loops to ensure that initiatives stay on track. They understand that good ideas can come from anyone, not just those with the highest status. They view their job as helping team members learn and take responsibility rather than telling every team member what to do and how to do it. An agile leadership team has to adopt such attitudes, or its pronouncements will ring hollow.

Bibliography

[1]   Wikipedia. Shoshin. [Online].; 2023. Available from: https://en.wikipedia.org/wiki/Shoshin.
[2]   Allchin J. Case study: Patagonia's 'Don't buy this jacket' campaign. MarketingWeek. 2012.
[3]   Explains K. "Don't Buy This Jacket" – Patagonia's Daring Campaign". Bettermarketing. 2020.
[4]   Bonakdar T. Olafur Eliasson, 'Eye see you' edition for 121Ethiopia. E-Flux. 2006.
[5]   Phil Lewis. "The most valuable skill in difficult times is lateral thinking – here is how to do it": Forbes; 2020.
[6]   Satran R. "How Alexandre Arnault is shaking things up at Tiffany & Co.". The Wall Street Journal. 2022.
[7]   Wikipedia. Adam Grant. [Online].; 2023. Available from: https://en.wikipedia.org/wiki/AdamGrant.
[8]   Robson D. "Curiosity: The neglected trait that drives success": Bbc.com; 2022.

[9]   Kashdan TB. "The Art of Insubordination: How to Dissent and Defy Effectively": Penguin Publishing Group; 2022.

[10]   Dhar J. "How to have constructive conversations": TED Salon: DWEN; 2021.

[11]   Liu A. "Making Joy a priority at work". Harvard Business Review. 2019.

[12]   Wikipedia. Maya Angelou. [Online].; 2023. Available from: https://en.wikipedia.org/wiki/Maya_Angelou.

[13]   Allworth J. "Empathy: The Most Valuable Thing They Teach at HBS": Harvard Business Review; 2012.

[14]   Sinek S. "The infinite game": Portfolio Penguin; 2019.

[15]   Peterson RS, Behfar KJ. "When to Cooperate with Colleagues and When to Compete": Hbr.org; 2022.

[16]   Galinsky A, Schweitzer M. "Friend & Foe: When to Cooperate, When to Compete, and How to Succeed at Both": Currency; 2015.

[17]   Steinhage A, Cable D, Wardley D. "The Pros and Cons of Competition Among Employees": Hbr.org; 2017.

[18]   Jones E. "Leadership: Lessons From My Life in Rugby": Macmillan Pub Ltd.; 2021.

[19]   IMDb. Chariots of Fire – John Gielgud: Master of Trinity. [Online].; 1981. Available from: https://www.imdb.com/title/tt0082158/characters/nm0000024.

[20]   Knowledge. HBSW. "Clayton Christensen: The Theory of Jobs To Be Done". Harvard Business School. 2016.

[21]   Viau G. "'Hire' this article about milkshakes if you're struggling to understand customer needs". UX Collective. 2017.

[22]   Capaldi E. "Understanding the Job": @Edwardcapaldi7915, YouTube; 2016.

[23]   Alton L. "How to come up with more truly innovative ideas": Inc.com; 2022.

[24]   Rigby D, Sutherland J, Noble A. "Agile at Scale": Harvard Business Review; 2018.

[25]   Rigby D, Elk S, Berez S. "The Agile C-Suite": Harvard Business Review; 2020.

[26]   Esser J. "The Secret of Adaptable Organizations Is Trust": Harvard Business Review; 2021.

Chapter Three
Building resilience

Do not judge me by my success,
judge me by how many times I fell down and got back up again.
Nelson Mandela

https://doi.org/10.1515/9783111335339-004

3.1 Life is a learning journey

Isabella is waiting for her friend. It is raining outside. She arrived just before the heaviest raindrops started clattering on the pavement. How lucky! She thought. She is now sitting in a cafeteria at Soho, where both friends used to meet. It is conveniently located for both of them for an after-office drink.

Kathy arrived and was trying to handle a drenched umbrella she had with her so she was safe too. All was good.

"Hi Isabella, what a nightmare; my bus was so crowded I had to walk. Easier this way. How are you? How did your event go? I am so curious!"

"Oh, of course, I'll give you the rundown. It didn't exactly work out as well as expected. Let me explain, and then hopefully, I can pick your brains for some advice".

"Yes, sure; what happened?"

"Remember I told you about this incredible event we organised with our colleagues at the head office in Europe? It involved a remarkable new collection launch we had been preparing for several months. For this magnificent presentation in Venice, key opinion leaders and celebrities would be attending it in person, and our best clients from all over the world would see the collection the next day – virtually. All regions connected simultaneously, so no one had a priority, and then we could organise the pre-ordering system. All this went perfectly; the collection is stunning, the technology worked out above expectations, everyone was in awe, and we got excellent feedback".

"What went wrong then?"

"Well, surprisingly, once the pre-orders reconciled, everyone internally expected The Americas to score highest for those orders – as always, but on this occasion, we only ranked third: behind Europe and China. Can you imagine the surprise?"

"Hmmm, what is your explanation, Isabella?"

"Well, when I say that we usually rank first, it is when the collection travels, and potential clients can view it personally. This time, with a virtual experience for the first time, and even though most of our clients are so digitally savvy, it was surprising that we fell into third place as a region. We have discussed it internally and found some possible explanations. When probing further with the Client Advisors who know these clients so well, some additional info came to light. Those are fascinating findings, I must say. Well, it will keep us on our guard to keep innovating and ahead of our customer's expectations. But what worries me most now is my team."

"Why do you say that Isabella?" asked Kathy.

"Well, we all kind of expected to get great results, and those just did not pan out. It was a setback for the many people who have been involved in this project over many months. It is disappointing. Of course, it keeps us on our toes, and this learning experience is great, but nevertheless, their morale is quite low now. As a collective retail unit, we will need to make up with higher sales elsewhere. I am sure we will manage. It's just that I need my team to get motivated again. What are your thoughts on getting them back on track and motivated?"

I want to start this chapter by sharing three learnings in my life and career that have proven fundamental. They are all philosophical by nature, shaping my mental strength and contributing profoundly to my self-confidence and life resilience. The first two are from adolescence, and the third came much later in life.

Early in my life, I learned that pursuing **perfection would lead nowhere**. In fact, Winston Churchill had a famous quote saying, "Perfection is the enemy of progress".

Wanting to pursue perfection is possibly a feminine trait, especially true for my generation and more so if you consider that I grew up with a German cultural background.

Luckily, I realised early that the quest for perfection should not be my primary objective since it would often lead to frustration and lack of progress and stifle my pursuit of freedom and happiness. Doing my best, yes; pushing myself, yes; being disciplined and kind, but not castigating myself if things did not work out quite as perfectly as envisioned. I learned to accept the burden of being imperfect, which would become my way for better or worse.

The other philosophical learning during my teenage years came from Sartre and the existentialist literary movement, summarised brilliantly by Albert Camus: **"Life is the sum of all our choices"**. It was key to learn that, in the age when approaching adulthood, when you start making your first major decisions that fundamentally affect the direction of your life.

For Sartre, humans define their meaning and have absolute control and freedom over their choices. He considers the following an introductory statement of fact: "I must be without remorse or regrets as I am without excuse; for from the instant of my upsurge into being, I carry the weight of the world by myself alone without help, engaged in a world for which I bear the whole responsibility without being able, whatever I do, to tear myself away from this responsibility for an instant."

Existentialism deals with the search to find meaning through free will and choice. Many existentialists believe humans should make their own worth regardless of rules, laws or traditions.

Let's go a step further in our choices in life and add a sense of positivity to strive for. The following saying may resonate with us: "May your choices reflect your hopes, not your fears", Nelson Mandela.

Later in life, I adopted the well-known phrase, **"Don't judge others by yourself"**. Very often, the opposite exactly had brought me into trouble – thinking that others would be and feel like me.

I believe there have been three key ingredients in my mental strength journey that I wish to share: the nonsense of striving for perfection, the awareness of judgement and the power and beauty of decisions and responsibility.

What about you? I invite you to take a break and consider your mental strength journey. When did it start? Where are you currently? Which were your main ingredients? Did you recognise any triggering factors? Or decisive moments in life?

Resilience – or how you shape your mental strength – can be learned and developed over time. Resilient people don't wallow or dwell on failures; they acknowledge the situation, learn from their mistakes and then move forward. We can adapt and bounce back when things don't go as planned [1].

According to the research of leading psychologists Susan Kobasa, Salvatore Maddi and their students at the University of Chicago in the 1980s, three elements are essential to resilience [2].

1. **Challenge** – resilient people view a difficulty as a challenge, not a paralysing event. They look at failures and mistakes as lessons to be learned from and growth opportunities. They don't view them as a negative reflection of their abilities or self-worth, which says that resilient people have a positive outlook. Their positive image of the future helps them to envision brighter days ahead. And maintain it through hardship.

2. **Commitment** – resilient people are committed to their lives and goals and have a compelling reason to get out of bed in the morning. Commitment isn't just restricted to their work; they commit to their relationships, friends and the causes they care about. These concrete goals and a strong desire to achieve those goals are what make resilient people so committed.

3. **Personal control** – resilient people spend their time and energy focusing on situations and events they control. Because they put their efforts where they can have the most impact, they feel empowered and confident. Those who spend time worrying about uncontrollable events can often feel lost, helpless and powerless to take action. Same for uncontrollable feelings. Resilient people don't waste time worrying about what others think of them. They maintain healthy relationships and are empathetic and compassionate but don't bow to peer pressure. Even

most importantly, resilient people never think of themselves as victims – they focus their time and energy on changing the things they control.

In my experience of recovering from several setbacks, I have learned that resilience is about how you endure and recharge. And this is very personal to each of us, but I will try to provide you with some patterns that you may find helpful. It is essential to underline that setbacks can be from professional nature or your personal sphere. In both cases, you – your body and mind – still need to cope. Setbacks do not differentiate between your two life personas. If you have built enough resilience, it will be easier for you to bounce back. Take the Nietzsche quote, "What doesn't kill you, makes you stronger" – true, it does not feel very positive, and nevertheless, it is so very true.

While writing this, I was recently robbed – my purse, with some valuable belongings, after a clever distraction manoeuvre. Exasperating and especially annoying to know you have fallen for a con trick. Of course, there was a mix of aggravation and anger, but I knew I needed to recover fast. The longer it took, the worse it would be. I handled it this way: stating the facts first. The thing is done; they have tricked me. I will not get my purse and valuables back; the insurance does not cover this situation. So, that will be that – it's over.

Moreover, I added how much worse it might have been. This mindset helped enormously. And then, you "talk to your mind" – literally. You have this conversation with yourself and be kind to yourself. You convince your mind that you could have done little to avoid the outcome. The tricksters are highly skilled, and you make an easy target if you are generally a trusting character. Lesson learned, and it's improbable they could pull the same trick on me again.

A week later, the event virtually evaporated from my mind. I am a visual person, and some flashes still come to mind about the lightning-fast moment of deception, but this is also a learning process. I know that with time the episode will move from trauma to story.

You must interpret setbacks as something temporary, local and changeable. Don't forget.

My lesson to share here is that it is crucial to learn how you endure hardships and find ways to take charge of your mind swiftly, thoughts and emotions. It is about you, and by knowing yourself well and how you react, you will be better able to test and find techniques that work best to overcome the distress.

In stressful situations that demand resilience, having a sound coping mechanism at the ready is advantageous. In the case of the purse robbery, where I lost some valuable jewellery, I realised these objects could be replaced if I felt the desire. But I could also apply a new technique of bouncing back from this loss to regenerate with a new direction. "In fact, I did not like that ring that much anyway; it was quite chunky, and the colour is not that great. I will find something better to replace it".

Admittedly, this example is simple to overcome; what about health problems? Uncontrollable events in your life? Losses of any sort?

I have experienced these as well, as everyone does over the course of a lifetime. I had a severe spinal disk herniation that immobilized me for several months. Other personal ordeals include finding the perfect partner too late in life to have kids, work colleagues undermining you to enlarge their power grip, a close family member troubled by now overcome mental health issues and another by cancer – all stressful life examples but by no means unique to me.

And all of these can be managed by how you endure first and then how you recharge after.

I am sure you have watched a professional tennis match sometime in your life. Whether you have or not, I would recommend you check out the Roland Garros 2022 Quarterfinal between Rafael Nadal and Novak Djokovic. Even if their preparation involves multiple team members, coaches, physios, psychologists and fitness trainers, in the end, there is the match, and they face their opponent alone. Sometimes, it can happen when there is a moment when mental fortitude can make or break the match. In the fourth and decisive set (Nadal was leading 2 sets to 1), Nadal returned when he was 3–1 down and won the set and the match. He showed his strong self-belief and fought for every ball and opportunity. A never-give-up mentality that he has shown throughout his career. More than ten years earlier, at another match in Roland Garros, he stepped up his game and refused to quit in the third set. He could easily have let it go for the opponent and concentrated on winning the fourth set. But he refused to give up at the moment he was 5-1 40-0 down and came back to win the set and the game.

What is even more impressive is to be able to have such a tempered mental strength at only 20 years of age. This is the case of Carlos Alcaraz – another impressive Spanish tennis player – at the 2023 Wimbledon final. Down after the first set and struggling simply to avoid embarrassment, Alcaraz rediscovered his unique combination of speed, power and touch and figured out the subtleties of grass-court tennis in the nick of time. He clawed his way back into the match in an epic 85-minute second set in which he was a point away from what figured to be an insurmountable two-set deficit.

The capacity of top athletes to overcome the pressure of the moment and immerse themselves in a prevailing mindset is remarkable. They can overcome the sometimes debilitating effect of the adrenaline rush and set themselves in a self-controlled mode of focus and calm. They have such a strong belief in their capacities – through all the hours of effort, dedication and preparation on the journey to get to that moment – they can dig deep, believe in themselves and channel moments of high pressure into almost superhuman abilities.

There is a similarity with the skills I already mentioned; talk your mind into a positive state, override the outcome you do not want and rewire your brain into success mode.

Sometimes it may be helpful to evaluate the cause of your anxiety. How to turn a difficult situation into a positive one – maybe a change of attitude towards whatever is causing the stress. This change does not mean that it will not re-occur, but when it does, you will be better prepared to deal with and cope with the situation. Often, the stress might be out of your control, so learning how to deal with it and make it work for you is a fundamental learning. Changing your perception of a situation or person and manipulating a favourable outcome is possible.

When it comes to your resilience and well-being, a significant contributor, both positive and negative, is relationships. I say positive and negative because there is an adage, "Who you spend time with is who you become". Relationships need constant vigilance and evaluation, and your judgement must be insightful long before they are called upon in challenging times. Consider this: if you are "the result of the five people you hang out with", Who are these people? How are they wired? Do they provide you with positive or rather negative energy?

Who you spend time with is who you become. Beware of energy vampires.

There is no question that relationships bolster our resilience. The people who know us intimately understand us and have no ulterior motive to say things that only they can say and that provide us comfort and reassurance, not pity. Let me share with you some very supportive and valuable comments I received from friends during such a period in my life: "You have many different possible options to evaluate", "it's a fantastic opportunity to revitalise yourself and consider alternatives", they also kept sending articles and links for inspiration, they joined for quality time together, and encouraged for new ventures, transformative projects and contacts.

There is no question that developing strong, trusting relationships, privately and at work, can only be of profound benefit. People with strong connections at work are more resistant to stress and happier in their roles. This also goes for your personal life: the more real friendships you develop, the more resilient you'll be because, ultimately, you have a strong support web to fall back on.

Building these relationships correctly as we progress through our careers is vital. But what is the right way? What is to be avoided? Relationships should not be undervalued resources, but we may sometimes lose sight of continuously building on them and keeping them up. Younger generations have understood the principle well, bolstered by social media and personal branding.

Regarding relationships, as mentioned before, our resilience tools are personal. Our unique history, personality and professional/personal context shape them. Having done some reflection and nurtured your self-awareness, you may have identified the top three sources of resilience you would most like to reinforce in your life. Please make a note of those that are most important for you and set out to work on their advancement. Once identified and developed, you should plan on how to expand your network. Here are some suggestions taken from the interesting article "The Secret to Building Resilience" [3]:

1. **Work Surge**: Connections that help us shift work or manage surges.
2. **Politics**: Connections that help us to make sense of people or politics in a situation
3. **Pushback**: Connections that help us find the confidence to push back and self-advocate
4. **Vision**: Connections that help us see the path forward
5. **Perspective**: Connections that help us to maintain perspective when setbacks happen
6. **Purpose**: Connections that remind us of the purpose or meaning in our work
7. **Humour**: Connections that help us to laugh at ourselves and the situation
8. **Empathy**: Connections that provide empathetic support so that we can release negative emotions

I want to end this Section by glancing at Chanel's Spring Summer 2023 Fashion Show on October 4th 2022. Kirsten Steward, actress and House ambassador, introduced the show with the following words: "It's no longer important to know who you are or even what you want. I think it's important to burn down your very best yesterday. Every day. So, you can start again".

These words resemble those I read around the same time about Juliette Binoche's life quest [4]. In an interview, the French actress stated that her life mission is "transformation". Literally, she said that we move forward in life through separations. As kids, we leave aside our first toys and separate from our friends, families and partners. Life is a continuous separation. Without separation, there is no evolution. She does not mean that every relationship needs separation but should allow the opportunity for each other to grow and flourish. Juliette Binoche has played mainly women who transform themselves in her acting career. She says that the role usually does not interest her if she doesn't see a transformation in the script.

And further on, she asserts that our true mission in life is to transform ourselves. For her, this means learning and understanding new things and leaving behind useless stuff. From those transformations, we come out lighter and more authentic. There is nothing better than to change, she declares. In a way, she is telling us that every ending is a new beginning. Maybe this view offers more hope.

But Juliette also recognises, as should we, that change demands courage. To achieve this, she recommends believing – this is the most important. She ends up saying that the fundamental aspect of being an actress is believing. "If one doesn't believe, one cannot transform the self".

Think about Carla Bruni as another example. She has always amazed me with how she transitioned from one incarnation to another seemingly effortlessly. Carla Bruni must have genuinely believed in herself, transitioning from a top model career to becoming a mother, then a very talented and recognised singer and songwriter, and excelling as a first lady of France for some years. Truly impressive.

Returning to the lessons Juliette leaves us in her interview, she expresses that as artists, they are allowed to do so because in art, 'the normal' should not exist. Artists must constantly move towards the unexpected and create unique and inspiring work. This sentiment certainly resonates with me. I see this as the precise message and raison d'être that our most iconic painters, musicians, dancers, sculptors, designers, architects, etc., have left us. We admire their courage to believe in themselves; we allow ourselves to believe what they believe. At least sometimes. This should be enough for us.

3.2 The secret to enduring in style

"Hi, everyone! My name is Lucy Cheng. It's a pleasure to be with you today to share some of my professional experiences. It has been some time since being here – at my university – so it is even more of an honour and pleasure chatting with you all tonight".

Lucy was delighted to have been invited. One of her former professors at the university connected with her only a couple of months ago. She felt that she wished to share and take time to provide orientation to young students in business and economics. Previously she had little time to dedicate to it or even chat with former colleagues who had decided to enter academia. This time, no excuse. She had been contacted by her favourite professor, who specialised in organisational behaviour, and she just couldn't say no. She ensured no other topic was on her agenda that afternoon, so she could at least prepare for it a couple of hours in advance.

It was the first time in more than ten years that she had returned to the benches on which she had spent so much time and countless lectures, and she was happy to have made it.

"I am Chief People Officer in Greater China for an American Hospitality company. Very proud to be contributing to this fascinating company, especially in times of post-pandemic customer behaviour shifts. The message I want to share with you today is: to be courageous. By taking measured risks, stepping out of your comfort zone, and pushing your boundaries of fear with considered but bold moves, you will surely grow, not only as a person but also as a professional."

"I view getting out of your comfort zone, trying new things, and walking unpaved paths as an adventure that offers unparalleled rewards. I adore taking adventures – especially on my holidays – and feel life is more fulfilling with this mindset. But it is something you must experience for yourself, really. Are you more of a risk-taker or risk-averse person? I would suggest that whatever your preference, you should hold it in high worth when it comes to fostering your career and your life. It is one of those building blocks. And, of course, your foundational values may evolve over time. So, even if you prefer to walk on the well-trodden path and like to have a familiar environment around you, I would suggest going out of your exploration envelope now and then. It will allow you to better understand the fast-paced world we all live in, be more empathetic with others, and open yourself up to new learnings. And this aspect is probably the most useful because whatever our personality may be, stagnation in life is never good. Evolution, learning, and progress is the advisable strategy. In which doses? Well, this is then up to you".

"Let me ask you all a question. And you don't need to answer it straight away. Please take a moment to think about it. It is the question of whether you feel more comfortable as a big fish in a small pond or a small fish in a big pond. Can you picture the illustra-

tion? Are you more like someone who lives in a well-known environment, where you know everyone, know the language, and how things work, not much change occurs, and you can plan your routines with ease? It pans out, you are not threatened and feel very comfortable and happy with it – this is the big fish in a small pond scenario. Or do you rather enjoy the thrill of an unknown environment around you, where you have plenty to discover, you may not know the language, the traditions, their people's set of values, where every day feels different, there is uncertainty around you, you cannot plan, but still this environment of endless possibilities speaks to you, and you feel happy there – so more like a small fish in a big pond. What would be your character? Or your natural tendency?"

The professor seemed excited and jumped in, "Ha, this is a great metaphor to visualise what you have just been introducing Lucy; thanks. We will now collect all your voices via a digital counting system, which interests me".

After the counting and viewing in which direction the class was oriented, Lucy continued:

"It is key for you to acknowledge for yourself what your preference is, whatever it is", and she looked over the whole audience, ensuring she did not forget anyone.

"But I will not leave the room before sharing this thought. The process of stepping out of your comfort zone (even if it is less often than an average person), this specific experience and attitude will provide you with additional fortitude, increase your resistance to setbacks, and provide you greater levels of resilience. This strength comes from learning, developing new skills or adapting your existing skills in a new environment. Forcing yourself to make that additional effort will pay dividends in the long run, either in success or experience and hopefully in both. From my humble experience, I can share that you can experiment with a virtuous circle. The more risk-exposed I am, the more resilience I will develop. I will feel more confident to endure risk. As easy as that".

Lucy finished with a smile and was happy to take over the Q&A session now.

"We need to accept that we won't always make the right decisions, that we'll screw up royally sometimes – understanding that failure is not the opposite of success, it's part of success". These are the wise words of a highly successful businesswoman – Arianna Huffington.

Resilient people are confident they will succeed eventually, despite the setbacks or stresses they might have to endure. This belief in themselves also empowers them to take risks. When you develop confidence and a strong sense of self, you have the strength to keep moving forward and to take the risks you need to get ahead.

One particular learning from being courageous, putting yourself out there and failing is that you realise the idea of failing is far more daunting than the failure itself. You fall, get up, brush yourself off and continue your quest.

Even if you don't feel naturally resilient, you can learn to develop a resilient mindset and attitude. To do so, incorporate the following into your daily life [5]:

1. **Practice positive thinking**.
    Don't let negative thoughts derail your efforts or energy. Listen to how you talk to yourself when something goes wrong. If you find yourself making permanent, pervasive or personalised statements, correct these thoughts in your mind. And edit your outlook. Practice cognitive (brain and thought) restructuring to change beliefs about negative situations and bad events.

2. **Choose your response.**
    Your reaction is always your choice. We all experience bad days or go through our share of crises. But we have a choice in how we respond: we can choose to react with panic and negativity, or we can choose to remain calm and logical to find a solution.

3. **Maintain perspective**. Resilient people understand that, although a situation or crisis may seem overwhelming at the moment, it may not make that much of an impact over the long term.

4. Remember, your brain is like a supercomputer. If you constantly program it with negative thoughts or outcomes, it will likely deliver them for you – **program positivity**.

5. How we **view and deal with adversity** and stress clearly **affects our chances of success**. This is one of the most profound reasons why having a resilient mindset is so important.

6. We're going to **fail from time to time** – it's **an inevitable part of living** that we make mistakes and occasionally fall flat on our faces. The only way to avoid this is to live a shuttered and meagre existence, never trying anything new or taking a risk. Few of us want a life like that!

7. Instead, we should **have the courage to go after our dreams**, despite the genuine risk that we'll fail somehow. Being resilient means that when we fall, we bounce back, have the strength to learn the lessons we need to learn and can move on to bigger and better things.

Overall, resilience gives us the power to overcome setbacks to live the life we've always imagined.

As Adam Grant – Professor at Wharton University – puts it: "Scars are more than evidence of trauma. They're proof of resilience. Sometimes it reveals strength you didn't realise you had. Pain is not just a teacher. It's a relic – a reminder of your ability to withstand adversity."

3.3 Five key resilience pillars to recharge

"Hi, how was your weekend? Did you manage to go hiking finally?" asked Lucy to her colleague Charlotte in charge of the Sales Department. "Oh yes, what a pleasure. We left our toddler with my parents and disappeared for two days; what a relief. Now and then, you have to do it . . . recharge those batteries. What about you?"

Both were sitting – as every Monday morning – at the board meeting room in Shanghai. The President for Greater China reunited the senior leadership team weekly for updates and discussions on ongoing projects.

What was different this time was that they had all undergone an MBTI test a few weeks earlier as part of a leadership program. The objective was to understand people's profiles better; make everyone aware of differences in personality, communication and leadership style and hopefully find better ways to align themselves. The outcome discussion was on today's agenda.

Before the President arrived, John – Head of Operations – entered the room and found Charlotte and Lucy. "So I see, we in Operations, Finance, HR, we all scored more as an introvert type, while you guys, from Marketing and the Retailers, you are all extrovert types. Well, is this of any surprise? How cliché is that"?

Charlotte took her time before answering. She knew that John was not easy to convince and always had his own strong opinions well anchored ahead of any possible discussion.

"From my understanding", started Charlotte, "but I suppose we will get an explanation in a while, it is less so the fact of being more of an extroverted or introverted character. The predisposition shows not how you behave but how you recharge your energy. This is, from my understanding, how it works. The key here is energy levels. Some of us pull our energy from interacting with others, and some of us avoid interaction with others, taking some quiet and introspective time for ourselves. I do not see any pros and cons for either aspect, just a certain preference. How do you see it?"

In my opinion, building resilience via your recharging strategies needs to be done with resolute effort. This will help you at the moment when you need it most. It is a kind of force or stamina that needs to be fully charged before it is called upon. To face the event, not to encounter the event, so to speak.

What do I mean?

Research has found a direct correlation between a slow recovery and an increased incidence of health and safety problems. In other words, the lack of a concerted recovery period dramatically affects our collective ability to be resilient and successful. Homeostasis is a fundamental biological concept describing the ability of the brain to restore and sustain well-being continuously. When the body is out of alignment from overworking, we waste many mental and physical resources trying to return to balance before moving forward. It is advisable to take a cognitive break every 90 minutes to recharge your batteries. My advice here would be to help yourself with an hourglass. I changed my habits in this regard following my spine issues. I no longer allowed myself to sit for prolonged periods and changed to a stand-up office desk. I also introduced an hourglass to prompt me to take regular breaks. I also introduced more stand-up and walking meetings with my teams.

But be aware that stopping does not equal recovering. Our brains need rest as our bodies do. I am sure you have recognised that it very often takes at least a couple of your first holiday days until you have a rested mind. Do you usually feel the change happening on day 2 or 3? Recovering is taking time off. A vacation, a weekend away, an evening enjoying a hobby, only this is a proper break and a recovery period.

Taking care of our minds and bodies will allow us to cope effectively with the challenges we face in our daily lives.

Rest and relaxation are vital elements to recharging energy. I have experienced people that need to learn to relax. It does not seem innate to humans anymore, and we all need to take stock. Our health and longevity depend on it. We often only pay attention when our bodies send us an alarm signal. I recommend developing a good sleep routine and learning relaxation techniques such as deep breathing or meditation. Use your bathtub and bath salts more often as a more immediate remedy.

1. A good sleep routine

Regarding a good sleep routine, I would like to share my learnings from Professor Matthew Walker, professor of neuroscience and psychology at the University of California Berkeley and author of the book "Why we sleep" [6]. He states that it is important to carve out a non-negotiable 8-hour sleep for our resting time to get better sleep. This is followed by a set of five suggestions for everyone to put into place:

– Try and maintain regularity – going to sleep and waking up at the same time, even on weekends.
– Since we are a dark-deprived (or light-polluted) society in this modern era, we need darkness in the evening to release melatonin. This is a hormone that regulates the healthy timing of our sleep cycles. Therefore, he recommends trying to dim down half the lights in your home and staying away from screens (especially those led blue lights) for at least an hour before bed.
– Keep it cool. Your bedroom should not be too warm. Around 18.5 degrees Celsius is the ideal room temperature to drop your body temperature and to initiate good sleep.
– Avoid excesses of alcohol and caffeine. You may think alcohol helps sleep, but it does not really; alcohol just knocks you down but does not relax your body; also,

alcohol will fragment your sleep. Caffeine is – as we know – an alerting chemical, a stimulant. Therefore, the depth of your sleep will never reach the levels you need if you had avoided caffeine, and you will most likely feel unrefreshed and unrested when you wake up. You will probably need 3–4 cups of coffee the following day, soon becoming an addiction.

– Do not stay in bed awake. If you wake up during the night and find it difficult to get back to sleep after some 20 mins or so, don't stay in bed. Your brain learns an association: bed = sleep, that you should preserve. That's why you should get up and, in dim light, read a book (no screen, no food) until you start to feel sleepy again and return to your bedroom. If you don't feel like leaving your room for some reason, meditation may help. You search here to relax your body and calm your nervous system to fall asleep again.

2. Keeping your body in movement

As crucial as rest and relaxation is movement. What do you do to keep your body in motion? And I do not mean walking or counting steps with an App; I mean the movement that brings your heart rate up and challenges your body to get every part going. This is what our bodies need in today's far too sedentary societies.

In his book 'Born to Run', Christopher McDougall researched the Tarahumara tribe in Mexico, who had a fantastic ability to run ultra marathons with apparent ease [7]. Whilst certain sections of the human population around the world have developed specialist skills, one thing we can be sure of is that we were all 'Born to Move'.

We have evolved over millions of years to move, and our bodies depend on movement for our health. Our ancestors had very physically active lives, so we never had to think about or engage in additional exercise to keep healthy. The concept of exercise for fitness is only a relatively recent one in our evolutionary history. It has become more critical as our lifestyles have become more sedentary.

Most people are aware of the benefits of movement and exercise. So, in this section, I will focus particularly on the benefits of movement for your business or professional life.

– Movement has been shown to have many beneficial effects on mental health. This includes a reduction of depression and anxiety whilst improving overall mood and self-esteem.
– Not unrelated to mental health is the effect of movement on reducing overall stress levels.
– Movement has been shown to increase energy levels, and equally important is the converse of that. When you are not moving regularly, the results can be lethargy and tiredness, which you must avoid when dealing with a challenging work environment.

- Movement helps with good quality sleep. Episodes of insomnia are reduced post-exercise.
- Regular movement has been shown to improve focus and concentration. This may be related to the increase in energy as detailed before.
- Movement has many brain and cognitive benefits. It aids concentration, as mentioned before, but also memory and analytical skills. Movement has also been seen to slow age-related cognitive decline, like the various forms of dementia.
- Your immune system gets a massive kick from exercise and movement. One key element of your immune system is the lymphatic system. The lymphatic system almost mirrors the blood circulatory system with one major exception – a pump, i.e. the heart. Movement of fluids through the lymph is almost totally reliant on the squeeze effect of contracting muscles – no exercise = no contraction and a stagnant and unhealthy lymph fluid.

Sometimes it might feel like you don't have enough hours to exercise and move. Knowing how important it is to your mental and physical health, it would be a mistake to ignore it.

Start with easy achievables – sometimes known as 'activities of daily life' you can suddenly improve your time doing movement just by changing simple daily habits. Walk the stairs rather than taking the elevator, run or cycle to work, do walking or standing meetings.

Balance is a great exercise – try standing on one leg on a bus or train.

Regarding more rigorous exercise, finding things you like doing to make consistent movement sustainable is vital. Take up a sport or physical activity. Even if you do gym or cross-training exercises, always try and think of improving your strength, stamina and skill for the sport you enjoy doing. Suppose you approach lifting weights to improve at snow-skiing, playing tennis or golf, hiking, swimming or cycling. In that case, it is easier to maintain.

3. Caring for a healthy nutrition
The next important step in how you recharge is nutrition. Let's stop here for a second: nutrition is part of rejuvenating the body. How do you think your body reacts if you feed it a sandwich or salad for 5 minutes in front of your computer screen? You may have saved yourself that trip to the canteen/salad shop/restaurant, but nutrition has been useless. For nutrient benefits to kick in, our bodies need to be rested. The best for office lunches is to walk away from your desk, enjoy time with others and take the necessary time for the body to unwind before eating.

The pace at which you eat is also essential; take your entire lunch break to eat slowly, calm yourself and socialise. It is important to remember that if you are stressed, you are in flight and fight mode. This means your whole digestive tract is shut down, and any good nutritional choices you have made are wholly wasted – they go straight through you. You must get yourself into the rest and digest or parasympathetic mode to properly absorb your food. So that is the importance of how you eat; let's now look at what you eat.

Here's a small research task for you: go onto amazon.com, go to the Books department next to the search bar, and then in the search bar, type *nutrition.* I tried this a couple of days ago and managed 70,000 search results – and that is only because I am sure the search engine got bored. Do a nutrition search on Google, and you'll get around 3.7 billion results. The point is that nutrition is one of our planet's most talked about, written about and controversial topics. Why, might you wonder? A leopard knows it should eat gazelle, and a panda bear knows it should eat bamboo shoots. Why is it so complicated for humans? The answer is that we have managed to inhabit every part of this planet and have had to adapt to the foods that were available in those environments. Then we decided to stop moving and domesticate wild animals and plants; the next phase was to start experimenting with cross-breeding these plants and animals. Now we have billion-dollar industries supplying urban populations with food. Some people have never even seen a cow, a chicken or a wheat field and have literally zero clue about what they are putting into their mouths.

Because nutrition is such a contentious topic, I will keep things simple and stick to known truths.

As humans, we have had to adapt and evolve. In general, our ancestors were omnivores. Evidence shows we were hunters, gatherers and scavengers. We would eat pretty much anything that wasn't poisonous. With the breakthrough of the ability to control and cook with fire, many items were added to our diet that would have been poisonous when eaten raw – potatoes (or their tuber ancestors) are a prime example.

The move from hunter-gathering to traditional farming to modern industrialised agriculture (which we need to sustain 8 billion of us) has been associated with the degrading nutritional value of our food.

All animals know that sweet food in the wild (generally rare) is energy dense. This means that a small amount provides us with a vast energy resource. But acquiring such energy comes at a cost; watch any mammal discover a beehive with honey – they will endure the wrath of the protective bees to get a mouthful.

With the discovery of sugar cane and sugar beet and the domestication of bees, sweet and sugary suddenly became very easy to attain, and food companies realised how addictive and lucrative sugar is.

Fat is also energy dense and, in the wild, highly valued. Hunting animals having made a kill will always take the fattiest organs first – the filet steak is left for those further down the pecking order or the scavengers who come after.

Unfortunately, fat has had a bad reputation in the past decades. Part of the problem is the name *fat* which is one of the three main macronutrients but is also the word used to describe people regarded as overweight or obese. Sadly, many assume that eating fat leads to being fat, which it does not.

Healthy fats are critical for our well-being, particularly for the brain and good cognitive function.

So what is healthy nutrition? I will just bullet point some key points below.

– Don't worry too much about micro-analysing the nutritional content of foods or superfoods. Eat food that is local and seasonal. An apple in season from 5 km away is more likely to have more nutritional benefits than a Goji berry from 5000 km away – plus, it's a lot better for the planet.
– Cook your own food. You will always make better choices of ingredients, and you will be in control of the amount of sugar and salt you consume. Research has shown that people who cook for themselves attain far more significant nutritional benefits than those who eat fast food, take-aways or pre-prepared meals.
– Eat variety. Humans thrive on a variety of foods; it's part of our evolutionary past. A variety of types of food, and when it comes to fruit and veg, choose all kinds and colours – they all have their unique benefits.
– Finally, and possibly the most important for your brain and body health, is looking after your microbiota. These trillions of micro-organisms in your digestive tract help break down and absorb the foods you eat. There are two main ways to help your microbiota. The first is actually to eat foods or supplements that contain good bacteria – these are known as probiotics. They are good but have a short-lived effect. The sources of probiotics are supplementation or probiotic foods, which include: fermented foods like German Sauerkraut, yoghurt, kombucha, pickles and some cheeses.

  The second is pre-biotics. These are foods that your gut bacteria love. They are often high in soluble and insoluble fibre and are perfect nutrition for your microbiota. Some examples would be many foods from the onion family, like all types of onions, garlic, leaks, chives and shallots—artichokes and Jerusalem artichokes, asparagus, bananas and oats.

Another good reason to look after your gut is that it is like a second brain with over 100 million nerve cells closely resembling those in your brain. Research in the past few decades has uncovered a fantastic connection between the gut and the brain. In fact, even in the few weeks and months of life, some of the chemicals produced by the gut microbiota can affect the brain's development.

The gut-brain axis plays a significant role in your overall health – including mental health. In short, a healthy gut means a healthy brain.

So that is it: trust your body and your ancestors (without them, you wouldn't be here) and keep it simple.

When it comes to our ancient ancestry, one thing to remember is that they didn't sit down to three meals a day or spend their days snacking on amazing comfort foods. They would eat irregularly, sometimes going days or even weeks without food. Their and our bodies were and are perfectly adapted to long periods of fasting, which has the bonus side effect of being enormously beneficial to body and brain health. So, let's talk about fasting.

4. Adopting intermittent fasting as a habit

What about intermittent fasting? I am sure you must have heard about it. I am not suggesting that you fast in the office every day, but what about one day a week? I do it. On Mondays – after the weekend.

Here are the scientifically proven health benefits intermittent fasting has for your body and brain [8]:

- Triggers Autophagy
- Improves Memory
- Brightens Mood
- Reduces Inflammation
- Fights High Blood Sugar
- Lowers Blood Pressure at Night
- Burns Excess Fat

It was brought to the fore in 2016 by a Japanese cell biologist Yoshinori Ohsumi – who won a Nobel Prize "for his discoveries of mechanisms for autophagy". Autophagy is a remarkable process the body uses to give itself what is essentially a good cleanout. Meaning "self-eating" in Greek, autophagy is often likened to a form of cellular house-keeping. Each cell can destroy or engulf old or worn-out internal components and take them to its waste disposal unit within the cell, called the lysosome. It's a marvellous example of natural biochemical engineering. This detox system doesn't require you to buy any special products – you just need to trust the wisdom of your body.

Some people have medical conditions that make fasting inadvisable – for example, those with diabetes. But for most people, the body can function without losing energy during a short fast. When food is not consumed, the body draws on its reserves. Glucose is stored in muscle and the liver in the form of glycogen. This storage is the equivalent of about 2,000 calories. When you fast, your body draws on this glycogen to provide energy. Energy may also be released from body fat. After an overnight fast, the body starts to burn fat and ketones, substances made from body fat. Ketones provide fuel to the brain in the absence of glucose. That is why intermittent fasting is so good for fat burning [9].

There's nothing new about fasting; it's what humans have done for millennia and for numerous reasons, from health to religious observation. There are also many ways to approach intermittent fasting; there are no hard-and fast-rules, and there are as many variations on this theme as there are reasons to try it.

It doesn't have to be complicated: a long overnight fast, beginning with an early evening meal and ending with a late breakfast, is an efficient and (for most people) manageable form of time-restricted intermittent fasting. Or you can keep your dinner timing and skip breakfast and lunch once a week, as I do. It is doable, and you will feel the benefits right away. When you give your body a break, the magic begins and the brain benefits.

5. Looking after your Soul

Last but not least, I recommend also dedicating enough consideration to your Soul.

What can you do to nurture your soul? Well, here we need, as humans, to take the time and dedicate energy to the topics 'that we are passionate about', the things we love and the activities that 'make us tick'. What can that be? Everyone is different, but some examples might be: inviting friends over for dinner, outdoor sports, nature, discovering art galleries, culture trips, cooking, teaching, dancing, listening to music, wine tasting and having fun.

Please remember to keep all these areas in balance. This means that all aspects need time and energy and require dedication and improvement at equal levels. Also, remember that dedicating time to what you love doing gives you energy so often – it's a straightforward win.

3.4 Getting along with anyone

"I no longer believe it's my place to change anyone's mind. All I can do is try to understand their thinking and ask if they're open to some rethink. The rest is up to them", Adam Grant [10].

This statement clicked with me. I couldn't agree more. It summarises many of my learnings in 20+ years of corporate life. I have developed enough self-awareness to understand my perceptions, triggers and behaviours. I have finally understood that it's only worth taking on the issues over which I have some control. And that I will not be able to change people, only myself.

What is possible, though, is to try to lean into the understanding of other people by being as empathic as possible, even with the seemingly most toxic people in your sphere. This will allow you to understand their position, motivations and general thinking. If you can accomplish this, an alternative approach is possible, which gives them the space and opportunity to rethink and reposition, as maybe you will yourself [11].

This is the best possible option for positive outcomes.

In the previous section, I have explained how I build resilience. All of them will allow you to deal better with difficult colleagues. In this case, your resilience reserves will be funnelled into interpersonal resilience.

At this point, I would like to introduce Amy Gallo. She has taught at Brown University and the University of Pennsylvania. She is a workplace expert who writes and speaks about gender, interpersonal dynamics, difficult conversations, feedback and effective communication. She works with individuals and teams to help them better collaborate, communicate and transform their culture to support dissent and debate.

The strategies I recommend considering – since they are positive and proactive – are the following three taken from Amy Gallo's book "Getting Along: How to Work with Anyone (Even Difficult People)" [12]:

1. Venting productively
Discussing conflicts with someone you trust is a healthy way of relieving stress. It will help prevent negative emotions from permeating interactions with your colleagues or other parts of your life. It is crucial to ensure you can trust the person you are opening up to. You may also consider venting in writing. Journaling is a good mechanism for some people, with similar effects to meditation.

2. Building a micro-culture
I find this one particularly helpful since I have actively worked on it, with very positive results for all the participants and me. Rather than allowing toxic relationships to dominate your work experience, determine what you need to be effective and happy

in your job and then build a coalition of people committed to similar goals and values. This can be project-based or with your own team. As McKee writes, "and while it may be easier to do this when you are the team leader, it's not critical that you be in a position of power". Even if your company may not advance in a toxic culture per se, there can be moments in corporate life, like a restructuring or a new boss arriving, that require this tactic to preserve motivation for yourself and your team.

3. Accept the situation

Part of interpersonal resilience is accepting that we can't always have the relationships we want. And we can't get along with everyone. Some people won't necessarily engage with this strategy even when you try to say what's on your mind with empathy and kindness. And while you assume the best of someone, they may not reciprocate. Disagreements are inevitable; this is a normal and often healthy part of relating to others. The goal isn't to feel comfortable every step of the way; it's to strengthen your relationship and take care of yourself in the process.

What I found very useful in reading Amy Gallo's book was to acknowledge that a complex relationship at work requires three entities: oneself, the other person and the dynamic between the two people.

For each entity, I would suggest focusing on two topics.

Starting with oneself, it is paramount to answer these two key questions:

1a)   Are you aware of your own biases?
1b)   Are you clear about your own goal?

Then take the other person: 2a) remember that your perspective is just one viewpoint, yours. Rely on empathy and humility and stay curious with a growth mentality. You should be able to understand other perspectives. And 2b) Only focus on what you can control. The other person is not included here.

And very important: the dynamic between you. 3a) A common mistake to avoid: "don't make it me versus them", and 3b) take the time and energy to experiment to find out what can work.

Let's start then with those six areas to work through:

1a) Are you aware of your own biases?
Interactions with our coworkers are not only influenced by our values and experiences but also by our biases. Even our definition of "difficult" behaviour can be shaped by the prejudices that we carry into the workplace. Two specific types of bias are ben-

eficial to understand when navigating complicated relationships: affinity bias and confirmation bias.

Affinity bias is the unconscious tendency to get along with people who are like us. In other words, we gravitate toward people with similar appearances, beliefs and backgrounds. When colleagues aren't like us – perhaps in terms of gender, race, ethnicity, education, physical abilities or position at work – we are less likely to want to work with them. That's why it's critical when we're struggling with a coworker to ask ourselves: "What role could our own bias be playing here? Is it possible I'm not seeing the situation clearly because we're different in certain ways?".

Another form of prejudice that often seeps into workplace relationships is ***confirmation bias***. This tendency to interpret events or evidence as confirmation of existing beliefs plays out with vexing coworkers in two ways. First, suppose your view of a colleague is negative. In that case, you are more likely to interpret their actions as further evidence of your belief about them – they're not up to the task, they're unkind or they only care about themselves. Second, suppose you've started to believe that your coworker falls into a specific stereotype. In that case, it will be increasingly difficult for that person to prove you wrong.

So how do you suspend these biases? For example, you may get to know your biases by taking an online quiz. Amy Gallo suggests the one from Project Implicit, a nonprofit started by researchers at Harvard, the University of Washington and the University of Virginia. Another exercise you may try is to explore different perspectives by learning through your own research, reading articles or books, listening to podcasts, attending conferences, etc. You may also consult someone you trust to reflect on how you might see the situation unfairly. You may also play devil's advocate with yourself. These are all tactics that you may apply to catch your own biases. And would you not like others to do the same towards avoiding biases against you?

1b) Are you clear about your own goal?
Whenever you are trying to address an issue with a coworker, it's essential to be clear with yourself about what you want. Identifying your goal will help you avoid getting pulled into drama and stay focused on constructive tactics. Do you want to move a stalled project forward? Complete the initiative you've been working on and move on? Have a healthy working relationship that will last into the future? Feel less angry and frustrated after interacting with them? Or do you want your colleague to stop undermining your success? Amy Gallo recommends making a list of the goals you'd like to achieve and then circling the one, two or three that are most important. Your intentions will subconsciously and consciously determine how you act and react. Refer to your goals before interacting with your colleague to stay focused on your destination. In a way, I see that as determining which are the goals related to the project you are working on together and which are on the table for everyone involved in the

meeting to tackle. Then there are those under the table that you act upon to bring the relationship to a better place.

2a) Your perspective is just one perspective

If you are stalled with a coworker in a difficult conversation, it may well be that you are facing the fact that there is rarely one objective truth. We all come to the workplace with different perspectives and sets of values. We may disagree on everything from whether it's ok to be five minutes late to a meeting or whether interrupting someone is justifiable to the appropriate consequences of making a mistake. It's unrealistic to think you'll work with people who always see eye to eye with you. There is a concept from social psychology called 'naïve realism'. It relates to the tendency to believe that we see the world objectively. If someone doesn't see it the same way, they are uninformed, irrational or biased. Similar is fundamental attribution error. This is the inclination to observe another person's behaviour and assume it has more to do with their personality than with the situation in which they find themselves. So, suppose your colleague is late for a meeting. In that case, you might presume they're disorganised or disrespectful, not because they were caught in traffic or another meeting that ran over. But you would do the opposite when it comes to yourself, right? It is important to remember those two biases since you are likely to make assumptions that aren't necessarily the truth. Please remember that you don't need to agree to get along. You must simply respect each other's perspective enough to decide on a way forward. Helpful questions to challenge your perspective may be: What if I'm wrong? How would I act differently? How do I know that what I believe is true? What assumptions have I made? How would someone with different values and experiences see things differently?

2b) Only focus on what you can control

We have all fantasised about saying or doing the perfect thing that persuades a rival to see the light, realise the error of their ways and vow to reform completely. But, no, the only control you have is over yourself. The suggestion is, therefore, to focus on the things that you do have the power to affect, no matter how insignificant they may seem. What is controllable might be pretty basic. Maybe you can't dictate how your coworker treats you. Still, you can build up your own defences by getting a good night's sleep, eating well, exercising and spending time outside. That is building on your resilience levels. Start small, focusing on progress in one area, since the more freedom you have over how you spend your time and energy, the less stuck you will feel. As said before, you may write down some thoughts or a great quote you like and read it aloud as a mantra when struggling with a nasty email or gearing up for a difficult conversation.

Here is where I would like to introduce you to the two human archetypes I found most challenging when confronted with them in corporate life. Both can be seen to be somehow connected, and the same person may even show traits of both archetypes. They are complicated cases, I must say. I am talking about the archetypes "The Passive-Aggressive Peer" and "The Political Operator". I invite you to discover the other six human archetypes that Amy Gallo describes brilliantly in her book. She also shares clues to understand them better and how to handle them. Her analysis and lessons are comforting, and for this book, I chose those that resonated the most with me. Still, I invite you also to discover the others. Those are: "The Insecure Boss", "The Pessimist", "The Victim", "The Know-It-All", "The Tormentor" and "The Biased Coworker". The names may seem daunting, but believe me, all those archetypes exist for real in the corporate world. As you know, we do not choose our colleagues; we will not change them, so we better prepare to handle them best. Voilà – my best advice.

Even if you cannot control these people, you should note that learning how they operate will avoid common mistakes that may worsen the situation.

The passive-aggressive peer

In this coworker archetype, we are dealing with someone who appears to comply with the wishes and needs of others but then passively resists following through. Sometimes the saboteur will do the task, but too late to be helpful or in a way that doesn't meet the stated goals. They may deliberately ignore deadlines after they've agreed to meet them, promising to send an email that never arrives, acting rudely toward you and then denying anything wrong when you confront them, claiming, for example, "I have no idea what you're talking about". What is often behind such behaviour is the avoidance of being honest about their feelings or trying to manipulate the situation in their favour without being obvious. Displaying body language that projects anger but insisting they're okay, implying that they aren't happy with your work but refusing to come out and say so or give you direct feedback. And very often, twisting your words in a disagreement so it seems like you're the one who's in the wrong.

We often assign hostile intentions to others where they don't exist. This is why it is vital to understand whether your colleague is genuinely out to get you. People's objectives aren't always clear; therefore, be generous in your interpretations and realistic about what's happening.

Here are some tactics suggested by Amy Gallo to improve your odds of getting along with a passive-aggressive peer:

–   **Focus on the content, not the delivery**
    Nudge them empathetically into being more productive in their interactions.

- **Open up a conversation**
Create a safe environment and make clear that you're interested in their perspective for the person to talk to you about what's bothering them.

- **Make direct requests**
Your colleague will probably deflect responsibility, so don't be surprised if you get pushback. They may even try to twist your words or take your comments out of context. However, by respectfully acknowledging your colleague's behaviour, you're letting them know that you've noticed their passive-aggression and that you are a straight shooter who doesn't intend to let them get away with it.

- **Get support from the team**
It's easier to get caught up in a never-ending 'who is right' war when it's just the two of you. By enlisting the help of your teammates and without ganging up on anyone, you will not have to deal with the situation alone.

- **Assess conflict avoidance**
People who fit this archetype are generally conflict-avoidant and rely on more subtle methods to communicate their thoughts or dissent. Working in a foreign country or organisational culture might be a factor too. If it is not the norm, or people feel vulnerable (layoffs, a merger or restructuring), people may have learned to get what they want by using this behaviour.

The political operator

Of course, everyone must engage in office politics to some degree. We compete with one another – for promotions, raises, assignments and C-suite attention. We need to advocate for our ideas and accomplishments to secure support and funding. But what if your colleague is fixated on getting ahead and has a ruthless approach? Here are some of the behaviours you might be dealing with from a careerist colleague: bragging about their successes, taking undue credit, currying favour with people in power or those in a position to help their career, acting like they're in charge, even when they are not, gossiping and spreading rumours, particularly about coworkers who they believe are standing in their way, pushing their agenda, often at the expense of team or company goals, hoarding information to appear powerful and purposely undermining you by not inviting you to a meeting or sharing critical details about your work. So how do you react to a hypercompetitive colleague who sees work as a winner-takes-all competition? Can you ever trust them? How do you avoid getting dragged into their game? And are there any lessons you can learn from the way they operate?

I once experienced a person who not only ticked all the boxes of the above behaviours but also appeared as an insecure manager micromanaging his team and exhibiting passive-aggressive behaviour. In fact, he even mentioned openly to his team that he had acute difficulties trusting people. His Machiavellian tactics ended up in a take-no-prisoners approach, with several executives ousted. This was followed by a deep imposter syndrome when his lack of competence became evident and a final fall into burnout and inability to handle the self-inflicted pressure. He quit the company only several months later, leaving behind an atmosphere of destruction and disengagement. How can this be possible or tolerated by his peers and superiors, you may ask yourselves?

I want to underline how tough multi-billion corporate Headquarters in a highly competitive industry might be. And it may not look or feel like it on the surface, but be warned that corporate life can occasionally be ruthless. Take it like a 'duty to advise'.

First things first: all offices are political. Now, to discern what's appropriate and what's not, I suggest applying the: "it is acceptable whilst it's not detrimental to others". Or, in other words, use the universal rule of: "treat others as you wish others to treat yourself". Speaking up in a meeting to share what's going well on your team's project is a great way to increase your visibility and enhance your reputation. As long as you avoid interrupting others to do it or speaking badly about another team, no harm should be done. But if your colleague intentionally takes up much of a meeting to laud their own opinions and prevent others from presenting their ideas, that's a different story.

One of the main factors that drive hyper-competitiveness is scarcity. If everyone got exactly what they wanted at work – the salary they dreamed of, the budget for all their projects, and endless attention from bosses – there would be little need to engage in politicking. But resources are finite, and we're often made to compete for them. Your colleague may focus on winning those resources to further their agenda and bolster their position. People who engage intensely in office politics sometimes do so because they're insecure or feel threatened. Many people play these games because it works for them. They keep their job as a boss, get promoted or achieve the funding they want.

Remember that it can be tough to hold a political operator to account precisely because they will likely have powerful connections at work and know how to make themselves look good. They also have little incentive to change their ways because overconfidence is very often rewarded. Instead of taking your colleague down a notch, which is probably unrealistic, start by removing yourself from the entanglement.

– **Make your good work known**
  During presentations at a meeting or via hard proofs. A paper trail can often stop careerists from undermining you.

- **Offer help**
  This can be surprisingly disarming for a political operator since they may not receive a lot of generosity or support.

- **Ask for advice**
  This may seem like a counterintuitive tactic. It makes you seem cooperative rather than competitive and can win someone over. If they feel you value their opinion, they may begin to see you as an ally instead of a rival.

- **Be wary of an attitude reversal**
  Proceed carefully if a careerist starts to take you into their confidence. It may feel like a relief but keep your antenna up. They might be using you for their own gain.

- **Bring up what's bothering you**
  Since power-hungry colleagues are rarely straight shooters, being explicit might catch them off guard. Holding up a mirror can give them a sense of how they're perceived and encourage them to change. In your conversation, it is imperative that you keep your language neutral and devoid of emotion or judgment. They may deny engaging in toxic politics, which is fine. At least they will know that you're aware of what's happening and that you're not an easy target.

Let's now tackle the dynamic between you with the two strategies to focus on:

3a) Don't make it me against them
The situation inevitably becomes polarised in a 'me against you' situation. This creates the consequence of someone who is being difficult and someone who isn't, someone who is right and someone who is wrong. Amy Gallo explains that this is part of our brain's natural response to negative emotions like anger, fear, pain or defensiveness. The 'victim versus villain' narrative can be comforting, but we are rarely blameless. Also, what can happen is that you trigger those negative emotions in someone without realising. You may inadvertently trigger resentment, fear or anger because you are performing well, have more innovative ideas, appear more at ease talking and exchanging with bosses and manage to get more exposure to C-level executives, etc. It would help if you were mindful of eliciting those negative emotions in others.

Another very destructive emotion can raise its ugly head: jealousy. And this one can be particularly toxic. Especially if you are not a jealous person and have no problem and even applaud the successes of others. Some people just radiate toxic jealous emotions around them.

Since you will be unable, as discussed previously, to change someone's personality, your best course of action is to handle those emotions yourself. No one will do it for you; ultimately, it is in your best interest. It would help to employ an altered mental model to get along with your colleague. Instead of seeing two opposing factions, imagine three entities: you, your colleague and the dynamic between you. Maybe that third entity is something specific: a decision you must make together or a project plan you must complete. Or perhaps it's more general: ongoing tension between you or bad blood because of a complex project. Either way, this approach separates the people from the problem, which is advice you might have heard before. This is one of the Harvard Negotiation Project's core principles for handling difficult conversations. Any leadership program you may attend or book on leadership you might read will approach the topic of difficult conversations. It is an important subject for personal growth. It would help if you remain aware of these matters amidst the teams you lead. What may help is to visualise yourself with your colleague in a positive image, working together on the problem at hand. Let's say, for example, sitting with the other person on the same side of the table, working on your unhealthy relationship together. In this proactive and more positive way, you need to find strategies to engage your colleague in problem-solving, which is inherently collaborative instead of combative. Allow openness and lateral thinking, with a dose of creativity, to start this collaborative path together.

3b) Experiment to find out what works

It is also worth considering that a difficult situation with your colleague may often have a unique context. This will impact which strategies to select and how to apply them. Consider thoroughly who you are, who the other person is, the nature of your relationship, the norms and culture of your workplace, and so on. Improving a relationship can be overwhelming, and it's not an easy undertaking. But it will feel far more manageable if you start by coming up with two or three ideas you want to test. Often, small actions can have a significant impact. Design an experiment: determine what you'll do differently, set a time window to experiment with your new approach and see how it works. Keep refreshing and adjusting your strategies, and be willing to abandon ones that aren't producing results. Conflict expert Jennifer Goldman-Wetzler recommends trying a 'constructive, pattern-breaking action', a simple act 'designed to interrupt the conflict pattern of the past'. In other words, try something you haven't tried before, even something the other person might not expect.

3.5 Tackling incivility at work

I was hesitant to dedicate a specific section to this topic. What changed my mind was seeing that Professor Christine Porath's Ted Talk had accumulated over 3.5 million views on this topic. I will share with you the main findings from her Georgetown University research [13].

First, I would like to introduce how she defines incivility at work because the topic is not easy. It lies in the eye of the beholder. The issue can be personal and relative. What seems uncivil behaviour to one person might be ok for somebody else. So, how to define it?

I like how she addressed it: "The crucial question about rudeness vs kindness in the office is about answering the following question: Do you lift people up or do you hold them down?". Some people would argue that one defining trait of good leadership would be the ability to lift people up, right? But not a selected few of your favourite people, no. The idea is to lift everyone you encounter by how you treat and interact with them. This is why this topic is vital in a book about leadership skills. As a leader, you should look out for your own behaviour, how you influence other people's behaviour and the kind of behaviour you inspire to flourish in your corporate culture.

The way a company's culture could be evaluated would be to examine the worst possible behaviour shown by the person who has recently been tolerated or even encouraged without any consequence. Did this person ever show an insensitive, abrasive, bullying style? This could give you a snapshot of what type of company culture prevails.

For those of you who might not have come across uncivil behaviour in your company or career, consider yourself lucky. Let me share with you some of my experiences. A president once told a colleague of mine that his "presentation was puke, nothing better than vomit". The deplorable part was that it was not even true; the work produced was perfectly fine. The comment was just designed to humiliate – especially in front of his colleagues. Even if the quality of the work was open for discussion, what was unacceptable was the phrasing and words used. On another occasion, an HR Manager told me that "respect is not a value here . . . ." I could not believe my ears; I was shocked and appalled. Listening to Christine Porath's findings, it turns out that this characteristic is what people expect most from their leaders (data collected from over 20,000 employees worldwide). I also remember a high-ranked executive addressing me this way: "I don't want to be an asshole, but . . . ". Well, my thought was if you don't, then don't.

In toxic environments, bullies win and may even manipulate reality and get away with blatantly lying about certain situations.

We spend way too much of our time and energy in our jobs, and so we need to make every effort to create a pleasant experience. We are also in charge of other people's motivation, so let's be clear: being civil is a powerful motivating mechanism for everyone. My recommendation is civility and kindness always.

Christine Porath stated in her talk that civility pays, because people will see you as an important and powerful unique combination of key characteristics: warm and competent, friendly and smart.

You may ask yourself: "Where can I start to contribute to promoting civility at work?" My answer here would be to start with the small things. The ones that nearly pass by unnoticed, but they need to be done consistently. This is key. The person who explains this best is Simon Sinek.

He insists that those small acts of generosity in the workplace, like saying "good morning" every morning to your colleagues, looking into someone's eyes when asking a question, and giving everyone full attention after asking "How are you doing today?". These small acts of simple courtesy should be done with complete authenticity and generosity of spirit.

What does that mean? Well, doing such acts genuinely. When we ask how someone is doing today, we need to really mean it, wait for and listen to the answer and not run away because we are supposedly too busy with more important things. This is the body language and message we convey. It is simple – if we ask a question, listen and hear the answer.

This genuine kindness may still not be enough. Simon Sinek states that consistency truly makes a difference and has the power to build trustworthy relationships. It is showing up with a behaviour that shows genuine care every day, every week, every encounter and at all times. A similar value of consistency might be observed in our attempts to get results with fitness workouts, dental care or romantic relationships, not with intensity, but with consistency. It's not that hard; in fact, it's about allowing humanity to unfold in the workplace on a daily basis [14].

Another great example comes from the former CEO of Campbell Soups: he encouraged his leadership team and employees to be resolutely tough-minded on standards and tender-hearted with people. One does not go without the other. And this approach and attitude are described as the primary action for the exceptional turnaround of the company. He walked the talk and steered the company from exhibiting an untrustful working environment close to bankruptcy to record profits and being the recipient of the best place to work awards [15].

Let us now address **gossip at the workplace**. It can be a destructive weapon used commonly by careerist colleagues. They will often intentionally spread rumours, burrow for information and strategically decide whether to keep intel for themselves or pass it along, often in exchange for juicy details from others. But, even if you refrain from spreading gossip and find it distasteful when exhibited by your colleagues, we all engage in it occasionally, and it's not necessarily wise to avoid it altogether. You may be missing out. Listening to office banter is a great way to learn what's happening at your company. The red line to draw, or the cues to help you decide whether to engage, would be to ask yourself if the chatter being spread can harm the subject of the stories or if it is at someone's expense.

I recommend interrupting negative gossip when you hear it; if an opportunist says something that could harm another person's feelings or reputation, speak up. This takes courage, of course, but doing this even a few times will put the person on notice. You may ask, "Have you told them you feel this way?" or protect the other person by mentioning something positive, like an impressive piece of work.

I will never forget a moment, particularly the person who intervened courageously in a gossip conversation and came to the defence of the person being denigrated, and he did not even know them. His action appeared so noble to me; from that moment, I would never have to question his integrity and kindness.

What about lying? It is wise to start pointing out mistruths by presenting contrary evidence privately, maybe by sending an email with proof included in an email chain. This can gently (or not so gently) expose deception and make clear that you won't let them get away with it in the future. A possible next step, if they don't respond, would be to correct your colleagues' lies when they occur in front of others. You might finally go and speak to your manager.

If you have persistently taken steps to get along with your co-worker but aren't seeing progress, there are a few things you can do before you throw in the towel. The strategies Amy Gallo suggests are to set boundaries and limit your exposure, document your colleague's transgressions and your successes, escalate the issue to someone who has the power to do something and eventually, if necessary, consider quitting. These strategies won't magically turn things around. Still, they will help you protect your career, reputation, and ability from doing your job without losing your mind.

To conclude with a positive note, inspired by Vala Afshar, Chief Digital Evangelist at Salesforce, these are some of the positive traits of your bosses or leaders people will never forget:

About The Use of Their **Authority**: they led by example and inspired us to stretch higher.
About our **Contribution**: they recognized and rewarded us and told us our work mattered.
About our **Mistakes**: they defended us when we needed it and forgave us when we made mistakes.

About The Use of their **Power**: they provided us with a safe place to grow and opened career doors for us.

Consider doing similar types of actions to be remembered as a calm and fair boss.

3.6 Embracing change

Liam has been General Manager for the digital business of a London Department Store for three years now. His job felt right to him, and his team and colleagues had become close, like part of a family. He felt confident in his results as well.

What he expected less is that a completely new paradigm, like the pandemic, would accelerate change at such a rate. It starts with customer behaviour and is followed by employees' preferences for organizing and managing their work schedules.

What was once considered taboo for a traditional brick and mortar retailer – enhancing ways to sell online – had finally collapsed. They would go for it! Embracing this change, finally.

Customers were stuck at home due to the pandemic regulations, so their needs had shifted completely. "What kind of service could we offer them to inspire their home entertainment activities in a fun way?" Liam's team had been dealing with this question for the last couple of weeks.

A new adapted catalogue showcased live, but remotely was the answer. From state-of-the-art kitchen utilities to all types of accessories for craft work, the latest DIY ideas, gardening tools, family games, indoor sports kit, etc.

Liam's team was very excited about this totally new creative format. Some of the products were a complete novelty in the assortments on offer on the website. His company, as a privileged e-Retail partner specifically, had been selected to test the customer's appetite and smoothness of operations by most of those brands.

For everyone involved, this project seemed so innovative. This was a tremendous acknowledgement of Liam and his team's accomplishments. An immensely successful online launch with most brands a few years ago, plus the integration of all the different innovation initiatives they had been testing during this period.

Everyone in his team was ready and set for the transformation and the operation to succeed.

Many people fear change; some are even confounded by change. Suppose you strongly believe the new situation may be worse than the existing one. In that case, you need a compelling argument to persuade you to embrace the change. But often, this visceral fear can be the first hurdle to understanding the necessity for the transformation. And even when changes are understood, there can be the fear of being excluded from new functions in the new paradigm or being judged negatively.

Surely you have heard the saying "everything must change for everything to remain the same". This is the famous phrase pronounced by Tancredi in the renowned novel 'The Leopard' by Giuseppe Tomasi di Lampedusa.

This can be regarded as the synthesis of a paradox: the ambition to preserve power structures only with apparent changes on the surface. It may be applied to some leadership practices in the current business world. Those that fear change. The most prevalent scenario is "It has always been done this way". This could be the phrase that best identifies resistance to change. This circumstance shows that some people resist with vigour any moves towards new ways of doing things. The causes could be fear, lack of commitment or simply laziness. If leadership asserts an interest in transformation and proclaims it in some meetings, then nothing significant happens; this resistance may be seen as a fear of becoming expendable or irrelevant once change arrives. This is the other paradox that nestles resistance to change by some business leaders. If everything changes, maybe they will be redundant in the new structure. There is safety in the status quo.

People who do not feel this fear – even if they can sense the anxiety or doubt from colleagues – their confidence and determination can override this sentiment because they also believe that they will be enriched by change.

Change is very often inevitable, so it is better to be prepared. And this preparation happens in our mind, particularly our attitude and outlook. Most times, preparation involves less our technical skills and more human skills. Suppose we apply a beginner's mind, curiosity and a continuous learning mindset. In that case, our mind will develop a positive outlook to protect us from concern and apprehension.

A phrase spoken by Ophelia in Shakespeare's Hamlet, "We know what we are but know not what we may be", is an excellent example of one of the play's most important themes – uncertainty. The future is unknown, so it's impossible to know how events will influence how one's life plays out.

Suppose we apply this idea to the corporate world. In that case, we may think leaders will change or adjust to the same rhythm as those changes happening inside the organization. And those leaders will be able to resolve transformation due to their capacity for vision and management. Something they have demonstrated in previous transitions. And suppose current leaders may be unable to adapt to the inevitable transformation in their organizations. In that case, an immediate and easy solution to overcome this mindset framework is to open the door. This fresh air that has been let in may come from new generations with less weight on their shoulders and capable of embracing change and leading that needed transformation.

The act of 'embracing change' must be trained regularly. Simon Sinek says, "It is not about winning the game all the time, but about staying in the game". In a world of continuous transformation, organizations should set their intentions to play a long game.

Here we can refer to a 'long game' strategy company like Chanel. Their way of embracing change is very selective and never as a pioneer. Let's wait and see what the experiences and learnings from others are, and then we decide how to proceed if it is appropriate. Prudent. This also worked well for late Queen Elizabeth when the purpose is 'remain in the game'. They will never have the innovator's first mover position, but this is not what the brand is about. Totally opposite from Gucci, a brand that is always ready in the starting blocks of a new revolution. Innovation and transformation are at the brand's core, and the company lives up to that standard. These are two very different and valid approaches since they perfectly serve the brand values and overall brand equity value.

How brands and companies react by adopting or rejecting change is often apparent. In my career, I have voluntarily transitioned from one of the most conservative to one of the most innovative corporate mindsets: Chanel to Gucci. I was inquisitive to understand how a contrasted way of doing business impacts brand building. And as you would imagine, the very different ways of embracing change. In one case, that of Gucci, embracing change was instinctive, stepping out of a gut feeling immersed in joy to try something new with a full-on challenging course of action. The innovation appetite was so evident at Gucci that a new initiative very often never required validation by the manager as if it came with each job's mission. A genuinely refreshing take and highly motivating when you are that type of person, of course.

In an environment where continuous transformation is encouraged, innovative ideas are expected from everywhere, each department, function and seniority level in the company: If the experiment does not pan out, mistakes are tolerated, the course of action is reassessed and eventually corrected – in the best fail fast manner.

In opposite environments, where preserving the status quo is pivotal, innovation must be tempered and remain within carefully guarded boundaries. Creativity is legitimized only for specific departments and trusted people: new ideas must follow an unwritten path to navigate and fully open their sails.

In today's ever-changing societies, context and uncertain world in general, I believe that we need to be able to embrace change. Then we may decide how to handle and manage it. I have illustrated two very different and contrary views and tactics towards change. Both are possible, depending on the long-term goal. But what is certain is that we all need to develop a fundamental skill, embracing change and not fearing it since it is somewhat inevitable.

If you wish to read an optimistic viewpoint on change from someone who may be seen as a role model in resilience, listen to what Nelson Mandela says: "As I walked out the door toward the gate that would lead to my freedom. I knew if I didn't leave my bitterness and hatred behind, I'd still be in prison." It is an excellent example of accepting complete transformation within yourself to face the next phase successfully.

Leaving negative emotions from previous incarnations behind and allowing the change of context to start with a transformed set of emotions and purpose.

We must unleash an open mindset for possible fast-paced and unannounced changes in our industry, verticals, distribution channels, providers, etc. It is critical not only to be open to face these changes but also to be open to unlearning current ways of working and thinking in the industry, listening carefully to new players, developments, success stories, trends and tech developments. Not only listening but asking questions to fully understand the impact of those changes. And after all, that is to decide if those transformations would be positive or not for the business. Said differently, decide if you want to take the ride on these novelties, even if it is just a test ride.

I like the thoughts on coping with uncertainty articulated skilfully by Vinita Bansal in her book 'Upgrade Your Mindset' [16].

"At times, I wonder what life would be like if we knew everything beforehand. Every decision we made turned out in line with our expectations. Every outcome was guaranteed. No unknowns. No unexpected conditions. No unwarranted circumstances. Pretty boring, right?"

"After all, as a species, we are designed to thrive in uncertainty. We don't find joy in the knowns. It's the thrill of navigating the unknowns that keep us inspired and motivated. What gives us pleasure is not the successful outcome, but getting past the obstacles and challenges we faced which led to that outcome. Without the ability to deal with ambiguity, we wouldn't have survived as a species. All the technology that's now a big part of our life wouldn't even exist. If you think about all the innovation of the last 200 years, it wasn't born out of our comfort zone. Every new advancement came with someone who was willing to step outside their comfort zone. Someone who made decisions without accurate information. Someone who stepped up and embraced unpredictability. Someone who navigated through change. Someone who led with a vision even without complete information".

She gives us the key to dealing with ambiguity: curiosity and flexibility.

"When faced with complex challenges and uncertain outcomes, many leaders rely on their brilliance or hard work to find the right answers. However, they fail to realize that navigating the unknown isn't about smartness, and putting in more effort won't solve increasingly complex business problems.

It's only by considering different perspectives, asking better questions, and learning from their own systems leaders can build the curiosity and flexibility required to purposefully cut through ambiguity".

3.7 Get comfortable learning and failing

Liam arrived at the department store; his journey had never been so speedy. It usually took him around half an hour by cab; today, he was there in 10 minutes. London looked like a ghost town; no one was around, completely deserted streets. "This is so surreal", he thought.

He had to get special permission to be able to get into their department store. Today is April 23rd, 2020. The launch of video shopping from the store was scheduled for 2 PM.

Sales teams have been in contact with their customers since the early days of the pandemic through remote communication devices such as WhatsApp and selling remotely without many complications.

But today would mark a new era: the company was testing to present their new home entertainment catalogue remotely, from the department store, in a one-to-one format, to their most loyal customers. Those will be viewing from the comfort of their homes and watching on a screen.

The marketing team had been preparing some guidelines. Additionally, they set up a specific kit in collaboration with the Operations team. The Training department took the advice, expertise and coaching of the most veteran Sales Associates – primarily those from the RTW (Ready to Wear) department and with the highest clienteling skills. Liam was attending out of curiosity for this new way of Retail Branding and Selling, the readiness of the technology, and to encourage his best-performing Sales Associates. He also wanted to ensure that the teams had everything they needed and felt reassured to go live with this new way of selling. The Merchandising and Visual Merchandising teams were also around to support when needed. The idea with this live test run was to check the feasibility of the first dry run done over Zoom, correct weaknesses and then prepare a guideline set for a roll-out for most product categories.

(Later that day . . .)

Everyone was tired. In just over 4 hours, they had only managed to engage with five customers. Result: no sales, conversion rate 0. What went wrong?

All teams involved were gathered around the big meeting table in the back office. From the different expressions, Liam could tell that solution to the less-than-successful experience would not be difficult to solve, even he had underestimated the difficulties experienced in a couple of areas of the trial but was confident that the solution could be easily implemented.

"So, what do you think? Is there room for improvement regarding our experience this afternoon? What do you wish to share? Does the setup need changes? Further training, perhaps? Let's start with you, Scarlett – thanks!"

Why is learning so important for us? It helps us to keep our minds young and alert. Developing new skills through learning improves purpose and self-confidence.

Here is what Henry Ford had to say: "Anyone who stops learning is old, whether at twenty or eighty. Anyone who keeps learning stays young".

And this statement comes from scientist and Medicine Nobel Prize winner in 1977, Rosalyn S. Yalow: "The excitement of learning separates youth from old age. As long as you're learning, you're not old".

Remaining vigorous in body and mind is a quintessential part of our resilience.

From my experience, the best way of learning is either **teaching others** or **developing a habit**.

If you have a yearning to teach, I recommend reaching out to your university or business school and finding your best way through the Alumni Association; another possible option is to share your knowledge through your corporate organization through mentoring.

You may also consider teaching others presentation techniques, unlocking analysis from financial reports, or even how to prepare a fabulous 3-course meal for eight guests, or sailing basics, or snowboarding. All of them will provide energy and reinforcement in a continuous learning journey.

Another option is to develop lifelong habits. Here are some requirements to follow [17]:

1. Articulate the outcomes you'd like to achieve.
    Picking one or two outcomes will allow you to set achievable goals to make the habit stick.
2. Based on those choices, set realistic goals.
    Monitor adherence to a concrete set of actions daily.
3. With goals in hand, develop a learning community, increase commitment and make learning more fun.
4. To focus on your objectives, ditch the distractions.
    Find a quiet place and leave your phone behind. And apart from physically eliminating distractions, consider training your mind to deal with them.
5. Where appropriate, use technology to supplement and facilitate learning.

Start with achievable goals that will provide you with a strong positive impact. Some healthy living habits could be to start meditating once a week, stick to 3–4 times a week workout session, and ensure you take a weekend break in nature at least once a month. Switching habits is more accessible when the price isn't a severe failure, and the reward is a significant success.

The ones mentioned would suit me personally but choose those habits that would benefit you the most, to begin with, in the context of your lifestyle. Once the choice is made, stick to the five rules laid out and start . . . tomorrow, no excuses.

"If you want to succeed at new habits, you must first learn to succeed at failing". Sociologist Dr Christine Carter says our success at adopting a new habit depends on our willingness to be bad at it initially [18]. I agree with her observation. If we think of a simple habit, like exercising more often or new exercise reps, it is good to take on failure with humour. Let's say that we do not manage to get the move right, that everything hurts, that we only get one session per week or that we fail our initial goals. But if we take those failures positively and maybe with a sense of humour, we would see it more like "Oh gosh, I totally overestimated myself, this move is tough to learn, but I will not give up right now", or "I must be so unfit . . . my leg muscles are aching . . . but it's a good sign, right? I am getting there . . .", or "I still haven't managed to step up to 3 workout sessions a week, when it does make me feel so well, I will pencil it in my agenda for next week, so no excuses . . ."

The best way to progress from couch to marathon is not by beating ourselves up each morning we miss a run. We undermine our motivation to continue when we shame or blame ourselves. Instead, track runs over time rather than assessing each day individually. By keeping a log of your efforts, you'll notice how far you've come over time.

Additionally, stop when you're at your peak — while you're doing well with your new habit and still enjoying it. Knowing you're stopping before your performance declines will provide you with additional motivational energy.

If we succeed at failing, then progress is possible. Learning new skills and adopting new habits necessitates a learning curve since improvement works in stages. The idea is that success in failing keeps the motivation up for the next level that needs to be conquered.

There is an old saying, "Practice makes perfect", which has some truth. Still, a more realistic and encouraging version of the phrase is "Practice makes progress", which we cannot argue with.

These examples are simple habits to change in life, but if we succeed in accepting failure as a successful learning curve for, let's say, a healthier lifestyle, handling a problematic colleague better, moving onto a new job challenge, settling into a new country, etc. might feel these are far more enjoyable tasks to take on and master.

You can immunize yourself against big letdowns by implementing experiments where you will fail in small ways. Don't like public speaking? Your voice wobbles, and you stumble over your words, feeling more self-conscious by the moment. Make your experiments small. Record yourself speaking one sentence and then watch the video, or simply ask one question aloud in a meeting where you don't have to speak up. By exposing ourselves in small doses to the skill we're trying to build, we are less likely to suffer severe consequences if we fail — and we might even triumph. With each step, we conquer our vulnerability to the shortcomings of a new habit, increasing our chances of acing it in the future.

How does learning benefit me there if we switch back to working life?

Quite simply, I wouldn't always cling to being right. When you realize you might be wrong and have learned from somebody else's point of view, you may have switched your views or even changed your opinion. You will have a gratifying sense of personal growth, of learning something new, or even stronger, to unlearn some misconceptions or non-adapted views in a new context.

Entrepreneurs would argue that you learn how to run a business by being wrong, not right. And whether you succeed in the end ultimately depends on how hard you're willing to work – and how often you're ready to fail.

Every mistake has the power to teach you something significant. It is crucial to look for the lesson in every such mistake. Something obvious may appear to be the lesson and may raise its head without too much excavation. But another less evident and deeper-rooted lesson could be waiting for you if you are prepared to be humble, question yourself and dig deeper into finding authentic learning from the circumstance. It is good to take the time to ensure you have gleaned the lesson and made the most of a difficult situation or mistake. Clearly, the first and 'ad minima' step is not to repeat the mistake and probably help others avoid the same mistake too. A deeper learning is when you can connect the dots to find a better solution for the next time.

What I would suggest also is to make sure that you understand the idea of 'post-traumatic growth'. Often people find that crisis situations, such as a job loss or the breakdown of a relationship, allow them to re-evaluate their lives and make positive changes when approached with a constructive attitude.

As Arianna Huffington puts it: We're all born with a natural curiosity. We want to learn. But work and personal life demands often diminish our time and the will to engage that natural curiosity. Developing specific learning habits — consciously established and conscientiously cultivated — can lead to continued professional relevance and deep personal happiness.

3.8 An uncertain future

"Hello, can I come in?"

"Hi Bob, sure. Apologies, but I had my ear pods on and couldn't hear you; in fact, I did not even see you arriving at my office – I was so concentrated on what I was doing . . . ."

"Sure, no problem. What did you want to chat about? I heard the latest remote shopping event has been selling the home entertainment catalogue off the shelf from our warehouse – well done, what an achievement!"

"Oh, yes, I am so glad. Even if this one was quite predictable, one never knows. Sometimes things just don't pan out, and then you must explain all those investments made, regain confidence with the teams, find new opportunities . . . . Anyway, the reason why I wanted you to join me for a coffee is really: where do we go from here?" Liam stood up, took his ear pods off, closed his laptop and poured Bob a cup of coffee.

"What do you mean?"

"Well, we have all these different options: shall we keep adding product categories to our online offerings, like home interior décor pieces, or shall we continue to play catalogue scarcity and drive desirability to offline purchases when we reopen? Shall we continue to prioritize local or also push foreign markets? Another option would be to experiment with the rental and preloved items. Maybe our loyalty program deserves more transparency. Shall we continue our service catalogue, like remote yoga lessons and mixology? With the huge shifts experienced during the pandemic, Pandora's box is open for every possible option to smooth and facilitate purchases. What do you think?"

"Hmm, these are all very different options in very different scenarios . . ."

"Yes, exactly, this is it. These are just possible options. As you know, customer purchase behaviour is evolving fast, competitors are unpredictable, and the context is forever changing. There is so much uncertainty out there that I wanted to pick your brains for ideas on how to proceed in framing scenarios. You guys in Finance do it all the time; maybe you could help me with some input".

"Yes, sure; where should we start?"

As mentioned in a previous section, it is fundamental to embrace change. Knowing that for some people, it comes more naturally since they are risk-takers and are comfortable going out of their comfort zones regularly. Even if you are less of that character, developing confidence and resilience for when the occasion arises is essential. Whether we accept it or not, our world and societies are getting more and more unpredictable. In an uncertain and ever-changing world, it seems prudent to be prepared and to stay on your guard – at all times.

I invite you here to listen to Bob Dylan's "Forever Young" song:

> May your hands always be busy
> May your feet always be swift
> May you have a strong foundation
> When the winds of changes shift

I would embrace Dylan's advice unequivocally. It is vital to have a strong foundation and always be agile to react successfully to the winds of change.

So far in this book, I have given some thoughts on how to be best prepared mentally and physically for you to remain the captain of your life journey and professional career. To lead your life, career and teams joyfully and resiliently.

Let's analyse now how and from where these winds of change may come to remain alert.

Usually, the changes will arrive from the circumstance. This may be in the Industry, the Markets, the Business Model, the Revenue Streams, Product Categories, Product Margin, Supply Chain, Distribution Channels, Media Platforms, External Factors, Customer Needs or Expectations, Social Values, People Engagement, Strategy Changes, Competitors' Moves, etc.

I recommend that you plan out possible critical changes that may occur and impact you and your business directly. A kind of risk assessment and management on your side that you may review with your team, boss and mentor to get further insight and have fruitful discussions.

You may find that you are not always just acknowledging changes in your environment. Still, it could also trigger a proactive response when you predict a change coming or a potentially innovative idea arising.

There is a pragmatic statement from the military: "Plans are useless, but planning is indispensable". This quote from Dwight D. Eisenhower is often used to illustrate the importance of flexible thinking in the face of change.

It applies to business decisions within an uncertain context. Louis Vuitton's former CEO – Michel Burke – used it when asked in December 2020 by 'The Business of Fashion' about his main takeaways on navigating the pandemic crisis. "I guess what that means is when the shit hits the fan, you need to have a plan, but having a plan before the shit hits the fan is not that useful. It's really a statement to the importance of resilience and agility. That's what we really stressed in those six months. That's how we got through it in better shape than when we entered it. Vuitton is a better company today than six months ago."

Moving to a very different context, I believe being a mother requires excellent preparation for swift and spontaneous changes in life. It is something I have not read anywhere or heard anyone saying, but I came to this conclusion by observing all the mothers I have known. Not being a mom myself – which was not a choice – I greatly respect mothers running a professional career alongside their motherly duties. I have observed that moms seem very inclined to adapt at an astonishingly fast pace to changing situations. How is that? My explanation would be that they have to deal first-hand with an ever-changing human being: their babies – then their children – then their adolescents. As dads, you will argue, yes, absolutely. Still, it is fair to say that overwhelmingly it is up to the moms to have the final word on the most unexpected of situations.

Nonetheless, their relationship with their kids is inherently different to that of the dads. Suppose you have to deal so closely on a daily basis with the most unpredictable situations with an ever-changing human being for which you are fully responsible. In that case, it is undeniable that you develop exceptional skills to adapt swiftly and successfully.

This could also explain why female political leaders excelled during the pandemic crisis and better navigated uncertainty (which was the same for all) in their countries.

Let me use this segway to drive into the pandemic experience of 2020–2021. We can all say that the pandemic has touched and changed us in many ways. A situation we had never experienced before. A high-risk situation paired with high anxiety levels for many people and an unpaved path to walk for everyone: in business, politics, government, schooling, parenting . . . .

Here is where we at the Gucci Global Brand and Client Engagement Department had a particular experience credit: we knew what remote and flexible working meant. We had implemented it a long time before the lockdowns hit. We also had the most updated tools to work this way. We had a slight advantage and were able to pivot fast. Nevertheless, that unpredictable context was new for everyone, and we all had to adapt. We felt a strong empathy for our sales colleagues on the front lines dealing with much higher levels of uncertainty, health exposure risk and environmental volatility. We felt a strong commitment together to support them as best we could. It was a wonderful sentiment of collaboration across distant geographies. The pivot here was for an immediate acceleration in using remote selling techniques and tools. What we had been advocating and preparing for clienteling suddenly became a frontline strategy. It was a tremendous transformational achievement. We felt the same empathy for our colleagues in the manufacturing areas. But there, sadly, we were less able to provide support. Where we had the most significant growth opportunities was obviously e-commerce, and we set our sights there.

The hard facts and skills developed during the unprecedented pandemic are personal to each of us and a great lesson to preserve. What has been more challenging to adapt in this circumstance are our soft skills: collaboration, teamwork, team motivation, handling anxiety, handling career and life balance, mental health, the special support needed for parents, singles living alone and burnout syndromes. Working remotely during the pandemic – and especially in the first months before the vaccine program – led to working longer hours and draining loads of energy from people; for every initiative we tried to implement worldwide, we had to lay out plans A, B and even plan C for every possible eventuality. This was enormously demanding for teams, especially when some needed to be covered if they fell ill.

Lessons from the pandemic to me are the following, and I invite you to understand and empathize with the new normal working life:

- Flexible work conditions and no obligation to full week working hours at the company office.
- Agreed to free agenda space without meetings to be able to focus on reflection, project advancement and coaching/mentoring.
- Commitment to no email exchanges late in the evening and at weekends (urgencies excepted).
- Continue to check in on people's emotional states as we have been doing during the pandemic.
- Also, share your feelings now and then and deeply care about how the team is doing.
- Make sure enough connection time exists among team members.
- More than ever, leaders must create a safe environment where people feel a sense of belonging.
- Leaders must constantly think ten steps ahead and make quick, informed decisions simultaneously. It is a regular priority to sit down and run through hypotheticals.
- Leaders must remain optimistic about the future and must over-communicate.

Let me finalize this chapter on resilience, quoting Arianna Huffington once again: "Resilience is not, as many of us thought in the early days of the pandemic, an end state we can reach. It is a constant process of becoming. In the presence of endless uncertainty, apocalyptic weather events, political instability and new variants that upend the best-laid plans, resilience is the quality we cannot do without – a constant process rather than a final destination. Not a marker to reach, but a mindset".

Bibliography

[1] Kobasa SC. "Stressful life events, personality, and health – Inquiry into hardiness". Journal of Personality and Social Psychology. 1979.

[2] Kobasa SC, Maddi SR, Greenberg D. "The hardy executive: Health under stress": Dow Jones – Irwin; 1984.

[3] Cross R, Dillon K, Greenberg D. "The Secret to Building Resilience". 2021.

[4] Vicente A. "Cuando uno es honesto consigo mismo, es muy difícil seguir toda la vida con la misma pareja". 2022.

[5] "Developing Resilience". MindTools.

[6] Walker M. "Why We Sleep: Unlocking the Power of Sleep and Dreams": Scribner; 2017.

[7] McDougall C. "Born to Run": Knopf Doubleday Publishing Group; 2011.

[8] "7 incredible things intermittent fasting does for your brain". Amenclinics. 2021.

[9] Cross M. "How intermittent fasting can benefit your mental health". Nutritionist Resource. 2022.

[10] Grant A. "The Science of Reasoning With Unreasonable People". New York Times. 2021.

[11] McKee A. "Keep your company's toxic culture from infecting your team". Harvard Business Review. 2019.

[12] Gallo A. "Getting Along: How to Work with Anyone (Even Difficult People)": Harvard Business Review Press; 2022.

[13] Porath C. "Why being respectful to your coworkers is good for business": TED, YouTube; 2018.

[14] Sinek S. "Why you only win with consistency": Motivation Elite, YouTube; 2018.

[15] Porath C, Conant DR. "The Key to Campbell Soup's Turnaround? Civility": Harvard Business Review; 2017.

[16] Bansal V. "Upgrade Your Mindset: How to Overcome Limiting Beliefs and Tap Your Potential"; 2021.

[17] Coleman J. "Make Learning a Lifelong Habit". Harvard Business Review. 2017.

[18] Nawaz S. "To build new habits, get comfortable failing". Harvard Business Review. 2022.

Chapter Four
Resolving harmony

Empty your mind, be formless, shapeless, like water.
If you put water into a cup, it becomes the cup.
You put water into a bottle, and it becomes the bottle.
You put it in a teapot it becomes the teapot,
Now, water can flow, or it can crash.
Be water, my friend.
– Bruce Lee

https://doi.org/10.1515/9783111335339-005

4.1 Finding balance

François was sitting in his preferred armchair at his favourite bar in Tokyo. On this Thursday evening, there was little else he wished to be doing: ordering himself a Gin & Tonic and waiting for Greg to arrive from his office. It is now a couple of years of being together since they met at a friend's party in London. Both dreamed of living in Japan for a while, and they just made it a couple of months ago. It felt like an accomplishment. François secured a promotion within his company to take over the General Manager position for Japan. Once they arrived and their flat was organised, Greg also found a job at the British Council in Tokyo.

While sitting there, François asked himself why he felt a milestone had been realised. Why is it? Does it feel like an accomplishment? There were different aspects: personal, social and professional. From a personal standpoint, to be living his dream in Japan had all the ingredients of a success story. He grew up in Paris from mixed French-English parents. The family has always preserved both cultures. Due to his dad's job as a high executive in the pharma industry, they travelled worldwide for several years. Unlike other kids, who hate changing school, country and friends every couple of years, François was comfortable with it and loved the sense of adventure and discovery that came with it. He dreamed of a similar life for himself.

Once at London Business School, unlike most of his peers, François was seduced by the challenges marketing faces to convince customers and their changing needs and desires. Attracted by the challenge of truly understanding the customer, he landed an internship at British Airways' Frequent Flyer Executive Club. He made his way from premium travel services into the Paris luxury world, from Marketing to Sales. At only 33, he had become a General Manager for one of those brands in Tokyo.

This led to his accomplishments in the social sphere: a General Manager role for a well-known brand from a specific country is similar to a country's ambassador's position – especially for brands in the luxury sector. You become the most senior representative of that brand – its values and the lifestyle it represents – in that country. Together, of course, with its business partnerships. Aside from the commercial aspect, both jobs are similar in nature. It was still quite unusual to see those jobs fulfilled by non-heterosexual couples. This is what François was so proud of too.

Regarding his professional accomplishment, he knew his leadership skills had been vital to getting the job compared to his opponents. He had been told there were internal and external candidates, and the process had been long, but he could now lay back and focus on his new mission in Japan.

While he was having this thought, Anne walked in. "Hi Anne, what are you doing here?". François had great respect and affection for her. What a great character she was. Growing up in Singapore, Hong Kong and Argentina – Anne spoke five languages and was comfortable in every environment. They met through François' relocation agent when he was flat hunting. Anne knew everyone in the Tokyo ex-pat society, which was helpful for François, who had just arrived. Being French, it seemed to Anne that doors opened easier for her in the closed society of Tokyo. Living here for nearly ten years as a journalist also helped.

"Hi, François! I know where to find you on a Thursday evening, so here I am. Have you heard the latest rumours?"

"Oh dear, news fly! Of course, I have. But never mind, it's Thursday evening and I wish to give myself a break now. You will get everything you need from tomorrow's press release. Is that a deal?"

"Absolutely, my dear François. That's fine!"

"Speaking about giving yourself a break from work on a weekday evening . . . in Tokyo . . . and . . . in your position", she continued, "I am curious: how do you manage? You must have the busiest agenda possible".

"Hey, that's a real interesting question, and I prefer it to the previous one", he said with a wink. "Can I buy you a drink? Greg is about to arrive; please have a seat".

"Un negroni, per favore", she ordered.

"Look, Anne, finding balance in life is crucial. Especially when you must recover from a complete loss of balance; this is where I found myself a couple of years ago in Paris. Out of balance. How does that feel? Well, anxious and stressed, always. But from these bouts, we must recover and make lifestyle changes as soon as possible. If we remain in that stressful situation, we risk burnout episodes. When we feel too accelerated, the remedy is to try and do the exact opposite and decelerate. As easy as that. A good place to start is during a holiday or a long weekend and make it an objective to change the behaviour that creates that stress. Very often, causes are external and not within our control; in that case, we need to take control of our mental activity. To decelerate there, nothing better than to empty your mind. Literally. Once you can achieve that, you will have done the first step to finding balance. Only unstressed and without anxiety, serenity is possible".

"Yes, you are right", Anne nodded. "Very often, we don't allow ourselves to decelerate when necessary. And only realize when it's too late, and your health has already started to suffer."

"Just before you arrived, I was thinking about a couple of successes in my life. I find it important to take time for yourself now and then – even at a busy bar like this one on a Thursday evening – and remind yourself of recent accomplishments. They can be big or small. Important to others or not, but should be kept to yourself. As soon as you do it regularly, these triumphs will introduce themselves into a bigger picture, and the effect *will cumulate. You will also know the empty areas or those still to fulfil. Because fulfil-ment is what gives you balance, don't you think?"*

"Yes, absolutely, you are right. Do you feel fulfilled right now, François?" asked Anne.

"In fact, yes. I set myself some objectives and feel that I have achieved them by being true to myself. The anxiety to achieve the objectives is calmed down; this is why I feel in balance".

"But difficult to stay this way, right François? There will be new challenges, ambitions, and targets to achieve. What do you think? How to remain in balance?"

"Well, this is exactly the greatest challenge of all: to continue our journey of insight and learning without falling into constant anxiety. To meditate, practice yoga or deep breathing, to walk in the countryside, to sing or dance. These are ways to empty your mind. To maintain a relaxed and acceptable activity in your brain, it is important to enjoy life, generate several small but meaningful happy moments, and cherish them fully. How? Practice what you love to do when you feel most connected with yourself. I feel that way when I am hiking in the forest. Shirin-yoku, or forest bathing, is what they call it here in Japan. Another option is swimming in the indoor pool at our tennis club. Greg loves karaoke evenings with friends. It's different for everyone. The next step is to be kind and reasonable with your mind and thoughts. This is probably the hardest part. Not to demand too much of ourselves or be harsh or judgemental. Raising the bar step by step, never too fast".

Anne seemed confused. "Oh, this is easier said than done. How do we achieve this when we are constantly judged in our jobs, hardly ever praised, and always feel the pressure of competition from others? How can I be compassionate with myself under these cir-cumstances?" she asked.

"Hey, people judge you much less than you would think they do. Believe me, I know about that. They have plenty of other things to worry about. And the more unworried you appear, the less judgemental people will be towards you. The only limit here would be developing enough empathy to avoid being identified as arrogant. Sometimes over-confidence can work against you".

"In other words, you are telling me, François, that I need to spare time in my agenda to breathe, sing, hike or other, to empty my mind now and then, and achieve a sense of relaxation and deceleration. After that, I should develop positive thoughts driven by my accomplishments and build on new areas of fulfilment with the next small steps to achieve. Is that right?"

"Absolutely; if you could do this regularly and consistently, you would feel less stressed and more fulfilled. Maybe writing things down would help you. Journaling in linear for-mat does not work for me, but as a mind map or a sketch, I find makes more sense – but again, it's personal".

"Hey, this is so useful. Does it work for you also when you are travelling? As you told me, you take a plane or a train every week".

François continued, "Yes, in my profession, you need to be able to develop strategies that also work away from your homey comfort zone. I spare time for swimming each morning and ensure the hotels I stay at have a pool or gym. When I travel, people seem to feel obliged to fill up my agenda; I maintain 'breathing areas' in my schedule – especially when I am away from home. And calm moments for oneself are key. The travel period is ideal: I find the moments in the aeroplane or train most useful for rewinding with positive thoughts".

"That's fascinating, François", Anne replied, completely engaged in the conversation, "but are you not more disciplined than the average human? I am not sure I can follow your example. What do you recommend?"

"Just try. And find your path. Japan and its traditions might be inspiring for you. It is a society that has a substantial number of rituals. I believe in developing our own set of rituals and traditions and sticking to those that work best. Like a learning journey through life".

"Hey Anne, hey François" – "Glad you are still here. Sorry I'm late, traffic was terrible". Greg just arrived at the lounge.

4.2 Listen to your fantasy heroes

François was sitting at his desk in his Shinjuku office. He had been preparing for the meeting with one of his team members. The person just arrived.

"Hi François, how are you doing today? Hope you had not too early a start today?"

"Oh no, I like arriving early and taking advantage of the office's quiet time before everyone else arrives. I have been reviewing the exercise I gave you last week. How was it? What do you think about it?"

"Oh dear", the colleague started, "François, we heard you had very creative coaching skills, but this was totally unexpected to me", he said with a laugh. "But I am curious, so I let myself in every learning option, no problem. What do you think? Is this what you expected? You wanted me to screenshot my fantasy heroes from when I was a child, is that right? The exercise was quite fun, really. I hope I didn't forget any of them, ha ha", he said to François.

"Ok, let's see what we have here: Peter Pan, Mowgli, Karate Kid, Asterix, Tintin, E.T., Phileas Fogg, fascinating . . ." answered François.

"It was great reviewing those characters – they sum up my childhood and the heroes I identified with most. What do you see in them about me?"

"Well, what I would like us to do, is to describe those characters best with keyword clouds. What do you think about: adventure, mystery solving, battling the bad guys, against the odds . . . ".

"Oh, yes, that sounds right to me. Is that a reflection of myself, do you think?"

"I'm not sure, you tell me".

"Well, in fact, it is. Kind of, maybe my ideal self. Where I wish to be or where I could have been in total freedom".

"Aha, you mean there are some constraints that may not allow you to be as adventurous as you wish or as successful against the odds as you had dreamt?"

"Yes, maybe. Life drives you in all sorts of directions, and you need to take decisions. Some dreams are put on hold . . .".

"Ok then. As your new manager, I would like to help you to feel more aligned with the feelings your fantasy heroes provide you. How could I do that? How could I help you?"

"Hmmm . . . what do you mean?"

"Maybe there is one adventurous dream that you wish to fulfil, some additional skills to master, or a challenge to address out of your comfort zone? What do you think? Might

there be any of those in your professional life? I might be able to help you accomplish those, which would be very satisfying. Let me know what you think?"

4.3 Manage your energy, not your time

It was exciting and eye-opening for François to discover that he would be most remembered and celebrated by his team for the pleasant downtime activities they enjoyed together.

Would you have thought? Not the accomplishments of the different projects and initiatives but the yearly seminar to a beautiful and inspiring place. To enjoy everyone's company, smiles, humour . . . .

François' boss also provided unique experiences twice a year that kept the group dynamics engaging and positive. Employees see it as a generous time spent without focusing 100% of the time on work.

In a way, those moments were there to recharge energy together, let go and manage time differently. Choosing an inspiring off-site location to live 2–3 days together, including some discovery and learning, was undoubtedly a great source of motivation.

It was – in a way – a lesson on managing energy and less about managing time.

As we know, time is a finite resource and the fundamental problem leading to working longer hours.

Energy is a different story. It comes from four primary wellsprings in human beings: the body, emotions, mind and spirit. Energy can be systematically expanded and regularly renewed by establishing specific rituals – intentionally practised and precisely scheduled behaviours to make them unconscious and automatic. To effectively reenergize your team, you must shift the emphasis **from getting more out of people to investing more in them**. Hence, they are motivated – and able – to bring more of themselves to work daily. To recharge themselves, individuals need to recognize the costs of energy-depleting behaviours and then take responsibility for changing them, regardless of their circumstances.

As an interesting set of actions, Tony Schwartz and Catherine McCarthy structured energy in four domains: physical energy, emotional energy, spiritual energy and mental energy [1].

This is what we can do to nurture each of them:

Physical Energy:
– Enhance your sleep by setting an earlier bedtime and reducing alcohol use.
– Engage in some form of exercise every day.
– Eat small meals and light snacks every 3–4 hours.
– Pay attention to the signs of flagging energy.
– Take brief, regular breaks from work at 90-minute intervals max.

Emotional Energy:
- Defuse negative emotions, such as irritability, through deep abdominal breathing.
- Fuel positive emotions in yourself and others by regularly expressing appreciation.
- Look at upsetting situations through new lenses:
  Reverse lens: "What would the other person in this conflict say, and how might they be right?"
  Long lens: "How will I likely view this situation in six months?"
  Wide lens: "How can I learn and grow from this situation?"

Spiritual Energy:
- Identify the sweet spot activities that give you feelings of effectiveness, effortless absorption and fulfilment. Find ways to do these activities more regularly.
- Allocate time and energy to what you consider most important in your life.
- Live your core values by practising them intentionally.

Mental Energy:
- Reduce interruptions by working on high-concentration tasks away from phones and email. Switch them off.
- Respond to voice mails and emails at set times during the day.
- Select the most critical challenge for the next day or the night before. Then make that your priority when you start work.

By focusing on managing employees' energy levels through an "Energy Renewal Program", the researchers at "The Energy Project" arrived at this conclusion in the paper published in 2007 by *Harvard Business Review*:

"We took a group of employees through a pilot energy management program and then measured their performance against that of a control group. The participants outperformed the controls on a series of financial metrics. They also reported substantial improvements in customer relationships, work engagement, and personal satisfaction".

"Most large organizations invest in developing employees' skills, knowledge, and competence. Very few help build and sustain their energy capacity, which is typically taken for granted. Greater capacity makes it possible to get more done in less time at a higher level of engagement and with more sustainability."

Or stated differently, in a very compelling way, by Professor Adam Grant: "Work-life balance sets the bar too low. No one grows up dreaming of a job that doesn't interfere with their life. We hope to spend our waking hours doing work that enriches our lives. A toxic job drains you. A decent job sustains you. A healthy job invigorates you."

In line with this statement, professors Emma Seppälä from Yale University and Kim Cameron from the University of Michigan found in their empirical research that leaders' greatest success predictor was not their charisma, influence or power. It was not personality, attractiveness or innovative genius. The one thing that supersedes all these factors is positive relational energy. The energy exchanged between people that helps uplift, enthuse and renew them [2].

The two researchers also found that energizers' greatest secret is that they lift up both themselves and their organisations by uplifting others through authentic, values-based leadership. Positive energizers demonstrate and cultivate virtuous actions, including forgiveness, compassion, humility, kindness, trust, integrity, honesty, generosity, gratitude and recognition in the organization. As a result, everyone flourishes.

You've most likely met people like this. They're like the sun. These people walk into a room and make it glow. Everyone becomes energized, enthused, inspired and connected. These incandescent people are positive energizers.

Here's what differentiates positive relational energy. Physical energy diminishes with use. Running a marathon exhausts us. We need recuperation time. We become fatigued and need to recover. The same is true with the help of mental and emotional energy. The only kind of energy that doesn't diminish but elevates with use is positive relational energy. We rarely get exhausted, for example, by being around people with whom we have loving, trusting, supportive relationships. Positive relational energy is self-enhancing and self-perpetuating.

It seems evident that when leaders display positive relational energy, it catapults the performance of all involved, to a new level, through enhanced innovation, teamwork, productivity and workplace cohesion.

There is a botanical term for these results: the heliotropic effect. That's the phenomenon whereby plants naturally turn toward and grow in the presence of light. In nature, light is the life-giving force; photosynthesis entirely relies on light's presence. Human beings have the same inherent attraction toward life-giving and life-supporting energy. This form of energy is what you receive — and give — in relationships with others. Decades of research show that this positive relational energy nourishes us and makes us come alive.

Research demonstrates that the need for positive social connection is so great that the lack of it is worse for your health than smoking, obesity or high blood pressure and reduces life span. In contrast, a positive social connection can lengthen our life span, strengthen our immune systems and lower rates of anxiety and depression.

At this point, you might ask yourself, what can I do or put into place to increase relational energy in your workplace? According to Professor Wayne Baker from the University of Michigan, there are four possible sets of actions that you may consider [3].

– **Build High-Quality Connections**. By definition, high-quality connections generate relational energy. At work, an effortless way would be to take on a challenge with a group of like-minded people.

- **Create Energizing Events**. Organize and run events explicitly focusing on creating energy, not just delivering content, products or services. Your executives will leave the event abuzz with energy because it's so contagious.
- **Use Tools That Promote a "Giver" Culture**. Helping someone at work creates energy in the form of positive emotions — the "warm glow" of helping. Receiving help creates energy in the form of gratitude. Gratitude for the support received encourages paying it forward and helping others.
- **Try Mapping Relational Energy**. Organizational network surveys map the invisible network behind the organizational chart – the natural way people interact. Energy maps help you target where to focus on building high-quality connections, creating energizing events and using tools that create an energizing giver culture.

4.4 Caring about your different selves

François had understood that we need to manage ourselves through the Three Selves in life.

I will reference the *Harvard Business Review* article that appeared in March 2021, written by Tony Schwartz, Emily Pines and Kashera Booker [4].

The first self, which appears as soon as we are born, is **our child self**: It's the most helpless, under-resourced and easily threatened of our three selves. It's also the most playful, curious and full of wonder. As children, we are often powerless, counting on others to care for us. As we develop more awareness, capability and autonomy, our child self's sense of powerlessness and vulnerability becomes increasingly intolerable to us. To cope with the threats we face, we form a second self: **our defender**.

It doesn't show up just when we feel threatened and display a fight-or-flight response. Instead, it's the primary self we inhabit for most of our lives. Unfortunately, our defender becomes the dominant player in our lives. Think of it as the persona we wear in the world. In the absence of stress, our defender can be focused and productive, even compassionate and winning. But it's also hypervigilant and highly reactive to any perceived threat to its value.

As soon as your defender self-moves into fight or flight, your capacity to think rationally and reflectively gives way to fear and defensiveness. Just think about the most recent time you felt triggered. How did you react? Perhaps you lashed out in anger, judgment or blame. Maybe you moved to harsh self-criticism or pushed your feelings aside by distracting or numbing yourself. These are all ways our defender seeks to protect us from our child self's experience of unsafety, unworthiness and fear.

Our most capable and mature self is our **adult self**. It shows up in moments when we're at our very best. Only our adult self, for example, can observe when our fear or anger increases. Still, rather than acting on those emotions, we can choose to treat them with care and compassion. The adult self is also in charge when we can sit with a colleague, a direct report or a friend struggling and hold space for whatever they're feeling without judgment.

But it's surprisingly challenging to access our adult self, especially under high stress, when we need it most.

Only our adult self has the capacity to see and accept all of who we are. By creating a safer internal environment, our adult self can free up our child self's best qualities: spontaneity, curiosity, creativity, wonder and joyfulness.

Four steps have proven to be key in this journey:

1. Be aware of how you feel in your body and mind when under stress. Any time you feel "less than" or "better than", for example, it's a sign that your child self is feeling threatened, and your defender has moved into fight or flight. Strong negative emotions such as fear, frustration, impatience and anger are other signs that your defender is activated.

2. When you sense that you are being triggered in your body, slow down to self-regulate. Take a deep breath. Name your emotions out loud, which helps you move from being at their mercy to observing them more objectively. Movement – especially oscillating or pendulating – can also help. Please think of how you instinctively hold and rock a child to calm them down.

3. Rather than judging or criticizing yourself, acknowledge and embrace your negative emotions and shortcomings. Yes, they are part of who you are, but they are not all of who you are. The more you accept yourself as who you are, the less you have to defend. As you self-regulate and bring your adult self in line, you'll be able to think more reflectively, compassionately and wisely about how to address whatever challenge you happen to be facing.

4. Get more comfortable with your discomfort. Discomfort is a prerequisite to growth and change, but we are taught to equate it with danger. Psychologist Resmaa Menakem makes a distinction between "dirty pain" – the chronic pain of seeking to suppress, deny and blame others for our fears and vulnerabilities – and "clean pain" – the inevitable discomfort that comes from questioning our assumptions, facing our fears and taking responsibility for our missteps.

4.5 Succeeding ambiguity and uncertainty

We have already addressed the importance of embracing change in Chapter 3. In this Section, we will go deeper into understanding how to succeed in continuously evolving situations and best walk untrodden paths.

Let's start by asking ourselves why it is important to be able to embrace change.

Examining ideas in Greek philosophy, Heraclitus pointed out that "Life is flux". Everything is constantly shifting, becoming something other than it was before. Like a river, life flows ever onwards. While we may step from the riverbank into the river, the waters flowing over our feet will never be the same waters that flowed even one moment before. Heraclitus concluded that since the very nature of life is change, resisting this natural flow was to resist the essence of our existence. "There is nothing permanent except change," he said.

If we accept that change is the essence of our existence, handling change well is the key to our happiness. Or at least avoiding being unhappy for a start – as Bertram Russell ('The Conquest of Happiness') would argue.

Also, 20th-century psychologist and author Carl G. Jung refers to this topic in 'The Stages of Life'. He states that refusing to embrace change as a necessary and regular part of life will lead to problems, pain and disappointment.

Stoicism is a school of Hellenistic philosophy. Its leading thinkers were Seneca, Epictetus and Marcus Aurelius. Stoics believe nothing is stable, and we must come to terms with that. The natural world is made up of a series of processes that are changing, but if we want to live happily with nature, we must live in harmony with it.

Stoicism is not so much about resisting change as facing up to it. "Since we don't have a choice, we should not fight it. If everything changes, then the question is: do we change with it?" says Sellars, Reader in Philosophy at Royal Holloway, University of London.

Sellars continues by stating that Stoicism recommends not fearing uncertainty, appreciating things now and understanding that they are not forever. This brings about broad parallels with Buddhism. "Things are changing; live in the present moment, and don't have strong attachments to external things. Like Buddhism, Stoicism also advises feeling compassion for all sentient creatures, having natural affinities, and not being unfeeling or emotionless."

In a way, Stoicism teaches us the following paradox: the more we allow ourselves to accept that change is inevitable, the more likely we are to change intentionally and adapt. In this sense, change can be an engine of progress [5].

In other words, embracing change helps us to be adaptable and flexible.

As Albert Einstein said, "The measure of intelligence is the ability to change".

In a forever changing world, we must look out for the skillset needed in the workplace of the future. Change will undoubtedly be more accelerated and more of a driving force than today. We'll have to continually contend with new technologies, rising automation, the rapidly evolving pace of work and vast business disruptions. In this context, we must all develop the mental resilience to thrive in times of constant change. Adaptability – the ability to adjust to new conditions – is critical to developing flexibility. Adaptable people are open-minded, curious and willing to learn new things because they focus on opportunities, not obstacles.

Whilst evolving in my career over the past 20 years, the business mantra was less about being able to deal with uncertainty and more about dealing with ambiguity. You may think that both point to the same outcome. I, too, was led to believe this until I realized there was an evident difference. In uncertainty, we know zero, absolutely nothing about the possible outcome of a situation. Therefore, we cannot lean into experience, data, or shared learnings. We walk into the complete unknown: a COVID-19 pandemic, the development of Web3 and its opportunities, the digitalization during the past decade, online luxury fashion shopping in the early 2000s, profitable Metaverse opportunities, AI outcomes, etc. Navigating this total uncertainty requires – what I call – the "equality factor". We will look in more detail into this on the following pages.

On the other hand, dealing with ambiguity demands powering up – what I call – the "adaptability factor". Ambiguity is not uncertainty. Here we have only partial information; we lack the complete picture, cannot rely on total possession of resources and may face mixed messages or changing goalposts. This is ambiguity. And those situations and contexts are much more frequent in business. In fact, it is a stable situation. A blurred environment, either due to external factors or internal and political ones. It is, therefore, crucial to master the skills necessary to cope with ambiguity. So, which are those skills?

First, I believe we can take insight from what Jeff Bezos – founder and former CEO of Amazon – describes as the critical skills for start-up entrepreneurs. These entrepreneurs evolve in a highly ambiguous context per the very nature of these potential businesses. Mr Bezos states, "the difficulty is not to have an idea, but to turn an idea into a successful product. There are many steps in between, and it takes stubborn relentlessness and as well as complete flexibility. And you have to know when to be which". Here is what he suggests: "Stubborn on your vision (otherwise it will be too easy to give up), but very flexible on the details". This is because you will realize – as you go along – that some of your preconceptions were wrong. And you will need to be able to pivot and adjust [6].

A leader needs to be adaptable and effectively cope with change; they need to be able to shift gears, decide and act without having the total picture and be comfortable handling risk and uncertainty. How do leaders achieve this [7]?

Great leaders cut through ambiguity using the **zoom-out and zoom-in techniques**. By zooming out, they map existing information to the demands of tomorrow, visualize how the various factors will play out and try to understand the consequence of their decision way into the future. This is also sometimes referred to as having a "helicopter view".

While zooming in, they try to face the current realities of their organization to determine what needs to change in the present to make that future possible. Very often, it is necessary to enter the most minute detail to ensure the situation or problem is covered and under control.

By combining the opportunities in the future with the challenges of the present, they can realistically carve out a plan, set deterministic goals and take small steps to turn them into success stories for their organization.

Ambiguity can often cause leaders to zoom out and/or zoom in on the wrong problems. To avoid sidelining the issues that often plague their organization, great leaders create a culture where people feel safe to speak up, actively encourage conversation and disagreement and lead with the mindset to get the correct information even if it misaligns with their current beliefs and expectations.

Uncertainty can be overwhelming if leaders don't realize that even amidst unknowns, there are always some knowns. Great leaders know this. They **separate what's absolutely clear from what's up for debate** to make the best use of their time and energy. Things they can rely on from the ones that can't be trusted. Information that's trivial from information that is crucial. Investments that are risky from the safe ones.

For example, every new product launch invariably comes with a degree of risk. How customers will react to the new product is always unknown. However, believing in your team and knowing you can count on them to overcome any challenge or setback can be known to you. This knowledge can be a great energy source to navigate uncertain times.

When deciding on two equally good opportunities, you might understand the added value each brings to your ecosystem but feel challenged when understanding their limitations. Knowing this can help you deep-dive into the limitations to make a more informed decision.

Undoubtedly, some problems are complex, but others, which may seem complicated at first glance, may turn out less so and are quickly resolved, especially if leaders are prepared to invest in **building cross-disciplinary thinking**. Cross-disciplinary thinking is the ability to gather knowledge and ideas from other domains outside your primary domain. It involves identifying creative solutions to problems by combining various types of information in your head in new and novel ways.

"Increasing specialization has created a system of parallel trenches in the quest for innovation. Everyone is digging deeper into their own trench and rarely standing up to look in the next trench over, even though the solution to their problem happens to reside there," writes David Epstein in Range.

He adds, "Modern work demands knowledge transfer: the ability to apply knowledge to new situations and different domains" [8].

Great leaders learn to deal with ambiguity by looking beyond all the complexity and uncertainty through diverse experience and cross-disciplinary thinking. They develop and apply a "situation-first" mindset.

Amazon Prime Membership and Fulfillment by Amazon, now highly successful programs, had a high probability of failure during the ideation phase. Jeff Bezos called them radical ideas and talked about **the importance of intuition in decision-making**. He said, "We invested in both of these ideas with significant financial risk and after much internal debate. We had to continue investing significantly over time as we experimented with different ideas and iterations. We could not foresee with certainty what those programs would eventually look like, let alone whether they would succeed, but they were pushed forward with intuition and heart and nourished with optimism."

He also said, "All of my best decisions in business and in life have been made with heart, intuition, guts . . . not analysis. If you can make a decision with analysis, you should do so. But it turns out that, in life, your most important decisions are always made with instinct and intuition, taste, heart."

It's essential to make decisions rationally and use data as a strategic decision-making tool. Still, not every situation at work is black and white or dictates a straightforward answer that can be resolved with data alone. Great leaders know that they sometimes need to rely on their expert intuition to make the right decision in times of uncertainty. This expert intuition, formed over years of learning, mistakes and experience, helps them navigate otherwise difficult and uncertain situations.

As Colin Powell writes in his book "It Worked for Me": "Superior leadership is often a matter of superb instinct. When faced with a tough decision, use the time available to gather information that will inform your instinct. Learn all you can about the situation, your opponent, your assets and liabilities, your strengths and weaknesses, the threats and risks. Select several possible courses of action, then test the information you have gathered against them and analyze one against the other. Often, factual analysis alone will indicate the right choice. More often, your judgment will be needed to select from the best courses of action. This is the moment when you apply your instinct to smell the right answer. This is where you apply your education, experience and knowledge of external considerations unfamiliar to your staff. This is when you look deep into your own fears, anxiety and self-confidence. This is where you earn your pay and position. Your instinct at this point is not a wild guess or a hunch. It is an informed instinct that knows from long experience which facts are the most important and which adverse facts, however adverse, can be set aside [9]."

Mark Twain said: "Good judgement is the result of experience, and experience the result of bad judgement."

Great leaders don't wait for perfect conditions to make a move. They know that every decision they make may not be perfect. But for a growing organization, the cost of inaction while waiting for an ideal opportunity is more costly than, at least, taking action, even if it might be sub-optimal.

They understand that taking risks does not mean flying blind. It involves the willingness to experiment, make calculated investments, to checkpoint, learn and make corrections along the way. This willingness to take risks and step into the unknown makes them stand out from many others who feel paralyzed with ambiguity, overthinking and indecision.

A new and uncertain context may cause leaders to invest in sunk costs – invested time, money and effort that is now irretrievable. This can impact their thinking and decision-making, leading to more wasted expenses and resources on an already failed cause.

As Annie Duke writes in her book "Thinking in Bets": "Our narrative of being a knowledgeable, educated, intelligent person who holds quality opinions isn't compromised when we use new information to calibrate our beliefs. There is no sin in finding out there is evidence that contradicts what we believe. The only sin is in not using that evidence as objectively as possible to refine that belief going forward" [10].

Great leaders embrace ambiguity with agility. They ensure that their team understands their intention, supports them in their vision and does not hesitate to switch gears when the outcomes do not match what they originally envisioned.

Instead of sticking to an already failed course of action, they are quick to reevaluate circumstances, shift direction and **are open to switching to a different plan of action**. Flexibility to adapt, either as a response to a wrong strategy or unexpected conditions, keeps their organizations strong and thriving.

Ambiguity can create a sense of loss of control, particularly when you start believing something is out of your control and is the reason for your shortcoming. Abdicating responsibility and blaming outside forces (other people, situations, circumstances) for an unexpected result only leads to evasion of responsibility and inaction. When leaders engage with a victim mindset, instead of putting effort into seeking clarity, they pull back. Instead of investing time in finding a solution, they spend more time complaining and feeding their frustration, leading to a toxic spiral of negativity and inaction.

Great leaders do not allow themselves to get trapped by a cycle of negativity. In this way, they feel more in control of their experience. They know that they can't control all circumstances, but they can certainly control how they respond to those circumstances. With an inner sense of control over their behaviours, decisions and actions, they lead with constructive action instead of blaming someone or something else for their situation. They **take responsibility**.

Let's focus now on what I called before the "equality factor". These are the required skills to elevate our ability to deal with uncertainty.

Let's look back to Spring 2020, at the initial months of the COVID-19 pandemic. When no one had yet figured out the best strategy, some female political leaders were acting slightly differently from their male colleagues. In general terms, women politicians were more focused on national well-being than on their personal political gain. They lead with a "people first" mindset.

An interesting piece of research from the University of Nevada on female leadership style during the pandemic shows that women leaders face a gender double bind: they are penalized for being too masculine but also penalized for being too feminine. Women leaders who flout gender expectations are labelled aggressive or pushy, and those who perform along gender expectations are labelled too nice or not taken seriously. With a radical change of context, like a pandemic crisis, women world leaders were offered an opportunity to reconcile this double bind: they could be both decisive and strategic, as well as compassionate and nurturing. This is how New Zealand's prime minister's actions presented when she decided to close borders and institute strict lockdowns. In a show of compassion, Norway's Erna Solberg made a unique appeal to children, saying, "It's OK to feel scared".

The researchers found that what matters more than the gender of the leader was a country's culture – power distance, uncertainty avoidance, individualist/collectivist, feminine/masculine, short/long term orientation and indulgence/restraint. The country's culture is more important – and those with more egalitarian societies tend to do better during these kinds of crises. Those societies that elect women also had fewer deaths per capita of population – so having **a more egalitarian society** and electing a woman leader has a statistically significant palliative effect on reducing the deaths from COVID-19 [11].

This is what I will call "the equality factor". It is not a gender-driven difference but more of a cultural mindset originating from a place enjoying a more egalitarian community conception.

Let's take prime minister Jacinda Ardern from New Zealand, for example. She clearly adopted a more compassionate touch during the first uncertain days of the COVID-19 pandemic when faced with the decision between saving human lives vs the economy. Kaja Kallas, prime minister from Estonia, demonstrated a similar leadership style during the first days of the Ukrainian war; she showed a similar female determination to protect the innocent by showing zero tolerance for bullying behaviour. They have both clearly understood what caring should mean and look like for politicians and how to lead with empathy.

The words for which Jacinda Arden has become famed and illustrate this exactly are the following: "One of the criticisms I've faced over the years is that I'm not aggressive enough or assertive enough, or maybe somehow, because I'm empathetic, it means I'm weak. I totally rebel against that. I refuse to believe that you cannot be both compassionate and strong."

I believe those traits are not gender specific, which is why I called them the "equality factor". We may find male political leaders showing similar reactions to Ardern's to the pandemic, e.g. Justin Trudeau or Boris Johnson, similar to Kallas's in the case of the conflict in Ukraine.

Therefore, this "equality factor" can be observed in businesswomen and businessmen. The following examples provide the intricacies of explaining the "equality factor".

During the first months of the COVID-19 pandemic, the world was facing an unprecedented calamity on a scale not experienced in many decades: not being able to control or cope with a new disease that was killing thousands of people. Under the pressure of this enormous uncertainty, leaders using their **moral compass** as the first guiding principle prevailed. This is so in politics and corporate arenas. When furlough schemes were put in place, and teams on the front lines were protected at all costs: from a health and financial point of view. Compassion and care were the guiding principles when the stakes were extraordinarily high and the situation was out of control.

Similarly, during the first months of the Ukraine war, Europe faced an unimaginable situation: to have war again on the continent in the 21st century. And here, the two political leaders mentioned above showed another ability: **reading the situation holistically**. To do this, Kaja Kallas could understand what was happening earlier than other politicians. She had first-hand information and personal experience to draw conclusions and make decisions. But she had also formed her opinion long before others by gathering exhaustive information about involved people, institutions and operations. She measured early what was at stake. This is undoubtedly due to the exposure of her country and its geographical location. But what about the UK? The country is close to the conflict but less than many other countries, and the difference in perceived support by the Ukrainians is evident. In an interview, I only recently heard

Boris Johnson say that what made him understand the best course of action were his learnings from when he had visited Ukraine as foreign minister years before the invasion and evaluated and understood the situation firsthand on the ground.

Gathering the best information, listening to all parties involved and understanding the situation and dynamics involved prove critical to gaining a holistic perspective to read a vital situation effectively.

Both approaches seem clear examples of what I would call "the equality factor". These examples of navigating uncertainty empathetically, with clear values, setting direction with conviction and without fear characterize this approach.

The question is: Why is it essential to have a section on the "equality factor" in this book? I believe there is still too little recognition in business for this way of working. Additionally, uncertainty is far from over; business ethics to regulate AI usage, behavioural alerts to avoid mental health disorders from Metaverse platform addictions, increased privacy hacks and cybersecurity risks, etc., are just some examples that are already being addressed. We need to be prepared on how to act best.

Let's take a great example of a company turnaround to achieve a higher market share within a new sector: cloud computing [12]. When Satya Nadella was appointed Microsoft's new CEO in 2014, he put Microsoft's cloud-computing arm, Azure, launched in 2010, at the heart of the business. Mr Nadella dethroned the Windows operating system as its core product. He brought Microsoft's software and services to other operating systems, including "open source" Linux, Google and Apple. This radical change in strategic direction for the company was paired with a complete makeover of its corporate culture. He sent his leadership team out to shift the culture – these were his words – from "know-it-alls" to "learn-it-alls" – a Learning Organization where empathy supports the transition from a static to a growth mindset for its people. Satya Nadella explained his choice for empathy like this: "If you say that innovation is all about meeting unmet unarticulated needs of customers, where is that source of your ability to get in touch with that unmet unarticulated need going to come from? In some sense, it will come from your ability to listen and understand the notions between the lines and extrapolate. And that's, to me, the deep sense of empathy [13]."

This is also what Simon Sinek believes. For him, empathy is king – when it comes to leading a transformation in an organization. The reason is that by putting ourselves as leaders in the shoes of our team, we will better understand their potential fears: the feeling of insecurity, being off their game, losing credibility, being humiliated, not understanding the jargon and recognizing that all is new and unfamiliar around them [14].

It is crucial for leaders not to assume that everybody knows about any given topic and that people evolve at a different pace. In extreme cases, people may resist change to the point of sabotaging themselves. This is when a leader needs to insist on having that difficult conversation, communicating that they get the sense that they are struggling and wish to find a solution with an empathetic personal conversation and allowing for patience.

What can we learn from this type of "equality-driven" leadership?

It is inclusive, encourages participation and shares information and power with those they lead. I have heard quite often: these leaders are driven by their impact rather than by power itself.

This type of leadership tends to create and strengthen group identities. They use their emotional intelligence to their advantage, generate high levels of empathy and are generally capable of considering individuals' "human" side. Influential "equality-driven" leaders are hugely self-aware; they know their strengths and can skilfully use language to connect with those around them emotionally. Various studies have found that they are equipped with better relationship-building skills. They are also found to be good at inspiring and motivating others. I would put that down to their naturally innovative communication capabilities.

Suppose we observe influential "equality-driven" leaders. In that case, we notice that they set a remarkable example to us all, with the courage and conviction to get behind their skills – and to inspire others. A greater purpose guides them. They regularly communicate their purpose and vision to their teams and encourage their colleagues to invest in themselves, ensuring that the company's vision trickles down into everyday tasks – creating a united sense of purpose and drive. In many ways, they are idealists who believe in making an impact and changing the world. Their passion is contagious. People want to be a part of it.

These leaders understand the correlation between a sense of fulfilment at work and experiencing happiness in the workplace. There is an A.T. Kearney survey conducted in December 2018 that explored people's workplace experiences across the Americas, Europe, the Middle East, Africa and the Asia-Pacific region. The sample included more than 500 employees of various ages in companies with more than $2 billion in revenues and multiple industries. Their findings were that joy stems from believing one's work is meaningful. Employees who believe their "company makes a positive societal contribution" and feel "personally committed to achieving the company's vision and strategy" experienced the most joy at work.

These leaders are emotionally resilient. They are strong and capable and focus on their abilities without getting distracted by others' opinions. Leaders with impact know that no risk means no rewards. They have the confidence to take calculated risks, and they can do this because they know taking risks is the key to innovation and achieving off-the-scale results. And whatever happens, they know that they will always glean valuable lessons from the process. They're not scared of failure. And they know this mentality can help them grow in confidence and ability in the long run.

These "equality-driven" leaders have the most appealing leadership abilities, especially in case of crises, contingency or an emergency of any sort. People development, the capacity to set clear standards and rewards, the ability to serve as a role model, the ability to inspire and participatory decision-making are all examples.

A "people-first" leader can accept that everyone perceives the world differently without passing judgment. They can relate to their team, openly interact with them and comprehend when they are experiencing difficulties. In brief, an empathic leader can listen to their team rather than fix, solve or dictate, thus preparing them for success. Empathy also requires being open-minded and understanding of diverse points of view. This facilitates the exchange of ideas and gives a fresh perspective on all manner of issues. As a result, there is often a clear and prompt identification of an effective solution to any particular problem. Using this form of leadership rather than the more authoritative leadership approach makes these leaders more effective at influencing others.

At this point, I would like to address the different options to fully improve our ways of embracing change. To become a change-maker, I suggest focusing your work on three areas: The Self, Others and The Organization [15].

It is crucial for oneself to display an open mind to new ideas and proposals and demonstrate a willingness to do things differently. Constantly and constructively challenge the status quo. It is actively making suggestions for improvement, taking a creative approach to change by challenging assumptions and not only enhancing existing practice.

In approaching other people in the organization, it is important to seek out diversity of perceptions and encourage experimentation and new ways of working. For a broader understanding and deepening commitment to change, it is vital to articulate its purpose and the context within which it is occurring and always communicate change positively through influence and persuasion.

Regarding the organisation, creating a climate favourable to innovation and receptivity to change is necessary. Leading by example in supporting the organization to break with traditional methods. Embracing new technologies, techniques and working methods is imperative, as is scanning the wider environment to seek opportunities to develop the organization. Last but not least, recognize that there may be a need to modify organizational strategy and governance to adapt to changes in the broader environment.

To finalize this section, I would like to summarize the main takeaways.

In dealing with uncertainty, we generally know nothing about the new situation, but no one else does either. It is an even playing field of uncertain rules and outcomes. For dealing with uncertainty, we should resist oversimplification and quick conclusions and should **apply prudence** and **avoid the temptation to go it alone**. With a pioneering approach, we must add some aspects of psychology to our skillset – the "equality factor", driven by **a "people-first" approach**.

In dealing with ambiguity, any doubt may be confined to us, our company, our team, a specific project or a moment. With limited information or changing goalposts or contradicting messages, this is where we might instead require a tactical approach – the "adaptability factor", driven by **a "situation-first" mindset** – for our decision-making. When dealing with ambiguity, we should rather focus on **Results** instead of Process and **Success** instead of Harmony.

4.6 Diversity and inclusion

Isabella was back at her office. She just returned from a roundtable organized by the American teams of The Business of Fashion. They would invite, every Quarter, a panel of Luxury Fashion experts to exchange over an exciting and pertinent topic relevant to the current state of business. This time, the subject chosen was Cultural adoption by Creatives amidst the evolving debate over giving a stronger voice to Diversity and Inclusion topics and professionals.

Although some of the companies in North America had already made considerable strides in this direction, Isabella felt there was still a long way to go. She accepted the invitation for the debate with great pleasure.

What she expected less was the honesty and generosity with which a colleague from a competitor brand shared their story of recovery after a colossal misstep. How the brand handled the situation would undoubtedly go into textbooks for others to learn.

Isabella had always believed that the teams at that brand in question had shown a strong sense of collective commitment and resolve to face that difficult situation. They did face the issue head-on, apologetically – with the unwavering support of their Head office in Europe – and started working immediately on a meaningful recovery plan.

The brand community had been hurt and needed public messages of reconciliation and respect. The general negative fallout from the brand had been far-reaching. The path was untrodden, but the company's leadership team realized they had made a serious error and needed to make resolute changes and evolve, so they enlisted the support of a group of experts in the field. Informal talks were held to learn and unlearn and reach out to expert voices to decide which changes and priorities needed to be put in place. Additionally, the brand took this misstep as an opportunity to reconsider attention to diversity at all company levels in an authentic, honest and transparent way.

If you adopt a humble mindset, with the eagerness to learn, step up and make the right moves in a timely manner to address the problem, recovery is possible. Customers will generally be willing to forgive.

The lesson shared by that professional colleague would resonate with other brands to mirror and evolve accordingly. An important learning point for the industry overall.

A couple of months ago, I was asked by some discerning female students what the most critical challenges of being a woman in business have been for me.

This was an interesting question. Since I have evolved in the Luxury Fashion Industry – which is female to a large extent – I could only answer the question from an industry-biased perspective. I would say this industry is quite female-friendly for all types of roles, including Manufacturing and Data. Another question would be Retail and C-level positions. During my Luxury Retail career, there have been marked improvements. What was a traditional male career path is now also open for women.

Nevertheless, male regional presidents still prevail in the organizations. This also goes for C-level and CEO positions. That is the reality. Nonetheless, as said, change is happening, and courageous and strong female leaders are being supported and developed in diverse areas, groups and brands. I hope they bolster the movement of change, which I have also been navigating.

Daily, female leaders face three main challenges in the corporate sphere. The balance between work life and personal life, the pay gap and the still relatively low recognition of intrinsic ways of working, like the one named the "equality factor" in the previous section, driven by a 'people first' mindset.

My take on how to overcome these three challenges is pretty straightforward: work together. For those leading the movement and for the generations who will follow – they are committed. Still, everyone should be concerned, including, of course, men. Especially men who have daughters. It seems unforgivable otherwise.

For the first challenge – the balance between work and personal life – there is an energy aspect to establish and accept. More than time management, I see it as 'energy management', which requires balance. This has already been outlined in Chapter 3 for both genders. Additionally, something that can come into play here is kids – the little nippers are notoriously energy-draining for their parents. Time, of course, but also energy; we should not forget that. As a manager, showing empathy to mothers and fathers is essential, specifically at significant moments in the day, week and year for the parents. Without prying or being nosey, it is helpful for a manager to be perceptive of the relationships of team members. Some may have a very supportive and helpful partner – others may not. Some might be single parents, and much of their energy may be sapped by juggling kids, work, babysitting, shopping and other domestic chores.

Women will need a supportive partner at home, with or without kids, especially as a family. Supportive for domestic tasks, but also and foremost physically and mentally. Therefore, the partner should support with love and understanding and not exacerbate the problem by sucking attention and energy. Again, especially for families with young kids. Michelle Obama stated in her recent book that "partnering well" is very important in life. Indeed, she is proud of her husband and partner in life. From what we know, the couple has been very supportive of each other's life choices and embraced those decisions fully. This is what everyone – women and men – need. Love at home is crucial to remain balanced. For a successful career, your other half will be a vital part of it. Over time, the most supportive and loving couples I know are not out of the same cookie-cutter. They are different, each with unique personalities, passions and talents. If we want a relationship to grow, we need to learn to fulfil ourselves inside this relationship. Each partner will complement the strengths and weaknesses of the relationship. I believe this is where the sweet spot resides, and this is possibly valuable for every relationship in life.

Returning to the subject of children. There is no question that they demand time and energy from parents with demanding corporate jobs. But I would add – and I have heard this so many times – that children also give immense energy and strong emotional support with the love and affection they convey. This is the extra vivacity parents can look forward to when they come home from work.

The pandemic has shown us the value of remote working; for some mums, it has become a revelation as to how to juggle kids' needs and work life better. For others, it has become more stressful with the blurry lines between work and home life and few boundaries to break the cycle. As a leader and manager of teams, I would say that one needs to be attentive to finding the best possible options for each team member. With the technological tools we have at our disposal these days (i.e. remote conferencing) and an enforced empathy sentiment encompassing the whole team, driving compassion for one another, a solution for every case should be found.

Regarding the second challenge – the pay gap – it should be every woman's duty to step up. A gender pay gap for the same job and outcome in the 2020s is totally unacceptable. If it is the case, you should address it and have the resolve to take your situation into your own hands, fight for it and shine a light on unfair treatment. This is not only a personal cause but a cause for all women suffering the same discrimination. Lead by example and ensure no gender inequalities exist within your team. This has always been the stance I have taken throughout my career. I have pledged and honoured this responsibility for my own remuneration and those of my female team members. And I can tell you with absolute conviction that it is possible. For this one, you don't depend on others but yourself; it's your fight.

Here is where the words from award-winning advocate Christine Michael Carter resonate with me: "No one has done you a favour by employing you; you were compensated with the expectation to deliver results. If you've exceeded those expectations, be self-interested and toot your own horn. Allies are wonderful, but they are not a strategy to secure the higher salary you feel you deserve. No one cares more about your career than you, and your strategy will determine if your family suffers from a significant amount of lost compensation during your working career".

The most difficult, however, is the third challenge: promoting and instilling new ways of leading and seeing those embraced and rewarded. Primarily what I call the "equality factor". That is, upholding a strong moral compass, reading the situation holistically, working in full collaboration with a 'people first' mindset and applying prudence in decision-making. Working methods catalysed during the pandemic and proved very successful in a high stake and uncertain context.

From my perspective, I have always tried to and continue to lead my teams and projects this way. It has become my quest, and I am always delighted to see and hear of others battling on the same grounds. Not only in corporate but also in politics, and other institutions, at the highest levels. Not to forget that startup founders and entrepreneurs have made some of the most significant breakthroughs. We increasingly notice the outstanding contributions made by role models leading "in a pack" with empathy and sensitivity, applying servant leadership . . . there are many ways to describe the new, more empathetic leadership style and it is undeniably a far cry from most leaders my generation has lived through for the past twenty years. I hope all of us who believe the same will notice the impact soon and have inspired others to lead this way.

Having female leaders in positions of influence will not only serve as role models for women's career advancement. Still, they will have a broader societal impact on pay equity, change workplace policies and ways of leading that benefit both men and women and attract a more diverse workforce.

Much work is still to be done to continue on a positive trajectory. One fundamental component is female mentoring. I have rarely experienced it myself as a mentee, and this is an oversight that I now look back on and regret in many ways. This is why I feel so passionately about leading by example and mentoring other women whenever the opportunity arises [16].

Here are some hints I would like to share on successful women's networking:

Consider that every time you say "yes" to one thing, it means a "no" to something else. Time is not infinite. Hence the importance of "generating space" in your calendar for networking and mentoring sessions. Prune non-essential meetings from your calendar, deflect low-priority topics, run streamlined meetings, insist on efficient email norms and set aside time for reflection and high-level thinking. You may even introduce a 'no-meetings' half day a week in everyone's calendar. I find this practice exceptionally efficient and productive. Only by implementing some or all these actions will you feel comfortable including and even prioritizing networking activities into your already busy calendar.

When networking, think carefully about whom you are networking with to help reach your goals. Either a political goal like gaining early access to opinion leaders, a developmental goal to supplement some skill gaps, an innovation-oriented plan when searching for new insights, or related to best practices, when you try to find people with expertise on specific topics. It is crucial to initiate new connections continuously. It could be as easy as approaching someone saying, "Could we grab a coffee and explore ways of working together?". Within corporate, reviewing necessary networking strategies when launching a new assignment or during performance evaluations is good practice.

What is also imperative is to connect with people from a wide variety of functions, geographies and business units. This will allow you to access new information, lead innovation and pursue the advancement of yourself and your teams.

The most successful women do not downplay their knowledge, skills and accomplishments; they show evidence that they can get things done. But they can also use humour, presence and small gestures to signal caring and positivity.

I cannot finalize this section without addressing the topic of bias. What needs to be fixed in business is pervasive bias, not women. As Tina Opie – an associate professor at Babson College – puts it: the professional environment is usually "Eurocentric, masculine and heteronormative".

Leaders must create a corporate culture for women, people of colour, the LGBTQ community and non-privileged backgrounds that address systemic bias, racism and elitism. Thus it is vital to create an environment that fosters a variety of leadership styles and in which diverse racial, ethnic and gender identities are seen as equally skilful, professional and successful as the current "Eurocentric, masculine and heteronormative" model. In this way, we will help those employees channel healthy self-doubt into positive motivation, best fostered within a supportive work culture.

I believe in collective intelligence and cooperation and that diversity helps us understand situations better, learn and grow and ultimately make better decisions.

To understand why diverse teams are smarter, I will take the lessons from a *Harvard Business Review* article by David Rock and Heidi Grant from 2016 [17].

Firstly, a diverse team will be **more fact-based** and remain **objective**. By breaking up workplace homogeneity, you can allow your employees to become more aware of their own potential biases – entrenched ways of thinking that can otherwise blind them to crucial information and even lead them to make errors in decision-making processes.

The researchers believe diverse teams may outperform homogenous ones in decision-making because **they process information more carefully**. Remember: Considering an outsider's perspective may seem counterintuitive, but the payoff can be huge.

Diverse teams are **more innovative**. Though you may feel more at ease working with people who share your background, don't be fooled by your comfort blanket. Hiring individuals who do not look, talk or think like you can allow you to dodge the costly pitfalls of conformity, discouraging innovative thinking.

Enriching your employee pool with representatives of different genders, races, and nationalities is vital to boosting your company's intellectual potential. Creating a more diverse workplace will help to keep your team members' biases in check and make them question their assumptions. At the same time, we need to ensure the organization has inclusive practices so everyone feels comfortable, appreciated and heard. All of this can make your teams smarter and, ultimately, make your organization more successful, whatever your goals.

A diverse workplace will also help employees to be more assertive. They will become more aware of others' rights and willing to work on resolving conflicts, only if, at the same time, the workplace is seen as a safe place to stand up for their interests and express freely their thoughts and feelings.

4.7 Preserving integrity

Lucy was sitting in a trendy bar at the French Concession in Shanghai. A friend had arrived a few minutes earlier, and they started chatting. This was their first catch-up since the lockdown. Nice weather outside, a great ambience in the bar and a sense of liberation in the air. Both friends felt great and were happy to be reunited again in person.

Not sure how the conversation turned; it probably addressed mental health issues that had been a hot topic for many people after the lockdown, especially regarding adolescents. The fact is that they ended up speaking about Lucy's burnout which she had experienced a couple of years ago.

Samantha, her friend, wanted to understand better how Lucy slipped into that state. "You were the last person I thought it could happen to, Lucy. You seem so strong to us all. And so happy in your job and your life. How could that happen?"

"Sometimes I do compare it to anorexia", Lucy answered. "It also presents itself unexpectedly to people we would not expect. People who seem to have it all, are satisfied in their lives and enjoying a happy lifestyle. When, in reality, the problem is simmering inside. The unexpectedness may be similar, but the source is very different".

"Did you feel it coming then? And what had been the source in your case?" asked Samantha worriedly.

"Well, I noticed myself slowly slipping into unknown territory; yes, I did in a matter of a couple of months. The reasons are commonly cited: a sense of not being acknowledged and rewarded fairly for your efforts. That's it, basically. And then, as the expression indicates, you feel your energy vanishing, exhausted, and without joy to continue. Luckily I noticed it quickly and took steps before it became too late. A quick identification and reaction was my salvation, and I am proud and grateful I managed it so swiftly".

"Was this the reason you quit your job?" Samantha asked.

"Yes, definitely. I wouldn't have been able to continue at that place. Because you need to understand that, the feeling of being treated unfairly is not everything. I was overcome with a depressing feeling of being misaligned with the company's values and way of acting – in total disarray. Clearly, there was no other possible choice for me. It became clear that this was my only possible option. After that, healing was then relatively fast."

"Would you then take this as a lesson that your integrity was out of balance in a way?"

"This is exactly how I felt. Exactly that. And since I know it is so important to me, I knew that first and foremost I needed to preserve my integrity, and so that's what I did".

How would you best define integrity? Living with integrity?

Well, it is undoubtedly living your life in accordance with an internal set of values and beliefs.

You value honesty in others; you are honest and transparent to others; you always keep your word and will not tolerate lies or deception from others. You would not lie to make a situation easier or to avoid scrutiny. You always believe in putting forward your best self. Hence, you refuse to cut corners or to fault others for things you know are your responsibility. You pride yourself on your compassion, so you will not just stand by silently as others berate the less fortunate or weaker ones or anyone for that matter. You also feel bound to act when you see injustice, to speak when others won't and to stand up for your beliefs by living them.

When we live our lives with integrity, we let our actions speak for who we are and what we believe. Integrity is a choice we make, and it's a choice we must keep making every moment of our lives.

Integrity is a highly valued trait, especially in leaders.

To develop and protect your integrity, start by identifying your core values. These are the values that, regardless of the consequence, you are not willing to compromise.

Next, analyse your choices to ensure you're doing the right thing. Often, people cut corners or make bad choices when they think no one is watching. Having integrity means that, no matter what, you make what you truly believe is the right choice – especially when no one is watching! If you are not sure what the right choice is, ask yourself these two questions:

"If my choice was printed on the newspaper's front page for everyone to see, would I feel OK about it?" or "If I make this choice, will I feel OK with myself afterwards?"

This makes me think about what must have gone through the head of Katharine Graham – owner and publisher of the *Washington Post* – when she decided to publish the Pentagon Papers in June 1971. She was risking the house – the company, the newspaper and her family's reputation. A great example of steadfast integrity. These were classified documents showing several American Administrations lying to their citizens. Still, she also faced Supreme Court's ruling and a possible prison sentence. Finally, as one of the Justices put it – "The press is to serve the governed, not the governors". This profound belief indeed guided Mrs Graham in her decision, well above private friendship with Defense Secretary Robert McNamara, who ordered the internal review of the U.S. military intervention in Vietnam.

Another strategy you can use when you are unsure about the right decision is to ask yourself what people you value as having high levels of integrity would do. I use the figures of Mandela, Jesus, Gandhi or Yoda (from Star Wars), and ask myself what they would do if they were in this situation.

Developing a culture of integrity around you and building your self-confidence and self-esteem is essential to help preserve your own integrity. Develop friendships and work relationships with others who demonstrate integrity and who will support your decisions.

People with integrity often display the same characteristics: they're humble. They have a strong sense of self, they have high self-esteem and they're self-confident. These characteristics are essential, because, sometimes, you'll be under pressure from others to compromise and make what you consider to be the wrong choice.

Sometimes I reflect upon two moments in corporate life where I did feel my integrity triggered but did not speak my truth. At least, I was aware of this, learned from it and found ways to avoid it in the future.

The first example was when a group of colleagues were gossiping about a senior leader who was to arrive imminently at the company. This had already been going on and on for several weeks. It had been relatively easy to avoid up to that point by just stepping away and not engaging in those conversations. But on one particular occasion, I was kind of trapped since it was during some cocktail drinks on a crowded terrace after a worldwide leadership meeting abroad. Tricky to leave your group when you are supposed to "turn up as a group" when all other Regions are present at that moment too. I have always relished the life lesson provided by this scenario. While I struggled, not knowing exactly how to behave best, since my feelings were uncomfortable and contradictory, someone else did the right thing. This person was moving around the different groups of people (as one does during cocktails), heard the gossiping happening and did the right thing: immediately pointed out the inappropriateness of the conversation. Quite unexpectedly, since it did not concern him directly, he did precisely the right thing. And chose all the most appropriate tone and words required for the situation.

The second example concerns another moment I could and should have spoken up more decisively. I did speak up, but I could have done better if it hadn't happened so unexpectedly. I found myself conversing with one of the company's senior leaders, defending an action from a former boss of mine, for whom the criticism was incorrect and unfounded. I plead my (or her) point of view but thought later that I could have been more courageous and gone further in the defence. These are examples of a feeling where my defence of a person not present in the room could have been better aligned with my beliefs and preserved my integrity. You will always know when you feel you have compromised your integrity – it's not a great feeling.

Sometimes you may find yourself making the wrong choice (the wisdom of hindsight). The point is to be self-aware in those moments, re-evaluate them and the decisions taken and then take the lesson to improvement if the occasion arises again. As long as the error is not catastrophic, you can move forward and grow with it. What is essential is not to jeopardize your reputation and preserve and develop your integrity wherever possible. Keep working on building and improving a strong sense of self so that you have the strength and courage to do the right thing when the time comes.

Remember, honesty and integrity aren't values you should live by when it's convenient; they're values you should always live by. This includes the big and little choices – the choices everyone sees and the choices that no one sees.

An excellent example of an outspoken personality always at the centre of the rights she wishes to defend is Bozoma St John, an American marketing executive and former Netflix CMO. In an Instagram post on October 26th 2022, she stated:

> My reason for speaking out when I see injustice or bigotry or any other social ills, isn't because it affects me directly. Y'all have heard me speak about the plight of Black women in corporate spaces, but that is not the only community I live in. What happens when our neighbours, friends, lovers, colleagues are attacked? We can't stand back and say, 'I'm not one of them' or 'They didn't say anything when it happened to me' . . . If it happens to one of us, it happens to all of us. And those who love far outnumber those who hate. And although there are more crimes against all of us than I have words to combat, my hope is that in the space I occupy, I can stand alongside those who are shouting for their cause and lend my voice too. If you have it in your heart, please lend yours. Collective silence is deadly.

And she accompanied her cry out by the well-known words of the German Lutheran Pastor Martin Niemoeller (1892–1984). "First, they came for the socialists, and I did not speak out – because I was not a socialist. Then they came for the trade unionists, and I did not speak out – because I was not a trade unionist. Then they came for the Jews, and I did not speak out – because I was not a Jew. Then they came for me – and there was no one left to speak for me."

If collective silence is deadly, personal silence can be devastating also. There is an episode I will not forget when a senior executive commented within a small group of people in which I found myself. Out of the blue, he stated that women who don't have kids are selfish. It was a side comment but it didn't go unnoticed. I decided to ignore it and kept calm. My mistake, I thought later. I should have made him repeat the comment, asked him if I had heard right, asked what made him feel so, etc. At that moment, I asked myself: would the other three people in the room have supported me? Probably not. His management by fear had taken its toll. Sadly. In a fear-ridden and toxic environment, preserving your integrity is more challenging.

Unfair treatment or any injustice, gossiping and lies, power games that become too prevalent and toxic people, in general, are all situations that may drive your integrity within the corporate environment to the brink. In fact, a toxic work environment has a high probability of leading employees to 'integrity misalignment'. That is when your values no longer align with the company or management culture. And that can result in the risk of descending into burnout.

How best to handle this and navigate those situations?

In the case of gossiping, you can always put a stop to it by saying that there's work to be done, and that this is no time to engage in pettiness. You may also praise the maligned individual's good traits or stand up for a friend or colleague. You can also walk away – but this is better done after you've made your point about not being willing to listen to such negativity about a person you both know. You might find yourself shunned or ostracized by this rumourmonger, or you can almost guarantee you'll be the next recipient of their vitriolic comments. Maybe, but you will be living with and feel comfortable with your integrity intact. You will be living according to your beliefs and values and with authenticity. And that trumps negativity every time.

It is also essential to understand when we are talking about a toxic workplace. It is a workplace with an ineffective culture. This is not the same as a workplace that doesn't appeal to you personally and is accompanied by a strong gut feeling. If we want a fact-based approach to assessing a workplace as toxic, I would suggest referencing Adam Grant's four deadly sins, as he calls them. As soon as one of these 4 R's is overemphasized within the corporate culture, there is a risk of toxicity for its members [18].

First R would be **Relationships**. If not stepping on toes or upsetting people is all that matters at a business, it's no surprise that getting things done falls way down the list of priorities. The result is mediocrity and a culture without accountability. "Even if you do a terrible job, you can still get ahead as long as people like you", says Grant of this first fundamental type of toxicity.

The second R would be **Results**. This is the other end of the relationships-versus-results tradeoff. Over on this side are companies that value relationships so little that they'll throw human decency under the bus in the name of performance. Grant and supporting research suggest this variety of toxicity is the deadliest of all company culture sins and can result in disrespect, abuse, unethical decisions and cutthroat behaviour.

The third R would be **Rules**. These are the companies which view even minor changes to the status quo with suspicion and hostility. Every business must balance the stability of rules against the rewards of risks. If you stray too far toward rules and regulations, you end up with creativity- and initiative-killing bureaucracy.

The fourth R would be **Risk**. The chaos of rules-free anarchy is at the other end of the spectrum from rules and bureaucracy. When everyone can do whatever they want without coordination or alignment, people end up working at cross-purposes, valuable lessons are rarely learned and a whole lot of effort gets wasted.

I find this analysis objective and pertinent to understanding a toxic workplace. From my experience, it is important to consider the following:

- Different moments in time in an organization might show different corporate cultures. A culture is like a living organism and may develop and change over time. There may be intrinsic proactive factors that may shape corporate culture instead in one direction or another.
- There may also be a difference within the organization, where culture differs at Headquarters vs. the Regional offices. Or toxicity exists in specific departments and not others. For both previous considerations, people who shape culture will provide those differences.
- Companies may rate on the extreme ends of more than one of the four deadly sins. This could have an even more substantial negative impact on its employees.
- Also, those toxicities will almost certainly affect some people more than others in the organization. Of course, those whose character and behaviour align better with those extremes will navigate more comfortably and advance their careers within those organizations.
- I have also observed over the years the degree to which the Human Resources teams can pull the strings within the organization and determine the direction of the company culture, good or bad. Some organizations allow excessive power of those HR teams vs other organizations where HR acts as a mere service department to the CEO and leadership team and the company.

It is also possible that even with excellent company culture and values in place, narcissistic leadership, sizeable egos and people with an excessive drive for power sometimes go out of their way to instil and promote toxicity in the workplace. This can be starkly apparent regarding who and why some people are rewarded or even promoted. Always ask yourself what the promotion is worth to you. Take a look in the mirror. Think about the kind of person you are at heart. If management value staff who will go to any lengths for promotion, then you are likely not on a level playing field regarding promotion and remuneration. An unlevel playing field requires new and well-thought-out strategies and alternative key allies. If, on the other hand, your boss values meritocracy and accomplishment, then you have a decent chance of getting selected for your integrity and performance. In that case, do your job well, make your boss and department look good and be noticed. Show that you're willing to invest in your own development – volunteer for extra assignments. Get on committees, make sure your work is outstanding and let company leadership (not just your boss) know about it. When promotions are based on merit, then out-merit your competing colleagues. Otherwise, consider switching elsewhere in the company or to a new employer altogether. Selling your soul for a promotion may simply not be worth it.

As Adam Grant states, "In toxic cultures, people are rewarded solely for individual results. How they treat others is ignored. In healthy cultures, people are valued for collective contributions. Pay, performance, and promotions depend on elevating others".

Or said in another way, also by Adam Grant, "Your worth is not defined by what you achieve or acquire. It's a question of who you become and how you contribute to others. Self-esteem should come from character, not success or status. The highest accomplishment is to be a person of generosity, curiosity, and integrity".

Whatever is valued in your company shapes your organisation's corporate culture; if you wish to succeed there, you must understand what is valued above other things. Easier said than done. Beware of your own biases and preferences; these may misguide you. Try to view situations unfolding in front of you with as much objectivity as possible.

The best way to find the answer to this question is, "What does my boss want?" Or better: "What does my boss really want?" Step one would be to observe your boss closely – observe their words and actions. Observe any differences in their words and actions depending on the context – i.e. talking to their teams or talking to their colleagues or superiors. There may be expectations on the surface, but more interesting are those behavioural expectations that lie below and need uncovering, especially if your boss shows signs of insecurity. You may find out by topics they request from you or by more indirect means, like requests they make to your colleagues or behaviours and outcomes they most value from you or your colleagues. These would all indicate the direction of what is expected from you and that you might not find written in black and white on your goals for the year.

Another way of viewing this is what I would call "managing your boss". As a leader, beware of leading your team and, equally importantly, leading your colleagues, your boss and yourself – a true 360 scope.

Here are some examples:

- If you realize that your boss values, trusts more or hands the power to people who have all the answers (correct or not) or act as if they have them, then what you need to develop more is your assertiveness – stating your ideas and suggestions with conviction.
- If you realize that your boss values, trusts more or hands power to people who are the most likeable, then what you need to develop is diplomacy, practising your poker face, and never roll your eyes in public (even if you feel like doing so). This will help you to develop trust in yourself.
- If you realize that your boss values, trusts more or hands power to people who are straight talkers, even appear aggressive, assertive, and who instil fear in others. You must develop a calm and forceful demeanour rather than a mean or aggressive communication style.
- If you realize that your boss values, trusts more or hands power to people who are more empathetic and collaborative than others, then what you need to develop is that style too. Making sure everyone is heard during meetings, all proj-

ects get supported by team members, disrespectful distractions (like scrolling on phones) are not tolerated during meetings, etc.

In these examples, you may find some behavioural adaptations easier than others, depending on how they align with your personality. It will be up to you to decide whether your position is worth the transformation and skills or not – if you find the required behaviour too out of sync with your personality, you will be anxious and disappointed. It may require a re-evaluation of whether you want to stick it out or not. In some environments or specific moments in your career, switching or navigating to "survival mode" can be helpful.

4.8 Being flexible in your own identity

To introduce this section, I would like to use the inspiration that revealed itself in an article written by Cyrille Vigneron, CEO of Cartier. He writes about time loops and trust in life.

Here is what he wrote:

> Leaders must simultaneously act in the present, learn from the past and prepare the future.
>
> There is not only one future to consider. One must consider several time loops.
>
> 1. Anticipate the immediate consequences and dynamics of what is in motion.
> 2. Anticipate mid-term scenarios and strategies.
> 3. Imagine what might disrupt the current business model and ecosystem and in which time frame. Being right too early is as equally misjudged as being right too late.
>
> Leaders must initiate actions in all-time loops at the same time. Deciding what might bring immediate changes and what might take longer to materialize, keeping in mind that the long term is as unpredictable as the short term and that best laid out strategies may fail.
>
> How to find the right balance between all these dimensions?
>
> There is no recipe. What is important is **to think in motion,** like playing music or performing ballet.
>
> Be determined yet pragmatic, patient but not passive. Accept mistakes, and do not think that it is always preferable to fail fast. If there is only a plan A, it should not fail.
>
> Forget about small mistakes. Learn from medium ones. Avoid big ones. Take responsibility for your strategic mistakes and, if necessary, resign.
>
> Above all, remember that even if fully committed to it, a job is just a job. Trust life and believe in love.

This flexibility in our consideration of time and the confidence in ourselves is what we need, to remain adaptable in a context that is not always under our control, and knowing that the environment may be shaped by external influences or evolving relationships.

Leaders must be agile, adaptable, open and able to switch modes and make swift changes while considering all the moving parts of the business . . . .

They know how to navigate the most complex situations, responsibly steer their teams and always keep those key responsibilities alive.

It is necessary to be flexible but undeterred. Resilient leaders understand that things change and that even the best-laid plans may, occasionally, need to be amended or scrapped. Trusting themselves and their judgement helps them most for good decision-making in changing and uncertain times.

At the end of the day, everyone will look to them to make the final call; it is ultimately their accountability, the reason why they have been given and have accepted the position of responsibility. Good judgement is what a great leader will need in the absence of clear-cut, relevant data or an obvious path.

Sir Andrew Likierman, former Dean of London Business School and former Director of the Bank of England, states: "Those with ambition but no judgement run out of money. Those with charisma but no judgement lead their followers in the wrong direction. Those with drive but no judgement get up very early to do the wrong things. Sheer luck and factors beyond your control may determine your eventual success, but good judgement will stack the cards in your favour" [19].

After talking to CEOs in a wide range of companies, Sir Andrew Likierman found that leaders with good judgement tend to be good listeners and readers – able to hear what other people mean and thus identify patterns that others do not. They have a breadth of experiences and relationships that enable them to recognize parallels or analogies that others might miss – and if they don't know something, they'll know someone who does and lean on that person's judgement. They can recognize their own emotions and biases and take them out of the equation. They're adept at expanding the array of choices under consideration. Finally, they remain grounded in the real world: In making a choice, they also consider its implementation.

Mr Likierman established six basic components of good judgement: learning, trust, experience, detachment, options and delivery.

1. Learning: listen attentively, and read critically.
Many leaders rush to bad judgements because they unconsciously filter the information they receive or are not sufficiently critical of what they hear or read. Good judgement requires that you turn knowledge into understanding. This sounds obvious, but as ever, 'the devil is in the detail' – in this case, your approach to learning.

This is the advice to improve your learning skills: active listening, including picking up even on what is *not* said; interpreting body language is a valuable skill to be honed and plenty of advice and resources exist. Beware of your own bias or filters and of defensive or aggressive conduct that may discourage alternative arguments. Ask questions and check conclusions if you get bored and impatient when listening. If you're overwhelmed by written briefing material, focus on the parts discussing questions and issues rather than those summarising the presentations you'll hear in the meeting. Look for gaps or discrepancies in what's being said or written. Think carefully about where the underlying data comes from and the likely interests of the people supplying it. If you can, get input and data from people on more than one side of an argument – especially people you don't usually agree with. Finally, look for discrepancies in the metrics and try to understand them.

2. Trust: seek diversity, not validation.

Leadership shouldn't be a solitary endeavour. Leaders can draw on the skills and experiences of others and their own when they approach a decision. Who these advisers are and how much trust the leader places in them are critical to the quality of that leader's judgement.

Leaders should have sources of trusted advice: people who will tell you what you need to know rather than what you want to hear. Don't take outcomes as a proxy for their good judgement when recruiting people whose advice you will rely on. Make judgement an explicit factor in appraisals and promotion decisions. Usha Prashar, who chaired the body that makes the UK's most senior judicial appointments, pointed to the need to probe *how* a candidate did things, not just what they had done. Dominic Barton of McKinsey told me he looked for what was not being said: Did people fail to mention any "real" difficulties, setbacks or failures in their careers to date? One CEO said he asked people about situations in which they'd had insufficient information or conflicting advice. Don't be put off by assessments that a candidate is "different." Someone who disagrees with you could provide the challenge you need.

3. Experience: Make it relevant but not narrow.

Beyond the data and evidence pertinent to a decision, leaders bring their experience to bear when making judgement calls. Experience gives context and helps us identify potential solutions and anticipate challenges.

Pertinent advice would be first to assess how well you draw on your own experience to make decisions. First, start by reviewing your significant judgement calls to identify what went well and what went poorly, including whether you drew on the right experience and whether the analogies you made were appropriate. Record and learn from experience, both positive and negative. This is tough, and it's tempting to rewrite history. It can be helpful to share your conclusions with a coach or colleagues who might take a different view of the same experience. Try also to recruit a smart friend who can be a neutral critic.

Second, especially if you're a young leader, work to expand your experience. That will not just do the young managers a favour; it will help both you and the company, because it will broaden the understanding from which you can tap. And as a CEO, a necessary experience you can offer high-potential managers is more varied exposure, so be actively involved in their career planning.

4. Detachment: Identify and then challenge biases.

As you process information and draw on the diversity of your own and other people's knowledge, it's critical that you understand and address your own biases. Although a passion for objectives and values is a wonderful leadership quality that can inspire followers to more extraordinary efforts, it can also affect how you process information, learn from experience and select advisers.

The ability to detach intellectually and emotionally is, therefore, a vital component of sound judgement. But it's a difficult skill to master. Research in behavioural economics, psychology and decision sciences has shown in recent years that cognitive biases such as anchoring, confirmation, risk aversion or excessive risk appetite are pervasive influences in people's choices.

The advice provided by Sir Likierman is to understand, clarify and accept different viewpoints.

Encourage people to engage in role-playing and simulations, which forces them to consider agendas other than their own and can provide a safe space for dissent. Suppose employees are encouraged to play the role of a competitor, for example. In that case, they can experiment with an idea they might be reluctant to suggest to the boss.

Leadership development programs are a great forum to challenge assumptions by exposing people to colleagues from different cultures and geographies who come to the discussion with different views.

Finally, people with good judgment ensure they have processes to heighten awareness of potential bias. Acknowledge that mistakes will occur – and doubt the judgement of anyone who assumes they won't.

5. Options: Question the solution set offered.
When making an important decision, a leader is often expected to choose between at least two options formulated and presented by their advocates. But smart leaders don't accept that those choices are all there is. In hindsight, many lousy judgement calls were inevitable simply because important options – and the risk of unintended consequences – were never even considered. This happens for various reasons, including risk aversion by people putting forward their solutions. That is why exploring the solution painstakingly is central to a leader's exercise of judgement. It's not the CEO's job to develop all the options. But they can ensure that the management team delivers the full range of possibilities, counteracting fears and biases that cause the team to self-edit. When all the options can be debated, the judgement is more likely to be correct.

A good starting point is to ask for clarification of poorly presented information and challenge your people if you think essential details or facts are wanting. Question the weighting of the variables on which their arguments depend. If timing is a crucial consideration, determine whether it's legitimate. Factor in the risks associated with novel solutions – stress and overconfidence – and look for opportunities to mitigate them through good piloting. Ask yourself what the personal consequences might be to them (and to you) if their solution works or fails. Consult those you trust. If there isn't anyone or enough time, imagine what someone you trust would do. Be unambiguous about rules and ethical issues because they will help you filter your choices. Finally, don't be afraid to consider radical options. Discussing them could make you and others aware of some that are less radical but worth considering and may encourage others to speak up.

6. Delivery: Factor in the feasibility of execution.
You can make all the right strategic choices but still end up in failure if you don't exercise good judgement in how and by whom those choices will be executed.

When reviewing projects, wise leaders carefully consider implementation risks and press for clarification from a project's advocates. This is as important for small decisions as it is for big ones.

A leader with sound judgement anticipates risks after a course has been determined and knows by whom those risks are best managed. That may not be the person who came up with the idea. More generally, flair, creativity and imagination aren't always accompanied by the capacity to deliver – so small tech firms often struggle to capitalize on their inspiration. Less-inventive but better-organized giants often buy them out.

When assessing a proposal, you make sure that the experience of the people recommending the investment closely matches its context. Participants should try to surface and expose what might cause a proposal to fail. If they point to their prior work, ask them to explain why that work is relevant to the current situation. Encourage advocates to question their assumptions by engaging in "premortem" discussions.

If you practice these fundamentals, you will give your judgement calls the best possible chance and remain responsible and supportive to your teams at all times; you will also allow yourself certain flexibility in your own identity.

How to shape your own leadership identity?

I would suggest considering these learning habits proposed by Warren Buffet, one of the world's most successful investors. He believes that "these habits separate the best from the rest":

- Master the art and practice of **setting boundaries for yourself**.
  Really successful people say no to almost everything. Have you ever noticed how you almost unconsciously raise your respect for those people? It is because they respect themselves first. Above all, they have learned this with experience and realized it has a positive outcome for their well-being. In our current accelerated frenzied life, finding ways to simplify our lives is vital. If you master simplification, you will be closer to mastering your life. And to simplify our lives, we must know what to shoot for. Remain focused and only say yes to the few things that truly matter.
- **Invest in your personal development**. Well, this is all that this book is about. Keep learning for yourself to reach the best version of yourself by being aware of your abilities, your values and your environment. Never stop acquiring knowl-

edge. It will surely help you grow as a person. Buffet calls it "the lifelong pursuit of learning", and I couldn't agree more. I place great emphasis on living this principle.

–   Buffet also reminds us that much of what you become in life depends on **whom you choose to admire and copy**. And when you give autonomy and delegate your authority, there is only one criterion to choose whom you hire: integrity.

–   Equally important is to build a **positive reputation**. How to achieve this?
    Establish trust, transparency and fairness
    Offer good value and high-quality products and services
    Treat people with dignity and respect
    Communicate clearly and promptly
    Provide service to the community.

Much introspection and learning should be practised to establish your leadership identity. To learn and find a positive way to deal with those people you do not get along with but need to treat as your allies. Why did I say "a positive way"? Because in my experience, this will be the most efficient way to maintain your own energy and identity and suffer the least stress or anxiety.

Here is a thought from investor and philanthropist Carmen Busquets that summarizes brilliantly, especially from the perspective of gratitude, what I meant by remaining in "a positive way": " I practice gratitude every day, at night and first thing in the morning, I even practice gratitude towards my enemies – the people who have envied, harmed or used me for their financial gain. Do you know why? Because now that I have built my barriers and surrounded myself with the best people, they show me the right path on which to walk on. The path of my heart, love, and forgiveness."

"Be grateful for everything that enters your life, including failure and the destructive deeds of your opponents, as they are your best teachers. Some of my professional adversaries engaged in pernicious disruption with the sole purpose of making things as uncomfortable and difficult as possible. In hindsight, I believe them to be lonely, lost beings, but I learned to feel both compassion and indifference as I walked away from them. Of course, I felt the rage inside, but then I am grateful because there is nothing and no one in this world worth losing my peace of mind and happiness".

Bibliography

[1] Schwartz T, McCarthy C. "Manage your energy, not your time". Harvard Business Review. 2007.

[2] Seppälä E, Cameron K. "The best leaders have a contagious positive energy". Harvard Business Review. 2022.

[3] Baker W. "The more you energize your coworkers, the better everyone performs". Harvard Business Review. 2016.

[4] Schwartz T, Pines E, Booker K. "To lead better under stress, understand your three selves". Harvard Business Review. 2021.

[5] Baker L. "Why embracing change is the key to a good life". BBC Culture. 2020.

[6] "Jeff Bezos advice for Young Entrepreneurs": @Fundabets.Shorts, YouTube; 2022.

[7] Bansal V. "How great leaders deal with ambiguity". Techtello. 2021.

[8] Epstein D. "Range: Why generalists triumph in a specialized world": Riverhead Books; 2019.

[9] Powell C,G. "It Worked for Me: In Life and Leadership": Harper Collins; 2012.

[10] Duke A. "Thinking in Bets": Portfolio.; 2018.

[11] Ostergard R,AP. "Are female leaders better during a pandemic?" University of Nevada, Reno Political Science. 2021.

[12] "How Satya Nadella turned Microsoft around". The Economist. 2020.

[13] "Satya Nadella, CEO of Microsoft". Stanford Graduate School of Business. 2019.

[14] Sinek S. "Overcome the Fear of Change". 2023.

[15] change E. University of Bristol. [Online].; 2022. Available from: http://www.bristol.ac.uk/staffdevelopment/professional-services/professional-behaviours/embracing-change/.

[16] Kashyap S. "7 reasons why we need more women in leadership roles". Proofhub.com. 2023.

[17] Rock D, Grant H. "Why diverse teams are smarter". Harvard Business Review. 2016.

[18] Grant A. "Beware the 4R's of toxic work culture". Inc. 2022.

[19] Likierman A. "The elements of good judgement". Inc. 2020.

Chapter Five
Empowering collaboration

If you want to go fast, go alone.
If you want to go far, go together.
– African Proverb

https://doi.org/10.1515/9783111335339-006

5.1 The importance of culture

"Bon dia, Nathalie. Que tal va tot ?" A greeting that I could only react to with a big smile. Not only had Mr Carcelle recognized me in the lift, but he remembered I am from Barcelona. He wanted to show his respect and appreciation by kicking off the conversation in the local language. Isn't that a great leadership quality? He made me feel acknowledged and valued. At the time – this must have been around 2006 – there were not many foreigners you could bump into the lift at the Louis Vuitton head office in Paris, but the international crowd had been growing, and some English could be heard occasionally. Yves Carcelle once told me that he held Barcelona in high esteem since the days when a very kind local family hosted him during a summer internship.

Nevertheless, remembering one of his thousands of employees by first name and some additional anecdote and being able to engage in a minute-long lift ride effortlessly says everything about a CEO's skill and leadership style. "Yves Carcelle was best known for his charm and charisma, no question". This is how Antoine Arnault – eldest son to LVMH owner and CEO of Christian Dior SE – described him when he passed away a couple of years ago, adding, "However, he was a fierce negotiator, and you didn't want to get in his way." A perfect example, therefore, of right and left-brain-fuelled leadership. I include this anecdote because the story didn't end after that encounter in the lift, an account I have shared with many people since. Amazingly, every year I received a Christmas card from his office, hand-signed by him, which continued even after leaving the company and working at Chanel. Every Christmas until he passed away.

What does this show us? These are not words; these are actions; this stands for behaviour. This shows clearly that it is not about what you say but what you do. This creates a sense of belonging and shared values and views. And this sticks with people and reveals a corporate culture. I am sure my previous colleagues at Louis Vuitton share plenty of these insider stories, as we also shared plenty of insider stories at Chanel.

An organisation's culture defines its success more than the teams, products and skills within it or the strategy that defines its vision. As the famous quote attributed to Peter Drucker goes, "Culture eats Strategy for breakfast". In that sense, the watershed that splits good companies from great ones will be the culture and the leadership behaviours that shape it.

How could organizational culture be described?

Two main approaches exist in academia:

–   The cultural web, described by Johnson and Scholes
–   The Three Levels of Organizational Culture, described by Edgar Schein

The Cultural Web, as described by Johnson and Scholes, has seven components [1, 2]:

At the centre of the web, and viewed as the starting point, we find the **"Paradigm"**. It stands for the working model of the organization.

Next come the **"Symbols"**. These are visible indicators of the organization, such as terminology, titles, perks, logo colours, office décor, etc. This is the material stuff that sets the tone for the organization.

Then, we find the **"Power Structures"**. These are reporting lines on how the work gets done, best described in an org chart. It shows formal hierarchies and who is in charge of whom. Interestingly, power structures may influence people's behaviour. We will analyse this in more detail in the next Section.

The fourth element is the **"Organization Structure"**. It is the diagram that is share-able with the outside world. It shows the formal relationships between functions and activities.

The fifth element is the **"Control Structure"**, which refers to how the organization measures and rewards performance. It also explains which attributes will be re-warded and which will be penalized. The next chapter will discuss how failed control structures can poison the culture.

Another cultural web element is the **"Rituals and Routines"**. These set out what we do and what we do not, and, more importantly, how we do it, and additionally, how we regulate processes and interactions between people.

The final element of the cultural web is **"Stories"**. These are the events and people that an organization remembers. The organizational culture will choose what events it will mark in its history and what personalities it will set aside as heroes or villains, creators or implementors. Also, what lessons we learn from the events are considered successes or failures. These are the stories told by people who are deeply immersed and stakeholders in the organisation's culture.

What about the three levels of organizational culture in Schein's model?

In this approach, Edgar Schein – a professor emeritus at MIT's Sloan School – speaks about three levels in terms of visibility. From the most visible to the least. They under-line that the most important things are the ones no one can see – a metaphorical ice-berg [3, 4].

The first, most visible layer contains the ARTIFACTS. These entities are easy to ob-serve but possibly difficult to understand. An example would be stories that are only recounted inside the organization. To better understand those stories, they need some interpretation, and their meanings must be found, which give rise to the following two levels: values and assumptions of the organization.

The second, less visible layer contains the organisation's ESPOUSED VALUES. These are a declared set of values and norms of behaviour the organization expects, in other words, what should be done and how. It is also about the choices we should make. It sets how people should interact, behave and represent the organization in the outside world. Statements or visible symbols can amplify these values and norms.

The third and least visible layer, which contains the SHARED ASSUMPTIONS, underpins everything. It is about the beliefs the people take for granted about the organization; they usually go unnoticed and are rarely questioned. The profound interpretations of the stories the organisation members tell about themselves.

Within the SHARED ASSUMPTIONS, there are six types to be found:

- The truth
- The importance of time
- Space – ownership and allocation
- Human nature
- Relationship with the environment
- Social power

Assumptions about Social Power dictate many organisational behaviours, such as how power and responsibilities are allocated within the organization. Also, the extent to which that authority is respected. Other examples could be the balance between cooperation and competition within the organization, the extent to which individuals are minded to collaborate or operate independently. Therefore the styles of leadership people expect are how people resolve conflict and make decisions.

As Edgar Schein mentioned, "Culture is always helping and hindering problem-solving. It is important to understand both".

Take another example. For instance, the deep underlying assumption that pitting employees against one another gets the best work out of them. That's not the kind of thing managers publicise; sometimes, they're even unaware that they are fostering this dynamic. And yet it's felt by leaders and employees alike. While it may result in healthy competition, it's just as likely to create a strong culture of envy, eroding trust and undermining employees' ability to collaborate.

We will analyze Social Power in more detail in the next section of this chapter.

A fascinating and inspiring paper I read recently is the one of Sigal Barsade (professor at Wharton) and Olivia A. O'Neill (associate professor at George Mason University), published by *Harvard Business Review* in 2016 [5].

They start by asserting that when people talk about corporate culture, they're typically referring to **cognitive culture**: the shared *intellectual* values, norms, artefacts and assumptions that serve as a guide for the group to thrive. Cognitive culture sets the tone for how employees think and behave at work – for instance, how customer-focused, innovative, team-oriented or competitive they are or should be.

Cognitive culture is undeniably crucial to an organization's success. But it's only part of the story.

The other critical part is what the two professors call the group's **emotional culture**: the shared *affective* values, norms, artefacts and assumptions that govern which emotions people have and express at work and which ones they are better off suppressing. Though the key distinction here is thinking versus feeling, the two types of culture are also transmitted differently: Cognitive culture is most often conveyed verbally, whereas emotional culture tends to be expressed through nonverbal cues such as body language and facial expression.

In their opinion, every organization has an emotional culture, even if it's one of suppression. What I found very interesting to consider is that leaders can better motivate their employees by allowing emotions into the workplace and understanding and consciously shaping them. One could conclude that managers should acknowledge their emotions to understand their teams better and funnel their emotions towards them, with the positive effect of achieving higher team motivation.

It's all about the small gestures rather than bold declarations of feelings. Facial expressions and body language are particularly powerful. For example, small acts of kindness and support can add up to an emotional culture characterized by caring and compassion.

Office décor and furnishings, too, may suggest what's expected or appropriate emotionally. Comfy chairs and tissues in small conference rooms convey that it's OK to bare your soul or cry if you need to. Photos of employees laughing at social events or action figures perched on cubicle walls can signal a culture of joy. Signs with lists of rules and consequences for breaking them can reflect a culture of fear. In a **culture of companionate love**, employees feel and express a degree of affection, caring and compassion toward one another.

This is a culture I discovered at Louis Vuitton Retail in the early 2000s when I was involved in several leadership positions at Flagship stores in Paris's Champs Elysees, Barcelona and Madrid. Motivation is vital to success in a very operational environment like this one, with teams that face a similar daily schedule and where a boring routine can eventually impact customer satisfaction negatively. It is a mega driver, and the best leaders show specific actions, ways of working and a thorough understanding of their teams' needs. This environment was a valuable school where I learned a great deal and where I was also allowed to experiment and try new things out. I felt affection for my teams. When I heard about this notion of companionate love, it totally struck a chord. This is it, I thought.

At LVMH, you are encouraged to spend time (enough time) in Retail. And it helps as a career accelerator, especially if you show signs of understanding the people dynamics and fostering performance and innovative leadership skills. There was no question, I absolutely hit the ground running, and my boss at the time referenced it as "a revelation". Yes, it was. And I continue to encourage every young professional in this business to get this experience. It is not for everyone, but it does provide many lessons: to understand not only the emotional dynamics in the purchasing path of a customer with luxury products but also the emotional dynamics of motivating a sales team day in and day out to achieve their goals. It is a lesson for life in many ways. Since then, I have also ensured that in the country, regional or worldwide offices, we always had people with operational experience to be "the voice of the client" within the Marketing offices. To lose that voice would have been a considerable risk, in my opinion.

In regards to methods to cultivate a particular emotional culture, Barsade and O'Neill continue explaining that there are three effective ones to utilize:

1. **Harness what people already feel**
This can work when such feelings regularly arise, and some progress is being seen. This would be a sign that the expected culture is being built. To help sustain that trend, you can try to incorporate some gentle nudges during the workday. You might schedule some time for meditation, provide mindfulness apps, space and trainers for yoga or fitness classes, and remind them to breathe, relax or simply laugh.

2. **Get people to fake it till they feel it.**
This option works on the premise that if employees don't actually experience the desired emotion at a particular moment, they can still help maintain their organization's emotional culture. If emotions are not expressed spontaneously, they could still be expressed strategically, imitating others out of a desire to be liked and accepted. In this case, the initial motivation is to be compliant rather than to internalize the culture. This is the reason why this particular behaviour is known as "surface acting". As you may imagine, it is not sustainable long term and may lead the employee to burnout. A second option still needs to be applied – "deep acting". With this technique, people consciously try to change into a desired behaviour because they genuinely believe it is the better option and wish to leave behind their default behaviour.

Here is an example: Imagine that an employee at an accounting firm has a family emergency and requests a week off work at the height of tax audit season. However, his boss's first thought is *No – not now – no!* She could engage in 'deep acting' to change her immediate feelings of justifiable panic into genuine caring and concern for her subordinate. By trying hard to empathize, saying, "Of course, you should go be with your family!" and using the same facial expressions, body language and tone of voice she would use when feeling those emotions, she could coax herself into the real thing. She would also be modelling a desired behaviour for the subordinate and the rest of the team.

3. **Model the emotions you want to cultivate**

In the previous example, an employee modelled a specific behavioural change because she was convinced it would better fit the desired culture. She modelled it with purpose, even if it didn't come spontaneously.

Another excellent option – and this would be my favourite – would be to hire and promote those people who adhere best to your culture or desired culture and then let them model the behaviour in front of others.

A long line of research on emotional contagion shows that people in groups "catch" feelings from others through behavioural mimicry and subsequent changes in brain function. Suppose you regularly walk into a room smiling with high energy. Your employees will smile back and start to mean it. In that case, you're much more likely to create a culture of joy than if you wear a neutral expression.

Like other aspects of organizational culture, emotional culture should be supported at all levels of the organization. The role of top management is to drive it.

Leaders are often insufficiently aware of their influence in creating an emotional culture. This is why they should be systematically reminded and speak explicitly about what is expected from employees. Because one of the biggest influences on employees is their immediate boss, the suggestions that apply to senior executives also apply to those managers: They should ensure that the emotions they express at work reflect the chosen culture daily. I would add that emotional culture values should be linked to operations and processes – including performance management systems. In this way, companies would ensure that evaluations, pay raises and promotions openly include culture-compliant behaviour. To avoid a sense of obscurity that too often surrounds culture topics.

Decades' worth of research demonstrates the importance of organizational culture, yet most of it has focused on the cognitive component. As we've shown, organizations also have an emotional pulse, and managers should track it closely to motivate their teams and reach their goals.

5.2 Ways to create and improve a great culture

Within the different luxury Houses, each has a specific culture that each company has built upon and developed as the brand evolved. Very often also tied to a particular CEO or CEO / artistic director tandem. If I look back at Louis Vuitton, Chanel and Gucci, what separates them the most is their different corporate cultures and values. It makes for a very enriching career path to have navigated them all, sometimes with ease and other times with difficulty. The same can be said about other iconic brand names such as Hermes, Cartier and Burberry.

It is undoubtedly also true to say that the fewer the gaps there are in corporate culture execution, the better the influence on the company's business performance. Let's say: the more the culture is adopted, the greater the results.

Without entering into details, what I wish to underline, though, is the strong team spirit that I have always felt within the Louis Vuitton Retail organization during the Yves Carcelle tenure. That clearly contributed to the strong motivation of every team member and to impressive growth results.

As mentioned in the previous section, we will now focus on the importance and influence of social power in corporations. Therefore it is vital to acknowledge and understand the different types of social power sources that exist. I would like to introduce you to an analysis provided by John French and Bertram Raven.

They affirmed that all power comes from the dynamic between individuals; power is social. You can only understand it in the context of the relationships among the people within an organization.

French and Raven identified five power sources; they then later added two additional ones, and others have been developed since. In their approach, they speak about two spheres of power sources: positional and personal [6].

Positional power sources

They derive from the position that an individual holds within an organization. It's the power granted to an individual by an organization.

– **Legitimate** Power
This is the power that derives from the organizational hierarchy. The higher up a person sits in the hierarchy, the more power the person has. Nevertheless, it must be acknowledged that even at the top position, someone can permanently remove you from that position of power, which would be the ultimate power.

– **Coercive** Power
The ability to coerce people to do something with threats and punishment are standard coercive tools. It is a problematic source of power and can be abused. You use coercive power when you imply or threaten that someone will be fired, demoted or denied privileges. While your position may allow you to do this, it doesn't mean you have the will or the justification to do so.

– **Reward** Power
Raises, promotions, desirable assignments, training opportunities and simple compliments are all examples of rewards controlled by people "in power." If others expect that you'll reward them for doing what you want, there's a high probability that they'll do it. When you use up rewards, or when the rewards don't have enough perceived value, your power weakens. Exceptions to this are praise and thanks. Everyone loves to receive them, and they are free to impart.

– **Resource** Power
It is about the ability to control access to resources that don't belong to you but to the organization and that other people in the organization need. Very often, people with low or medium-pay grade status jobs have the power to control access to resources, people and services; they have a tremendous amount of resource power for people within the organisation. These people usually act as gatekeepers of people's time and attention (e.g. CEO's PA) or as managers for additional resources within the organization such as travel booking, providing printing and stationary, hardware and software.

Relying on these positional forms of power alone can result in a cold, technocratic, impoverished leadership style. To be a true leader, you need a more robust source of power than a title, an ability to reward or punish or access to resources.

Personal power sources

Those are the ones an individual earns by themselves. They are their own personal power base, regardless of whether their organization grants them power.

– **Information** Power
Control over information others need or want puts you in a powerful position. Access to confidential financial reports, being aware of who's due to be laid off and knowing where your team is going for its annual "away day" are all examples of informational power. Information is a particularly potent form of power and control in the modern economy. The power derives not from the information itself but from having access to it and from being able to share, withhold, manipulate, distort

or conceal it. With this type of power, you can use the information to help others or as a weapon or a bargaining tool against them.

– **Expert** Power

When you have knowledge and skills that enable you to understand a situation, suggest solutions, use solid judgement and generally outperform others. People will listen to, trust, and respect your words. As a subject matter expert, your ideas will have value, and others will look to you for leadership. Moreover, you can expand your confidence, decisiveness and reputation for rational thinking into other subjects and issues. Expert power allows you to use information power and deploy it and get things done (even if somebody wants to cut you off with information, your expertise still has value). Expert power takes a long time to gain, which is vital to maintaining your level. This is an excellent way to build and maintain expert power and improve your leadership skills.

– **Connection** Power

You gain connection power through the people you know and the relationships you maintain with them. People who respect and like you are more likely to help you get things done. Suppose you influence other people because of your relationship and the investment you have made to build that relationship. In that case, that ability to influence others gives you power.

It can also be seen as the influence a person attains by gaining favour or simply acquaintance with an influential person. This power is all about networking. "If I have a connection with someone that you want to get to, that's going to give me power".

People employing connection power usually build necessary coalitions with others.

– **Referent** Power

The ultimate form of personal power, however, is what French and Raven refer to as "referent" power. It means the power we have as a result of the person to whom the power refers, as a result of our personality, character and everything about us. People come to trust us due to our credibility, reliability, trustworthiness, gravitas or simply a combination of the other forms of personal power: the ability to make and hold connections, expertise and knowledge; it comes down to character and trust. If you are credible and reliable, people believe and trust you and think you work for them as much as yourself, then you have a great deal more personal power.

Referent power comes from one person liking and respecting another and identifying with them somehow. Celebrities have referent power, which is why they can influence everything from what people buy to which politician they elect. In a workplace, a person with referent power often makes everyone feel good, so he tends to have much influence. Referent power can come with great responsibility because you don't necessarily have to do anything to earn it. As a result, it can be abused quite easily.

Someone likeable but who lacks integrity and honesty may rise to power – and use that power to hurt and alienate people and gain personal advantage.

Relying on referent power alone is not a good strategy for a leader who wants longevity and respect. When it is combined with expert power, however, it can help you to be very successful.

The simplest referent power definition is a type of power that stems from a leader's ability to inspire and influence others. This authority comes from the extent to which people admire, respect and like a specific leader. It is the ability to convey a sense of personal acceptance or approval. People with charisma, integrity and other positive qualities attain it. It is the most valuable type of power.

Considering the different sources of power within an organization, it is essential to note that whatever power you maintain as a leader, you will be influencing the corporate culture. How? Primarily by your behaviour. How you act, what you do and what you don't do.

And because of this impact and the critical role every leader in an organization plays in shaping culture, it is important to consider this seriously daily. Never forget: "culture eats strategy for breakfast". It is a critical element to a company's success.

What is it, then, "a great culture"?

Melissa Daimler has led Global Learning and Organizational Development at Adobe, Twitter and WeWork. Her career's focus has been to create systems that leverage both individual and organizational capacity. She states, "The best companies I've worked with have recognized that there are three elements to a culture: **behaviours**, **systems**, and **practices**, all guided by an overarching set of **values**. A great culture is what you get when all three of these are aligned and cohere with the organization's espoused values. When gaps start to appear, that's when you start to see problems — and see great employees leave [7]."

These gaps can take many forms. A company might espouse "work-life balance" but not offer paid parental leave or expect people to stay late consistently every night (a behaviours-system gap). You might advocate being a learning organization that develops people but not giving people the time to take classes or learn on the job (system-behaviours gap). Maybe your company tells people to be consensus-builders but promotes people who are solely authoritative decision-makers (behaviour-practices gap).

Melissa Daimler continues by explaining that "a common culture-building practice is the creation of value statements. But the real test is how leaders behave, enact these values, or don't. People watch everything leaders do. If leaders are not exhibiting the behaviours that reflect the values, the values are meaningless."

Given your organizational values, the question is, which **behaviours** consistently get rewarded? Which behaviours lead to promotion? Which behaviours are expected and encouraged at one company vs another?

Clarifying expected behaviours for employees holds leaders accountable as well. When desired behaviours are explicit and clear, people can focus on practising those behaviours rather than wasting time and energy trying to identify them. Accountability becomes easier to measure, and success easier to attain.

Five systems are essential to the overall cultural system: hiring, strategy and goal setting, assessing, developing and rewarding. Every process created, every system installed, every technology used, every structure designed and every job title assigned will reinforce or dilute the culture.

I find the last three systems critical to analyse.

How are behaviours assessed? How often are they reviewed? Is feedback shared consistently, and is it weighted based on who said it? Lack of trust or questions about what behavioural standards will be used will create political and fear-based environments.

When employees feel that professional development, feedback assessments or engagement surveys are irrelevant, it's usually because the questions don't tie back to what the organization actually reinforces and rewards. Culture problems can also arise when a "safe learning environment" turns into a way to punish employees for low scores rather than a way to help them grow.

What are the criteria for becoming a manager, director or vice president? What are the expected behaviours that earn a person's said title? What technical and leadership skills are needed? These are all expressions of culture and values, but they are often perceived as ambiguous and random. Employees do not have to be concerned about being friends with the CEO, competing with each other and other political challenges when these processes are viewed as transparent and fair.

A good culture sets these processes up to feed into and off each other.

The third element to be considered is **practices**. These are dynamic and may evolve as the company grows and transforms. Practices include everything from company events, running meetings and the feedback processes to how decisions are made. Do you have repeatable decision-making processes in place? Are meeting participants expected to be collaborative and consensus driven, or is some conflict OK? What should managers talk about in performance reviews?

Melissa Daimler ends by stating that great organizations and leaders know that the culture stuff is the hard stuff. Culture takes time to define. It takes work to execute. Yet, if the time is spent (1) really understanding the behaviours expected throughout the organization; (2) identifying the systems and processes that will continue to help those behaviours be expressed and sustained and (3) shaping practices that help employees and the organization improve, then you can close your culture gaps.

And by closing potential culture gaps, you avoid disappointing your employees by stating one thing but, in reality, doing the opposite or exposing a completely different reality.

Employees feel disappointed and leave when these culture gaps are not addressed and solved.

A toxic corporate culture is by far the strongest predictor of industry-adjusted attrition and is ten times more important than compensation in predicting turnover, as found by Donald Sull, Charles Sull, William Cipolli and Caio Brighenti, and published in March 2022 by *Sloan Review*. Their analysis found that the leading elements contributing to toxic cultures include failure to promote diversity, equity and inclusion; workers feeling disrespected and unethical behaviour [8].

Nearly 10% of employees in the sample grumbled about uncooperative teammates or the lack of coordination across organizational silos. When employees talked about colleagues actively undermining one another, their comments strongly predicted a negative culture score. Employees who cited a cutthroat culture talked about coworkers who "throw one another under the bus," "stab each other in the back" or "sabotage one another."

You might think that toxic culture is someone else's problem, something your organization doesn't need to worry about. Unfortunately, cultural toxicity is widespread. Even in companies with the highest employer ratings, hundreds or thousands of employees might experience the culture as toxic. Women, underrepresented minorities or older employees, for example, might have a much more negative view of the culture than other employees. In most large organizations, distinctive microcultures coexist within the same company, often across business units, functions, geographies or acquired companies. Individual leaders also create subcultures within their extended team. Whatever their origin, microcultures can diverge from the broader corporate culture, which means that even the best cultures can contain pockets of cultural toxicity.

This begs the question now: how might a corporate culture be improved? What can be done and how?

Business leaders believe a strong organizational culture is critical to success. Yet, culture tends to feel like some magical force that few know how to control. So most executives manage it with just their intuition.

Lindsay McGregor and Neel Doshi, co-founders of Vega Factor, wished to reverse this and set out to find a solution so that culture, instead of remaining a mystery, could be handled as a science [9].

The two academic researchers' main conclusion was that "why we work determines how well we work".

In other words, culture alone is insufficient to explain and drive individual and team performance. Culture needs to be coupled with a missing link: our motives. It is the motives that drive performance. Again: why we work determines how well we work, and culture shapes our why.

Culture drives motives, and motive drives performance. In other words, when the reasons we work are connected to the work itself, we perform better.

Some reasons to work seem to matter more than others, however.

McGregor and Doshi found six fundamental motives: play, purpose, potential, emotional pressure, economic pressure and inertia. The first three boost performance, and the latter three destroy performance.

Play is the strongest motive since it's the work itself. You work because you enjoy it. Play is our learning instinct, and it's tied to curiosity, experimentation and exploring challenging problems. Being at play is "being in the zone".

Next **Purpose**: "Does the direct outcome of your work fit your identity?", "Do you value the immediate impact on your team, customers, etc?" If so, then your work has a **purpose**.

Potential is when the outcome of your work benefits your identity. In other words, if your work is a stepping stone to a longer-term success.

Since these three motives are directly connected to the work itself in some way, you can think of them as direct motives. They will improve performance to different degrees. Indirect motives, however, tend to reduce it.

Emotional pressure is when you work because some external force threatens your identity. Fear, peer pressure and shame are all forms of emotional pressure. When you do something to avoid disappointing yourself or others, you're acting on emotional pressure. This motive is entirely separate from the work itself. Some examples are family traditions, fear of your boss and itching to be liked in the workplace.

Economic pressure is when an external force makes you work. You work to gain a reward or avoid punishment. Now the motive is not only separate from the work itself, but it is also separate from your identity.

Inertia is when the motive is so far removed from the work and your identity that you can't identify precisely why you're working. When you ask someone why they are doing their work, and they say, "I don't know; I'm doing it because I did it yesterday and the day before," that signals **inertia**. It is still a motive because you're still actually doing the activity; you just can't explain why.

These indirect motives reduce performance because you're no longer thinking about the work—you're thinking about the disappointment, the reward or why you're bothering to do it at all. You're distracted, and you might not even care about the work or the outcome's quality.

The researchers found that a high-performing culture maximizes the play, purpose and potential felt by its people and minimizes the emotional pressure, economic pressure and inertia. This is known as creating total motivation (ToMo). The highest performing companies have a high ToMo in common, which is the best part since you can determine the health of any organisation's culture factually.

In another piece of research, McGregor and Doshi measured a correlation in some industries between a strong workplace culture and high customer satisfaction. Cultures that inspired more play, purpose and potential and less emotional pressure, economic pressure and inertia produced better customer outcomes. This was the case amongst airlines, retail, banking, telecommunications and the fast food industry.

We can conclude that culture drives performance; it can be measured and continuously improved.

McGregor and Doshi continue by defining a high-performing culture as the set of processes in an organization that affects the total motivation of its people. In a high-performing culture, those processes maximize total motivation. The gap between a poor and an excellent process can determine a vast difference in total motivation scoring, individually or for the company. In descending order, these processes would impact total motivation the most: role design, company identity, career ladders, community building, workforce and resource planning, leadership, compensation, adaptive governance and performance review.

Looking at all these processes together, it's clear that culture is an organisation's operating system. Senior leaders can build and maintain a high-performing culture by teaching managers to lead in highly motivating ways.

Here are some pragmatic steps that leaders can take, even without redesigning processes, to start improving the total motivation of their employees.

1. Organizing a reflection huddle with your team once a week. 1) Play: What did I learn this week? 2) Purpose: What impact did I have this week? And 3) Potential: What do I want to learn next week?
2. Explaining or finding out together the *why* behind your team's work.

3.   Considering how you've designed your team's roles. Does everyone have a space to play? Think about where people should be free to experiment and make that clear.

A great culture is not easy to build – it's why high-performing cultures have such a decisive competitive advantage. Yet organizations that build great cultures can meet the demands of our fast-paced, customer-centric, digital world. More and more organizations are beginning to realize that culture cannot be left to chance. Leaders must treat culture building as an engineering discipline, not a magical one.

5.3 Navigating toxic leaders

When it comes to defining what toxic leadership is, I find one of the best illustrations is the one Simon Sinek gives. He uses the lesson he learned from exchanging with the Navy Seals. You may not be familiar with this group, but that doesn't really matter. You only need to know that they represent the highest-performing teams in their field – military preparation. Using this organization as a benchmark for hiring their team members, he helps us understand the characteristics the best profiles need to embody. To do so, Simon tells us that the Navy Seals draw two lines: a vertical and a horizontal axis. Vertically they would measure "performance", and horizontally they measure "trust". The Performance Axis refers to the valuation a Navy Seal gets on the skills he has to do his job at best. This can be measured by clear metrics such as speed, point systems, rankings, etc. The Trust Axis values the trustworthiness of the person. Metrical systems cannot measure this, but more by subjective emotional questioning like "Would you trust your money / your wife to this person? [10]"

In such an illustration, no one wants to hire someone who obviously scores on the bottom left square – low performance and low trust. The best candidates to hire would be the ones scoring at the top right square – high performance and high trust. But the real value of this exercise is pointing out the Navy Seal organisation's clear preference for hiring a candidate with relatively lower performance but a somewhat higher trust ranking. The upper and mid-right square candidates would be considered for hiring, while those positioned in the top left square would not make it.

In the Navy Seals organization personal trust ranks relatively higher than job performance. As said before, this is an organization that embodies the highest level of performance in their field.

If a business organization wishes to become a benchmark in its industry regarding business performance, it could be inspired by the Navy Seals organization. Hiring, promoting and bonusing using relatively higher importance apportioned to personal trust vs business performance.

What do you think? Would this work? As Simon Sinek mentioned in his talk, we have infinite ways to measure business performance and rank people in the workplace relative to those metrics; it is straightforward. But what happens with personal trust? Here it gets much more complicated since no metric has been developed and is currently used to measure a person's trustworthiness. Since it is such a subjective topic, it also allows for misuse.

How to measure trustworthiness in the corporate environment? Which questions could be applied in corporate, similar to those used at the Navy Seals? Well, Simon Sinek comes up with a very simple one: "Who is the ****ole in the team?" It seems everyone would point to the same person. As easy as that. And equally, it is easy to find out which team member always has your back, takes time and energy for other people and shows loads of empathy and respect.

In summary, if we use this benchmark from the Navy Seals organization, we could apply their methodology to point out toxic team members and toxic leaders. The cursor to use would be trustworthiness at a personal level.

As Bill Gates said at the World Economic Forum's 2008 meeting in Davos, "There are two great forces of human nature – self-interest and caring for others." In many organizations, those forces come together with damaging effects. With thoughtful management, however, they can be yoked in such a way that caring for others becomes the best strategy for the most ambitious, and givers can become comfortable asking for favours as well as granting them. Time can be spared for others' projects but also protected for one's own. Generosity can be guided in the direction of greatest impact.

At this point, I would like to integrate the notion of "givers" and "takers" in an organization. First introduced by Adam Grant in his 2013 book 'Give & Take' he wishes for a world where givers succeed [11].

While "givers" look for ways to contribute to the organization, such as by sharing knowledge or offering to take on challenging assignments, "takers" have the opposite approach. They are typically self-serving and even narcissistic. They frame every interaction with the same question: "What can you do for me?"

Within the corporate world, the "zero-sum" mentality results from takers playing a dominant role in an organization's culture. In a classic zero-sum decision-making process, somebody wins, and somebody loses. The net sum of a positive outcome and a negative outcome is zero. Immediately, you can see the problem with this type of approach: the expected value of any zero-sum game is precisely zero. For that reason, takers are always on the lookout for the ways that they can "win." If that comes at somebody else's expense, so be it. As they see it, there is only a limited amount of value to go around, and they want to ensure they capture as much of that value as possible.

Unfortunately, this zero-sum mentality still dominates much of the thinking in the corporate world today. We think about market share in terms of somebody winning and somebody losing. If somebody gets promoted, somebody wins (the person getting the promotion), and everybody else loses. Forced-ranking performance evaluations, now widespread within the world of sales, also dangerously promote this way of thinking. For someone to be ranked at the top of all performers, somebody else needs to be ranked at the bottom.

The big takeaway lesson, then, is that any organization should be looking to hire givers and weed out the takers. While all of us are probably guilty of "taker" behaviour now and again, there appears to be a default mode that everyone falls into when interacting with others. You can recognize givers very easily – they share knowledge, make introductions for others and assist other employees. Givers realize that giving just 5 minutes of their time to help someone else can have a huge multiplier effect on performance. And, best of all, they aren't ensnared in the outdated "dog-eat-dog" and zero-sum mentality that is the exclusive domain of takers. Hire as many givers as you can, and you'll see not just how your organizational culture improves but also how your organisation's overall performance improves.

Takers have a distinctive signature: they like to get more than they give. They tilt reciprocity in their favour, putting their own interests ahead of others' needs. Takers believe that the world is a competitive, dog-eat-dog place. They feel that to succeed, they need to be better than others. To prove their competence, they self-promote and make sure they get plenty of credit for their efforts.

In the workplace, givers are a relatively rare breed. They tilt reciprocity in the other direction, preferring to give more than they get. Whereas takers tend to be self-focused, evaluating what other people can offer them, givers are other-focused, paying more attention to what others need from them. Givers and takers differ in their attitudes and actions toward other people. If you're a taker, you help others strategically when the benefits to you outweigh the personal costs. If you're a giver, you might use a different cost-benefit analysis: you help whenever the benefits to others exceed the individual costs. Alternatively, you might not think about the personal costs at all, helping others without expecting anything in return. If you're a giver at work, you simply strive to be generous in sharing your time, energy, knowledge, skills, ideas and connections with others who can benefit from them.

Most people act like givers in close relationships. In marriages and friendships, we contribute whenever we can without keeping score.

In the workplace, things change and get more complicated. Professionally, few of us act purely like givers or takers, adopting a third style instead. We become matchers, striving to preserve an equal balance of giving and getting. Matchers operate on the principle of fairness: when they help others, they protect themselves by seeking reciprocity. If you're a matcher, you believe in tit for tat, and even exchanges of favours govern your relationships.

Despite that, we develop a "primary reciprocity style" at work, which captures how we approach most people most of the time. It becomes the way people see us or judge us. Perception is a key element. And that style can play as much a role in our success as hard work, talent and luck.

What would you say if you were to guess who would end up at the bottom of the success ladder? Givers? Takers? Matchers?

Research demonstrates that givers sink to the bottom of the success ladder. Across a wide range of important occupations, givers are at a disadvantage: they make others better off but sacrifice their own success in the process.

But if givers are at the bottom, who is at the top? It's the successful givers. Successful givers are every bit as ambitious as takers and matchers. They simply have a different way of pursuing their goals.

Givers are win-win, people. When takers win, someone loses. As venture capitalist Randy Komisar remarks, "It's easier to win if everybody wants you to win. If you don't make enemies out there, it's easier to succeed." Or, as Charlie Munger says, "The best way to get success is to deserve success."

Givers, takers and matchers all can – and do – achieve success. But something distinctive happens when givers succeed: it spreads and cascades. When takers win, there's usually someone else who loses. Research shows that people tend to envy successful takers and look for ways to knock them down a notch. In contrast, when givers win, people root for and support them rather than gunning for them. Givers succeed in a way that creates a ripple effect, enhancing the success of the people around them. You'll see that the difference lies in how giver success creates value instead of just claiming it.

Suppose you consider yourself more of a taker in an organization. In that case, you may survive toxic leadership more easily or at least develop traits of a "taker" character. Contrariwise, if you are more of a "giver" character, you will find it hard to thrive under toxic leadership.

Think for a moment how some insecure people behave under threat; and think also how lies repeated over and over again become semi-truths in politics. Trustworthiness is hard to fact-base. What if, on top of it, that person holds more personal power than you? Would this not put you in an untenable and challenging situation? This will depend on your corporate culture and the values leadership wishes to embrace.

A go-to approach that seems prevalent nowadays is to admit nothing, deny everything, blame other people and develop an alternative narrative. Another situation could be somebody in your organization using malicious tactics to recover from a mistake. But these tactics are simply diversionary and manipulative: the real goal is to turn the facts on the other person and make them look more like an instigator than the victim.

Unfortunately, sabotaging colleagues because of jealousy and resentment happens a great deal. I feel grateful that I don't and have never had those sentiments of jealousy, and it took me some time to realise how widespread it can be. Resentments can be extremely destructive in organizations and should be identified and dealt with swiftly. "Jealousy is like taking poison yourself and waiting for the other person to get sick". The point is that the target person may never notice nor be aware. Still, the jealous colleague may be deeply poisoned with a bitter sentiment and would do better trying to manage it pragmatically themselves. Nevertheless, the reality is that envy can lead to toxic behaviour.

Your stress levels are another emotion to watch closely and keep under complete control. In this case, the sabotage is often self-induced, you are the one in control (or not) of your stress levels, and only you offer the remedy and can make sure it does not happen again or is at least kept within acceptable limits.

Fast Company published a piece of research which demonstrated that it takes only a few toxic behaviours on the excellent reputation of a leader's team to evaporate and perish completely [12].

They interviewed 50 outstanding individuals with remarkable personal histories, passion for their work, thoughtful philosophies on leadership, and seemingly, all the correct answers. Somehow, though, these leaders had managed to undermine the confidence of their direct reports, who – usually after a couple of failed attempts to address their manager's toxic behaviour – suffered in silence. How could this be?

Their teams had submitted them as "bad bosses" for their behaviours when they were under stress, frustrated or insecure. It turns out that stress turns us into different people and stokes our dysfunctional tendencies, which harm other people's experiences with us.

The researchers were able to identify seven of the most common courage-destroying behaviours:

1. **Micromanagement**. When we micromanage the people we lead, we tell ourselves that we're helping them stay on track and manage challenging tasks. In reality, we're creating a recipe for frustrated high achievers who lack trust and will switch teams at the first opportunity. The people left are those who wait to be told what and how to do every little thing, afraid of being proactive because they feel they might not achieve their expected level of perfection.

2. **Reacting with anger and judgment**. We might tell ourselves, "I'm passionate about this work, and anger or judgment is the appropriate response to this situation. We must hold people accountable." But what we get is employees who fear setting you off, so they withhold telling you about their mistakes or offering you the critical feedback you need for making good decisions.

3. **Caring only about the deliverables and not about the team as people**. When we do this, we tell ourselves, "I am driven to do great work and get great results. I hope my hard work will inspire my team." But instead, your staff feel you don't care about them, so they don't care about you or your goals. They believe appearing productive is more important than focusing on doing the *right* things.

4. **Not reinforcing positive performance**. When we fail to reinforce positive performance, we tell ourselves, "They know what their strengths are. I don't need to reinforce that for them. Plus, we should be intrinsically motivated." What do we get? Frustrated employees who feel like their efforts and strengths go unrecognized and lose the motivation to try harder or help their teammates. They may also resent others whose strengths are recognized.

5. **Withholding negative feedback**. When we withhold negative feedback from our teammates, we tell ourselves, "I don't have time for a feedback conversation, so I'll just fix it for them and wait until their performance review to bring this up." Your attitude and body language tell them you're not entirely satisfied, but they can't know for sure what they did wrong. They wish you believed in them enough to invest in their learning and growth. They think you're too passive-aggressive to say what you actually believe and have the necessary hard conversations.

6. **Ignoring their suggestions**. Your rationale might be, "I don't have time to consider their suggestion and determine whether or how it will work. It's on me to keep folks focused on priorities." But the danger is that employees who feel ignored will either seek other ways of pushing their idea forward (e.g., having someone else suggest it, going over your head) or become disengaged from the work.

7. **Not dealing with an underperforming or toxic teammate.** We tell ourselves, "That team member is a little hard to deal with, but they have the strengths we need. Plus, I've talked to them, and they are making small improvements. It's not that bad. I wish the team wouldn't take it so personally." But employees think less of you as a leader for not dealing with the employee who is bringing down the whole team. They feel hurt that you don't believe them when they tell you how bad the situation is. They may overreact or take seemingly minor transgressions personally because, to them, that small transgression is part of a much larger systemic issue.

We, as leaders, have an important choice to make: We can either destroy our teams' confidence and courage or supercharge it. A great way to take the temperature of our leadership style (especially under pressure) with our team (as well as with peers) is a 360-degree feedback analysis.

Finally, a golden rule to avoid getting yourself into trouble through your behaviours or the behaviour of others and their lies and manipulation: try not to be disliked by anyone. This would be the key to success in any given environment and independent of how much personal power you hold.

Returning to the eight different sources of power mentioned in the section before, you may ask yourself which ones you need to develop further in the near future and how. I encourage you to give it a thought – it is an essential survival strategy.

By analysing over 80,000 360-degree reviews Jack Zenger and Joseph Folkman – CEO and President, respectively, of Zenger/Folkman, a leadership development consultancy – the authors found that three elements predict whether a leader will be trusted by his direct reports, peers and other colleagues. These are positive relationships, consistency and sound judgment/expertise. When a leader was above average on each of these elements, they were more likely to be trusted, and of those elements, positive relationships appeared to be the most important of all; without it, a leader's trust rating fell most significantly. Trust is an essential currency in organizations, and any leader would be wise to invest time in building it by focusing on these three elements [13]:

Positive Relationships:
- Stay in touch on the issues and concerns of others.
- Balance results against concern for others.
- Generate cooperation between others.
- Resolve conflict with others.
- Give honest feedback in a helpful way.

Good judgement/expertise:
- They use good judgement when making decisions.
- Others trust their ideas and opinions.
- Others seek their opinions.
- Their knowledge and expertise make an important contribution to achieving results.
- They can anticipate and respond quickly to problems.

Consistency:
- They are a good role model and set a good example.
- They walk the talk.
- They honour commitments and keep promises.
- They follow through on commitments.
- They are willing to go above and beyond what needs to be done.

"We are not a team because we work together. We are a team because we respect, trust and care for each other" is possibly one of Simon Sinek's best quotes that summarize very well the notion discussed above.

At this point, it may be worth considering how these sources of power manifest and interact in the working environment. Unfortunately, toxicity is quite widespread. It may not be within a whole company. Still, if it resides in your department or surroundings, it is bound to provide a challenging environment. These keys should help you to better deal with it.

In the previous section, we explored the idea that a toxic working culture should not be defined subjectively but considered an overexposure of the 4 R's: relationships/results or rules/risks.

This is the best way to analyse a whole working culture that has become toxic.

What if this toxicity originated and was spread by people around you? How should you best act?

Two possible scenarios may appear:

1) When toxicity is circulated by **people with more *positional* power** than you. Essentially, the most difficult person you will have to deal with is your **boss** or someone N + 1 to you in the organization.
2) When toxicity is spread by **people with more *personal* power** than you. Your colleagues are the most difficult people you will have to deal with.

In the first scenario – you need to handle a toxic boss.
The fact that they, quite obviously, benefit from more positional power than you and can significantly affect your working life and career can make it quite a frustrating and anxiety-provoking situation for you.

Seven different hostile leadership options exist with which you may be confronted.
This leader does some or all of the following:

1. Hires talented people and then micromanages them to the point of making them ineffective
2. Withholds critical information from employees
3. Maintains power over employees by pitting them against each other
4. Rewards submissive, marginal employees and punishes productive, vocal employees
   People who comply with the leader are yes-people
5. Views employees' relations as expendable relationships
6. Makes resource allocation decisions based on power and control issues (employees favoured by the CEO or compliant and silent employees to keep in place) rather than on business benefits or needs
7. Doesn't share credit where it's due. Keeps employees busy and hidden.

On a positive note, you will learn from these behaviours what you wish not to do or endure to others, especially your own team or project teams. All of them will mark the corporate culture of the group being led. This will result in reduced Total Motivation levels and performance.

Building a cohesive work group is nearly impossible when behaviours that divide and conquer take over. Suppose your supervisor tends to pit people against each other in what they think is merely a friendly competition for more sales or better customer service. In that case, they may not know they are tearing the team apart. Dividing coworkers can cause deep divides that are hard to bridge. I found this the trickiest to handle, and it frequently happens when senior executives need to preserve their power and status.

Bringing up sensitive issues in a team meeting (like what's-his-name's inability to meet deadlines), ignoring tension, playing favourites and using sarcasm to make a point are all ways that can stir up issues at work. Those specific behaviours do nothing to create a happy and productive workplace.

No one likes to feel small in front of their peers, even if you think it's the push they need to improve. If you're looking for ways to motivate an individual, start by seeing them as individuals. Private discussions about shortcomings or areas for improvement will help them hear your message. At the same time, you tailor your comments to their specific situation. Let's be honest; public displays that result in winners and losers are only fun for the winners!

And, then, there's gossip. It's the ultimate way to divide and alienate people and one of the most common behaviours in which even the best of us have participated. If you do it, it's time to stop it. If a coworker comes with a juicy bit of information or you notice he's good at throwing gibes at others when he has an audience, don't participate. Instead, say something like, "I'm not sure how necessary that was," or "I think I'll pass on this conversation." A good response that works almost every time is, "Oh," followed by a prolonged silence. That sends a clear message that you have no intention of participating in destructive behaviours that divide, rather than unite, the working relationships around you.

In the second scenario – you may need to handle a toxic colleague.

In this case, the situation is also highly exasperating. Even if those individuals don't have to hold more positional power than you, the fact that they maintain more personal power than you (or you think they do in your head) makes the situation problematic.

Even if it is arduous and may feel unpleasant, there are some people that you will need to have on your side. These will be the people who hold the most power. There is little point in trying to understand how and where they may get it from. Very often, it is down to ridiculously insignificant contexts and may even be irrational and be part of a circumstance that is way beyond your control; that's why it's unnecessary to delve any deeper into it. People who wield more power than you may feel like they are "untouchable". And this is the primal emotion we get as a signal or red flag to alert us. Use it. Use the message and take some control by adapting your own behaviour. Don't fight the message; live with it, flow with it. This will be the winning strategy.

I find there are three types of **difficult people with more power than yourself** to consider when finding the best possible strategy to cope with them and to keep them on your side:

– Toxic people
We have spent some time discussing them already. These people have adopted toxic behaviour for many different reasons. Still, the traits they all have in common are their own insecurities. They appear to be aggressive combatants (the personification of a bulldozer), but don't be fooled; they are frightened by the situation, environment or yourself. Just be cognizant of that. It will be the well-known "swallow the frog" situation, but ultimately it will be worth it. Never confront them head-on. This doesn't work, and you risk big time doing so. They might well use underhand tactics like lying or manipulating. The best and most effective option is to ask many questions if necessary. Questions are never perceived as aggressive, and this will help you diffuse and understand the confrontation. Another invaluable tactic is to make the required moves to avoid them rallying allies against you. If this happens, they will be more challenging to tackle. To keep a reasonable dialogue open, following up calmly and constructively engaging with them will be essential. The best is to act upon the well-known saying: "Keep your friends close; keep your enemies closer." You'll be safer if you know more about your enemies than your friends. Look after your enemies better than you look after your friends. Sun Tzu – the author of this saying – went even further in his book "The Art of War": "If you know the enemy and know yourself, you need not fear the result of a hundred battles. If you know yourself but not the enemy, for every victory gained, you will also suffer a defeat. If you know neither the enemy nor yourself, you will succumb in every battle."

– Non-supportive people
For these types of people, you will undoubtedly have to ask yourself why they show this lack of support. Very often, it even will not make sense to you. But again, the hidden reasons may be irrational and founded on an emotional discord. These are people frightened by the context they find themselves in. They are intimidated by their bosses or their lack of charisma or authority. In this case, they might decide not to support you as a bizarre form of rebuke or retaliation. Others may suffer from paranoia that may have its roots in a traumatic situation they may have experienced or just be applying the "divide and conquer" strategy. You will need to follow up and check in with these people constantly. Having a regular coffee moment, for example. This will allow you to understand quickly and anticipate in time if there is a possible change of mind, confrontation or other unhelpful situation brewing. This way, you

can counter-act in time and ensure to get them on your side as soon as possible and before it is too late. Nishan Panwar shares how to handle your naysayers, "In life, when you encounter mean and hurtful people, treat them like sandpaper. No matter how rough they may scrub you, you end up polished and smooth." You can't stop people from talking about you, but you can choose who you listen to.

– Over-competitive people
These people have an always-win attitude. Or said differently, the "winner takes it all" attitude, nothing is left for the others. They are second to no one – don't forget. To deal with them is very tiring. This is why it's best to have them on your side and support their competitiveness with efficiency and foresight. The best tactic is to attain their respect through knowledge. I would even recommend that you try and develop the respect of their N + 1 to be more effective in your strategy.

Matt Higgins, CEO and co-founder at RSE Ventures, says handling a pernicious employee is one of the hardest things any founder or manager has to deal with. You need to do something about it and fast. If you don't – he says – energy vampires will suck the life out of your company and either poison your employees or make them run for their lives.

"I'm so glad we waited a few extra months to fire that toxic taker", said no one ever, right?

Cyrille Vigneron – CEO of Cartier – stated in November 2022: "Positive and kind cooperation bears more fruit than wasting energy in useless fights. Being kind does not mean being candid or weak. It includes the risk of delusion and, as such, implies strength and self-confidence. Accepting this allows for receiving kindness, respect and goodwill in return. It also entails being grateful for the kindness received and not feeling entitled at any point. Some prominent leaders think differently. There have been many examples over the decades of aggressive and belligerent leadership. Sometimes they can have some success in using this approach. Even if these leadership styles have some success, one should not conclude and think it is the only way. As a matter of fact, kindness in business is more sustainable over time. Return on kindness multiplies the positive energy of the world."

How do you survive, preserve your positive attitude, expand your energetic vibes and succeed if you need to be so close and handle those problematic colleagues all the time?

Having a positive and pleasant gang of people to hang out with is equally important!

The ones who are collaborative and show a real team player mindset. Surround yourself with those. There are plenty, but they don't tend to shout out as loud.

And my last piece of advice here is to keep learning from the most likeable people in the organization. This can be different from one organization to another and will be influenced by culture.

Be aware, at this point, that those people will not necessarily be the most efficient, knowledgeable and powerful. Here we are speaking of the most likeable. There is a big difference. And in some cultures, they might even be the most valued people. So, make sure to hang out with them a lot, learn from them, let it rub off you and even celebrate them and become one of them! Think that colleagues will rarely say anything derogatory about those people, something that should not be underestimated in a work environment. It may not necessarily be true that those people are the kindest and most authentic, but it's the perception that counts. And this is extremely valuable: always polite, taking care of everyone, calm, always in control, sometimes funny, cracking jokes, you get the point?

5.4 The beauty of building human magic

To start this section, I would like to recollect the recruitment strategy employed by the Navy Seals we spoke of earlier, where personal trust overrides organizational performance.

The ultimate challenge would be how to find the ideal personality sweet spot and be able to measure **trustworthiness in the workplace**.

Trustworthiness is a feeling, and as such, falls into the area of emotional culture. Therefore, an organization and its leadership must be adept at managing its emotional culture. Techniques for measuring the emotional culture should be adopted, finding out which feelings are dominant and propagated. Feelings are interpreted primarily through verbal expressions but also through facial expressions and body language.

In emotional terms, you would read (even subconsciously) non-verbal cues from colleagues and other leaders in the organization, which would trigger specific hormones in your body and tell you if you can trust or not this person. The more untrustworthy people are in your organization, the lower the trustworthiness is in your workplace. And vice versa.

In cognitive terms, you could read trustworthiness by analysing people's behaviours. Indicators of high trustworthiness would be high levels of autonomy and accountability given to employees, clarity in defining responsibilities and transparency about vision and progress. Regular check-ins with the team and allowing downtime for socialising, drinks, and play with the team.

Less straightforward are the hormonal triggers elicited by the emotional culture in your organization. For trustworthiness, it would be the secretion of oxytocin and serotonin.

Oxytocin is produced in the hypothalamus and secreted into the bloodstream, stimulating the oxytocin receptors throughout the body. It is a hormone that develops the feeling of love, friendship and trust. It allows us a sense of belonging and means we feel safe in that environment. As we have already explained, business is not a rational entity; therefore, acts of physical contact, like shaking hands after a deal or a hug after an illness or other hardships, are human signs of connection and belonging. Acts of human generosity, like giving up your time and energy and expecting nothing in return, will also stimulate the release of oxytocin, as does doing nice things for people that require some level of personal sacrifice (either time or energy). The release of oxytocin has many additional benefits: it inhibits addictions caused by dopamine. It will boost our immune system, make us healthier and happier and increase our creativity and problem-solving ability. One aspect to consider when stimulating oxytocin is that it takes time to develop. Trust does not appear at day one but is developed over time through the consistency in small actions of our behaviour. Examples of such behaviour could be; a friendly smile each time you cross someone, a genuine good morning greeting to everyone while arriving at the office, bringing a sense of humour and good vibes to the office. Additionally, taking the time to help others, walking to people's desks to speak to them about feedback or share your opinion, encouraging, mentoring or complimenting other people, being honest in your assessment and information sharing and making other people feel heard, by giving them your full attention.

Serotonin is a leadership chemical that fills you with pride and status. It can also come through public recognition and allows confidence to increase. It reinforces the relationship between parent and child, boss and employee and coach and player. Every time a relationship is strengthened because of this feeling of pride, a level of trustworthiness has developed.

What does it mean for an organization to exude high trustworthiness towards its workforce? As Simon Sinek puts it in his famous "Leaders eat last" talk, "If we trust in our companies, we will do our absolute best". He compares it with the situation of our caveman ancestors since we remain social animals. Naturally, we are designed to work together and make things together. Let's look at our societies and the civilisations we have built. We can say that we have survived astonishingly well and are certainly not the strongest nor fastest of species. We have survived because we have built social systems of collaboration. In that sense, during the Palaeolithic era of our species, we could fall asleep around the campfire at night, knowing that someone would always be on watch and alert us if some danger appeared [14].

Do you feel the same around your colleagues at work? What if someone told you that he has a shoulder problem that required surgery but had been avoiding it all this time because a couple of days/weeks of absence would jeopardize his position in the organization? What if, in your organization, politics and competitiveness came before health? How would you feel about that?

What about you? Have you experienced excessive levels of politics in your organization? If you get metaphoric banana skins thrown by colleagues, have to worry about someone stealing your credit or don't always feel your boss has your back, surely you will not trust others to go out of their way for you. This demonstrates a flawed system since it is not a safe environment. In such an organization, people will waste much valuable energy that will be geared toward protecting themselves from one another. Whereas that energy could have been better used to innovate, experiment with creative ideas, outperform the competition, etc.

Another side effect of a precarious work environment is the risk of burnout for these employees, not due to lack of recognition but exhaustion from using their energy for no valuable purpose.

Overly responsible leaders tend to bear quite a weight on their shoulders and too often ignore their own fragility and limitations. Self-care is a mandatory prerequisite for taking care of others in the long run, overcoming difficulties and driving change. Self-care is the opposite of narcissism or complacency. It requires discipline in many aspects: health, hygiene, exercise and enough sleep. It requires adequate allocation of time to rest and recover, to think, to read and to listen to others.

The biggest concern for any organization should be when their most passionate people become quiet. As a team leader, you should focus on preventing continued stress for people around you and in your care. Mithu Storoni, the author of "Stress-proof", speaks about three golden rules for smart leaders to prevent burnout [15]:

A. **Protect self-identity** by clearly defining roles, scope and responsibilities. Be fair and reward effort. Take time to explore your employee's goals and find alignment with the team's goals and values. Be there.

B. **Maximize control**. Everything outside your organization is beyond your control, especially the danger zones. But inside your organization – especially within your team and people in your care – you are in control and therefore bear the responsibility. Protect your people's well-being by generosity towards them, like giving them your full attention and listening actively. Employees who feel their voices heard feel more in control of their situation. Share decisions with transparency. If you see an imminently stressful project ahead, tell your team and involve everyone in the decision-making and planning process. They will feel more in control of a heavy workload they have voluntarily taken on than one forced upon them.

C. **Minimize exhaustion**. As mentioned before, the most critical area is creating a safe and trustful working environment. Also, allow for an objective and impersonal approach to criticism or feedback – demand sprints, not marathons. Frame the workload as short, high-intensity sprints rather than a continuous, high-intensity marathon. Constantly remind employees of the next breather day so that they can visualize the light at the end of the tunnel. Put in circuit breakers. If your employees sweat over the same problem, day after day, break the circuit of monotony so they use a different set of cognitive skills or work in a novel environment at regular intervals. Check on sleep. For a better night's sleep, enforce daylight exposure at intervals throughout the day, daily exercise and later starts in the morning during periods of intense pressure.

Coming back to the level of trustworthiness towards another person – If you are unsure, you could do the following: assess whether you are more or less "alpha" than that person. As Simon Sinek puts it: "If you are nervous while meeting someone, you are not the alpha, and if you can sense they are nervous while meeting you, then you are the alpha" [16].

Leadership consists in creating a safe environment within the organization for people to thrive. In that case, it can be achieved in two straightforward steps:

First, recruit people who believe what you believe, the ones who share your values, and second, manage the circle of trust, ideally, by expanding it to the very periphery of your organization. The more people in the organization you can encircle, the higher the degree of collective trustworthiness and the greater the sense of belonging.

In the animal world, the alpha male/female gets the privileges that others accept willingly, like eating and mating first. This happens because the privileges come with responsibility and sacrifice, harder work and risking themselves to look after the others. These are the expectations. Do the leaders in your organization sacrifice themselves when needed for the group and show that they deserve the perks and privileges they have? Or would they instead sacrifice others to save themselves?

The type of culture (cognitive and emotional) you will develop as a leader is also shaped by what kind of attitudes you tolerate in the workplace. Here are some points to consider:

- *Hire people with the right values and attitudes*
- *Communicate the behaviour you want*
- *Model the behaviours you want to see*
- *Be observant: pay attention to behaviour*
- *Reinforce the right behaviours*
- *Understand the cause and motive*
- *Respond to behaviour consistently*
- *Inspire others*

You can shape culture by action – by using the measures outlined above – but also by inaction. Gruenert and Whitaker stated that "the culture of any organization is shaped by the worst behaviour the leader is willing to tolerate" [17].

What has best-selling author Hubert Joly to say on corporate culture building, when he writes about 'Human Magic'? He states: "I want to use my energy and experience to help contribute to the necessary re-foundation of business around purpose and humanity" [18].

Joly is a CEO who believes in and practices the approach that it is critical for leaders to understand what drives the individuals around them – and how it connects to the purpose of the organization. He believes business is fundamentally about purpose, people and human relationships. When common purpose aligns with individual searches for meaning, it can unleash a kind of human magic that results in outstanding performance.

Hubert Joly supports a new capitalism formula: purpose first, people at the centre, and then profits. In his book "The Heart of Business: Leadership Principles for the

Next Era of Capitalism", he explains how to put them into practice, in both the best and hardest of times.

His thesis is that companies have three imperatives: people, business and finance.

These three imperatives are linked. Excellence with regard to the first imperative – the development and fulfilment of employees – leads to excellence in the second – loyal customers buying your company's products and services again and again. This then leads to excellence in the third imperative, which is making money. There should be no real trade-off between these imperatives; the best companies achieve excellence in all three simultaneously.

He shares with us a good practice to get started: begin your monthly business reviews by first discussing employees, then customers, before getting into financials. And this is, to remind everybody, that humanity – not financial results – is at the heart of the business.

The centrepiece of Hubert Jolie's book is 'the purposeful human organisation'. At the very top is a noble purpose. The reason the company exists: it is the positive impact it is seeking to make in people's lives and its contribution to the common good. 'Engaged employees' – at the centre – rally around the noble purpose, and 'delighted customers' profoundly relate to it. It becomes a guiding North Star against which strategy is formulated and every decision made and measured. In order to do great work for customers and deliver great results, employees also connect and collaborate with 'vendors as partners'. Business also needs 'thriving communities' to flourish, and employees who come from those communities and contribute to them are central to that connection. Finally, the connection between the company and its 'rewarded shareholders' is fundamentally a human one. So, employees pursuing a noble purpose are at the heart, and relationships are the blood that flows through the entire system and make it thrive. In this approach, all elements are connected in a mutually reinforcing system. This approach is a declaration of interdependence. Profits are an outcome of a successful strategy and the quality of the human relations that drive it. But they are also essential to fulfil the mission, as they make it possible to invest in employees and innovation, create growth, support the community and of course, reward investors.

Hubert Joly stands for this approach, since it makes sense, both philosophically and spiritually, and it works. It is not just theory or wishful thinking; he has seen it work at several companies over 25 years.

Simon Sinek states a similar reasoning: "People don't buy what you do, they buy why you do it." Good examples are brands that have evolved to sell a cultural phenomenon, like Apple, Lululemon and Aesop.

Instead of driving the behaviour of a collective workforce, it is much better to seek to inspire people by connecting with what matters to each one of them. Unleashing human magic means creating an environment in which individuals flourish. Because when people are doing what matters to them and what they believe in, they will give it their all.

Hubert Joly's business "recipe" has five key "ingredients":

1. Connecting individual search for meaning with the company's noble purpose.
2. Developing authentic human connections.
3. Fostering autonomy.
4. Growing mastery.
5. Nurturing a growth environment.

Business – as we all know – has unprecedented power, resources and reach to carry a movement forward. This is why it can – and must – be part of the solution and help address the challenges that society and the planet are facing.

The actions delivered by Mr Chouinard and his family through their company Patagonia is another very inspiring lesson.

What does purpose mean in today's society? Bill George, in a new CEO program he leads at Harvard, gets this number-one question: "When should I speak out on public issues?" It comes down to whether the issue relates to the mission and values of your company. At Medtronic, we had to speak out on healthcare. In Minneapolis, every CEO had to take a stand after George Floyd was murdered. People remember what you do during crises. Did you step up, or did you duck?

Similarly, many mid-level managers who come to postgraduate classes at Harvard have bosses who manage in the old style that creates friction. Bill George tells them to keep their heads down and create the culture they want on their teams, then let the top management see the impact it has. "Show them the outcomes, whether it's productivity or higher revenues, but also tell them what you are doing to inspire people. For far too long, we have looked to the top to solve problems". These are his words: "Don't wait for your boss to change – do it on your team, bloom where you're planted, and you have an opportunity to stand out. The top CEOs I know are all looking for people like this, who are willing to change the culture and get results [19]." I couldn't agree more.

I would like to share the summary of the email Brian Chesky, CEO of Airbnb, sent to his employees on April 28th 2022, to explain their ways of working moving forward [20].

The first assumption he shares is that the world is becoming more flexible about where people can work. The second assumption is that the company wishes to hire and retain the best people in the world. The best people live everywhere, not concentrated in one area. And by recruiting from diverse communities, Airbnb will become a more diverse company. The third assumption is trust in the people. These assumptions and learnings are based on my successful accomplishments while working remotely during the pandemic: we went public, upgraded the service and reported record earnings.

The company's leadership added that the right solution should combine the best of the digital world and the best of the physical world. "It should have the convenience and efficiency of Zoom while providing the meaningful human connection that only happens when people come together."

The design for Airbnb's employees' way of living and working has five key features:

1. You can work from home or the office
2. You can move anywhere in the country you work in, and your compensation won't change
3. You have the flexibility to travel and work around the world
4. We'll meet up regularly for gatherings
5. We'll continue to work in a highly coordinated way

Brian Chesky finishes his communication by saying: "I've always believed that you design the culture you want, or it will be designed for you. I'm excited about this new design and giving you the flexibility to live and work anywhere. I think it will unlock some amazing creativity and innovation – and make working here really fun. The past two years have been some of the most defining in our history. I'm so proud of each one of you and everything you've accomplished. Today marks the beginning of a new chapter together. It will be just as defining as the last one but a whole lot brighter".

As a leader, you'll spend much time making decisions that many people won't agree with. If you lead with your values, you might still get some details wrong. You'll still make mistakes, but it's much easier to know that you're doing the right thing when you know who you are and what you believe.

Tim Cook, the CEO of Apple, gave a speech to a crowd of graduates at Gallaudet University in May 2022 [21]. Cook talked about the most important principle of leadership: Cook didn't say to lead from your strength. He didn't say to lead with your heart or with your passion. Many people talk about leadership with those qualities, but Cook takes a less conventional approach to leadership. He says to lead with your values.

Your values are your core guiding principles that inform every decision you make. "By leading with your values," Cook said, "what I mean is that you should make decisions – big and small, each and every day – based on a deep understanding of who you are and what you believe."

"Working closely with people from all walks of life, I had found that people, emotionally, feel much the same about work: they derive the most satisfaction from doing the best they can". This statement comes from Isadore Sharp, founder of Four Seasons Hotels and Resorts. Motivation to go that extra mile and reach excellence will only be done in a trustful work environment with supportive leadership. He continues saying the following about success: "To me, that's what success is: it's not what you do on your own, it's how many people have come along with you to reach higher than their expectations ever were." And his book finishes with this premise: the greatest challenge for leaders in the 21st century is to align corporate values with human values [22].

A CEO from another generation and another industry – Christian Klein, CEO of SAP – states: "It's very important to assign clear responsibilities and accountability while also making sure that everyone works together as a team. The strategy can only work if the company works in harmony, and it's my responsibility to make sure that happens. It's very important to me that people are honest and transparent, that they speak up, and that they have the courage to say they need help. And maybe that includes asking me to make the call [23]."

A culture is simply the collection of beliefs on which people build their behaviour. Learning organizations – Peter Senge's term – classically focus on intellectually oriented issues such as knowledge and expertise. That's plainly critical, but an authentic growth culture also focuses on deeper issues connected to how people feel and how they behave as a result. In a growth culture, people build their capacity to see through blind spots, acknowledge insecurities and shortcomings rather than unconsciously acting them out and spend less energy defending their personal values so that they have more energy available to create external value. How people feel and make others feel becomes as important as how much they know.

A performance-driven culture often exacerbates people's fears by creating a zero-sum game in which people either succeed or fail, and "winners" quickly get elevated above the "losers." Results also matter in growth cultures, but in addition to rewarding success, they also treat failures and shortcomings as critical opportunities for learning and improving, individually and collectively [24].

A performance culture asks, "How much energy can we mobilize?" The answer is only a finite amount. A growth culture asks, "How much energy can we liberate?" The answer is infinite.

Building a growth culture requires a blend of individual and organizational components: an environment that feels safe, a focus on continuous learning, time-limited experiments and continuous feedback.

As Tony Schwartz, CEO of The Energy Project, says, "Perhaps the most fundamental lesson we've learned is that fueling growth requires a delicate balance between challenging and nurturing. Think about a young child beginning to venture into the world. The infant crawls away from its mother to explore the environment but frequently looks back and returns periodically in order to feel reassured and comforted. We are not so different as adults. Too much challenge, too continuously – without sufficient reassurance – eventually overwhelms us and breaks us down. Too little challenge – too much time spent in our comfort zone – precludes our growth and eventually makes us weaker."

5.5 Demystifying a successful career

When walking into a room full of unknown people, have you ever considered who was wielding and demonstrating the most power? Who was clearly the alpha male or alpha female in the room? What do you think? How would you recognize this person?

Indeed, you must have thought of good posture and maybe how this person carries themself, or even how this person comes across to the group, right?

As Caroline Goyder – voice coach, puts it in her Ted Talk "The surprising secret to speaking with confidence": "The most powerful person in the room has the most relaxed breathing pattern" [25].

Let's think about high levels of confidence. We need to ensure that we understand that this comes from within our bodies and is not a reflection of the external signals of our bodies. Confidence does not exist on the outside.

In our highly visual culture, where we mostly interact by visual exchanges, we might be tempted to believe that we need to spend time perfecting how we are perceived on the outside, and this is the most important aspect to master. And this is especially important for women, where additional pressure weighs on their shoulders. It is undeniable that beauty and ageing burden still prevails over one gender.

As said, confidence will have little to do with external appearances but is rooted deep within our bodies; it is visceral stuff. The bits within us that we don't see. And as such, we need to find that area, cherish it, train it, and get hold of it whenever we need it in a stressful situation.

The exact location is our **diaphragm**. Experts in using this tool to best effect are actors and singers. We should learn from their techniques. Ancient Greeks had already discovered its power and called it the centre of all expression. We may view it as the key to regulating your system. Therefore, we could insinuate that the diaphragm is the king of confidence. By feeling your diaphragm and training your breathing daily, you will develop in getting into the unconscious and calm yourself down.

Training breathing every day may not be enough; what we should also **practice** daily is using our **voice**, this great communication instrument we all have. The air against the vocal cords is all we need. The simplest way to improve your communication instrument is probably singing – under the shower while cooking in the kitchen . . . . Another practice I often use and highly recommend is memorizing and reciting poetry.

Last component of confidence: never run out "out of breath". Why does air matter? Because "we breath our thoughts", as Caroline Goyder poetically says. All speech is our breath, like all song and all poetry is our breath, whilst all in-breath is thought.

With this idea – breath is thought – it is simple to understand that you can control the emotion of your voice. Think about an emotion while breathing in; this is the emotion you will breathe out. It also ensures you get a positive message out while thinking about a feeling-good moment. Especially in moments you risk getting it wrong and upsetting someone. Remember this trick.

And by just closing your mouth and focusing on your in-breath, you will build clarity and confidence in speech.

In summary, you can gain a charismatic outlook when stepping into a room by building confidence through the power of breath.

The next topic to analyse on top of great breathing techniques will be your awareness and utilization of your informal power in the workplace. What does that mean exactly?

As corporations become more and more customer centric, workflow is migrating from specialized verticals to the white spaces between the verticals. It is crucial to comfortably and efficiently work in cross-functional teams and matrix structures. Even smaller organizations are increasingly project driven. Being able to "build bridges" between siloed work environments is becoming an essential skill and a trend that will stay. You will gain more confidence by switching frequently to different departments and organizations, even within your company.

When you have to work across your organization and deal with different teams, your formal title, direct reports and formally granted authority do not always carry you far. It is a humbling and critical fact to bear in mind. You should ask yourself, "Do I have the informal power to generate value and get things done?"

To answer this question pragmatically, I recommend using the power audit elaborated by Maxim Sytch, associate professor of management and organizations at the University of Michigan's Stephen M. Ross School of Business [26].

He suggests proceeding in three steps:

– **Step 1:** List your top 10 contacts enabling you to finish your work. These contacts can be either internal or external to your organization.

– **Step 2:** Assign a score from 1 to 10 for each contact, indicating how much you depend on them. Think broadly about the value your contacts offer. This includes career advice, emotional backing, support with daily activities, information and access to resources or stakeholders. If a contact provides much value and is also difficult to replace, assign a high score.

– **Step 3:** Do the same in reverse. Assign a score to yourself from others' perspectives. Approximate how much value you offer your contacts and how difficult it would be to replace you. Be honest.

Next, look for red flags in your power audit. These could indicate that you lack informal power and are replaceable. A couple of critical questions will help you get into more detail:

Do all of your contacts work in a single team, function, product unit or office building? This could indicate a limited ability to generate value beyond the basic requirements of your job description. This might signal, therefore, a limited potential for evolution within the organization.

Do your contacts provide you with more value than you return? Such relationships are difficult to sustain in the long run. Asymmetries in dependence indicate that others hold the power in a relationship. In this case, you should also be careful and take action; you may become expendable.

Are your dependence scores low throughout? This could indicate the prevalence of transactional relationships often driven by *quid pro quo*. In contrast, high-dependence relationships can be imbued with values and relational dynamics that are not simply calculated. This situation may prevail, especially in corporate cultures with an overrated relationship dependence. Be aware of this (the 4 R's analysed by Adam Grant and explained in previous chapters).

Is all the value you give or receive concentrated in a couple of contacts? You could be vulnerable if you lose these contacts or your relationship changes. Imagine if two key contacts drive the value in your network, and then one leaves for a promotion elsewhere and the other moves to a different region. In this case, your informal power is shut down overnight. Lesson: not only to watch out that your informal power does not remain highly concentrated but also to be aware of people's potential moves in plenty of time before it hits the rumour mill.

Maxime Sytch suggests that one excellent way to rectify unfavourable power audit scores is to earn relationships by delivering value to your contacts. Ask yourself: what value can you provide to them? One way is to develop and continuously improve upon a skill set that leads others to value your contributions. Then proactively use your skills to help others above and beyond the demands of your formal role.

Second – he states – let your job help you. Manage your job description to contribute to the workflows of multiple functions inside the organization and customers, outside partners or regulators – volunteer for cross-functional initiatives. View lateral transfers as great opportunities to develop your informal power. By positioning yourself at the intersection of workflows, you position yourself to meet, learn from and deliver value to a variety of diverse groups in the organization.

Lastly, Maxime Sytch suggests getting to know your stakeholders and collaborators better as individuals. You may be surprised how something relatively easy for you to do carries significant value for them. Sometimes we believe that we have to offer momentous contributions or do massive favours for others, which may not be necessary. Good to find out by yourself directly.

This power audit is beneficial and adds an additional view to the four personal power sources studied in Chapter 5.2. We are exploring here what could be called "the dependence" power, which means the level of dependence we have on other key people in the organization to get the job done. Using a two-way point of view that highlights possible dependence gaps between people to alert us to act upon them. This dependence power may be added to the four other sources of personal power – information, expert, connection and referent.

At this point, and from my experience, there is still a sixth source of power missing. It is what I would refer to as "the inner circle". I have encountered it on many occasions, and it also needs to be considered. It could undoubtedly be embedded as a type of connection power; the difference is that the source is not proactively held by building alliances with people of interest in the organization. The source of this power is based on the intrinsic belonging to the "circle of trust" within the organization, providing you with some level of protection. This may rely on having been recruited and introduced to the organization by someone with substantial power and authority. Another criterion for acceptance could be the possibility and appreciation of belonging to a specific community, whether gender, religious, cultural or beliefs based. Yet another criterion might be to be in possession of some sensitive information that needs to be preserved in silence. All these possibilities may culminate in the power to influence and provide protection for a particular individual who has managed to be "in the circle". And this protection power can easily be within or outside the organization. You may find that these circles can be difficult to gauge and identify, to begin with when you start out in a new organization, and that is undoubtedly true. But it would be best to always keep a close eye for clues that could reveal these microcircles. And then, consider these critically in your power map. An example I became aware of was when a relatively junior person was observed speaking to a person of significant seniority in a very familiar and, in my view, somewhat disrespectful way and even took an overfamiliar and even impertinent tone in some emails. This small flag of lack of respect can put you "on garde," then watch out for more clues to raise their improper and surprising heads. It seemed very likely that this junior had managed to gain some 'inner circle' power.

At this point, we have analysed our eight sources of power – four positional ones and four personal ones – then reflected on our informal or dependent power map and also considered the potential additional protective power. Once all this is done, we will have a pretty good view of where we stand, our strengths and weaknesses, the gaps that have been flagged and the areas where action needs to be taken.

What comes next? There are techniques to inspect further and expand your "range of power".

But first, why is it important? Why do I need to understand my range of power? The effectiveness relies on the scope, which dictates what acceptable vs. unacceptable behaviour is. There are always absolute red lines. This is the reality in corporate organizations, but in fact, also in life in general.

For some reason, some people are granted more leeway in their behaviour. It can be the case where untrustworthy behaviour is tolerated for some successful people in areas of pure performance. Maybe you can think of someone in your organization who swung power in one direction or another. What about you?

Just think about it for a minute: "What does power look like daily?"

Here are some examples provided by Adam Galinsky in his Ted Talk "How to speak up for yourself" [27]:

Let's take negotiation as a possible scenario: the range of power will depend on how many alternatives you have. The more potential cards you have up your sleeve for negotiating with your counterpart, the broader and more significant your range of power. This will also imply that your tolerable range of behaviour and how you negotiate will promote a wider variety of options.

When you are the new kid on the block, you clearly have less power than the seasoned old-timers. If you are new to a country, an organisation or a life experience – like having a baby – then you are much more dependent on advice given by others and how much they care for you.

In the scenario of a business organization, clearly boss vs. subordinate has a different degree of power. But this is also true in any relationship; don't forget that business organizations rely upon relationships; that's it. In any form of relationship, one might be more invested than the other. Think about it. What is your degree of commitment? Visualize it on a power map for a business organization and maybe as a dependence map for other relationships in your life, like your kids and your partner, for example.

What is pointed out by Adam Galinsky – American Social Psychologist and Chair of the Management Division at Columbia Business School – is that when you have lots of power, you will have a broader range of what is considered acceptable behaviour. You have more leeway, or said in another way, a higher degree of protection within a given organization. And vice versa, when we lack power, our range narrows. This may even spiral downwards and lead to a low-power "double bind". In one case, you don't speak up, you remain unnoticed, and in another, you do speak up and get rejected, even more so if gender bias comes into play.

We may conclude then that power determines your acceptable range of behaviour and that to build up a successful career within an organization, **continually expanding your range of power is vital.** This is especially true for women.

The next question will be how to achieve this. How to expand your range of power?

My answer is to try and always be likeable, whatever the circumstance. Whatever it takes and whatever the complex situation you may be navigating. Especially towards what feels like the most unlikeable people within your network but are necessary to get the job done. This might mean swallowing frogs and confronting painful situations more often than less and sooner than later. But don't forget that the dividend you will achieve in the long run is increased power and, therefore, a higher range of acceptable behaviour and additional protection granted by the organization itself. It will also reduce toxicity potential and allow you to enjoy more pleasure and freedom at work.

I find mastering assertive communication skills so essential – and have included those skills at the beginning of this book as an absolute fundamental – because they can lift you in your career but may also serve as a pebble in your shoe if you neglect to master them. Using an adapted communication style can help you gain power inside the organization, maintain your power or expand it. Including here also non-verbal communication, of course. The most successful people I know in this domain have struck me as always able to maintain that never failing "poker face". Other people are known by this French saying "elle/il cache bien son jeu". This saying would translate into "she/he hides her/his game well".

Two things are fundamental: to appear powerful in your own eyes, to provide you confidence and to appear powerful in the eyes of others so that others grant you greater leeway.

The tools to achieve this are these four:

A. **Use Empathy**. You may unapologetically endorse yourself and your ideas but do it with a considerate attitude. That is, looking at the world through the eyes of others. Once you know what the other party wants, you are more likely to get what you want.
B. **Signal Flexibility**. By offering choices among different proposed options, you lower your opponents' guard, allowing the acceptance of your proposals more likely.
C. **Gain Allies**. Gaining allies for your cause is critical to advocating for others and offering social support. You may also ask other people for advice. This will flatter them and show humility.
D. **Build Expertise**: Your credibility is built upon excellent evidence. A great way to enhance your expertise is to communicate it well. If your expertise comes across with passion, it will gain traction and help you enormously.

Chapter 1.5 addressed the importance of developing key traits you detect in genuinely likeable people. They will always ensure a great first impression and engage in conversation truthfully and agreeably. There is a lot, as said, to take on.

Let's go a step further in the pursuit of being genuinely likeable. We may wonder if the ultimate goal should be to become extremely popular on top.

The example that comes to mind is the late Queen Elizabeth II of England. Her goal seemed not only to become likeable but also to be popular. Her favourable ratings were consistently above 60% throughout her reign (besides only the period following Lady Diana's death) and as high as 75% in her last months. As Neville Wran – Australian Labor Party leader (and advocate for an Australian Republic) in the early 80s – said, "The biggest problem we've got is the Queen! Everybody loves her". It has to be said that when it comes to these ratings, it is difficult to distinguish between the Queen herself and the monarchy since she felt it was her duty and purpose to represent and embody the institution of the monarchy. This is why I see the British monarchy operating very like a brand and the late Queen Elizabeth II more like a personal brand.

Suppose some of you wish to grow your personal brand value. In that case, maybe it's worth considering taking the additional step and moving from likeability to popularity.

In the case of Queen Elizabeth II, she had indeed become the monarch her people wanted and expected of her. This was the most significant asset she provided her monarchical institution. Embodying the motto of the royal family, "never complain, never explain", she lived by her steadfast and superhuman ability to give absolutely nothing away. With this discipline, she pressed herself into the form of a blank slate onto whom onlookers could project practically anything (but rarely criticism).

As Tina Brown stated in "The Palace Papers": "Because she's not showing any emotion at all, she's not dividing the audience. She's not on one side or the other. And that must be exhausting for her." In another section, she says, "Celebrities flare and burn out. The monarchy plays the long game. There is no time stamp on the public's interest in you, as long as it's clear that your interest is the public's". An apparent reference to servant leadership that was so remarkably embodied in the Duke of Edinburgh's funeral during the pandemic lockdown, where she refused any preferential treatment for her or her family. Also very similar to President Zelensky refusing preferential treatment in the early days of Russia's invasion of Ukraine. He also enjoys enormous popular approval thanks to his servant leadership style.

In the words of former UK Prime Minister Tony Blair, the Queen's political genius is due to her "extraordinary ability to balance the mystique of the Monarchy whilst moving with the culture of the country over time." In terms of iconic fashion designers and brand-building geniuses, her Majesty could be seen as a mix of Karl Lagerfeld and Alessandro Michele.

She was able to do both for the Royal brand: playing the long game and surfing on the Zeitgeist. This may be expedited by respecting the institutions and representations of the Monarchy, like the legacy and symbolisms left by Mademoiselle Chanel. Understanding equally the evolution in the emotions of the nations she headed. Her focus of allegiance is understood and felt by a vast diversity of people from different social, cultural and political backgrounds, like Alessandro Michele's sensitivity to a necessary shift in luxury fashion to become more inclusive.

Over the past decade's flurry of royal weddings, gossip and scandal, the queen's blank slate allowed onlookers and admirers to ally her with whichever camp they pleased imaginatively. In Prince Harry and Meghan Markle Netflix films, the Queen is a staunch ally to her grandson and his mixed-race wife. The anti-Meghan camp, meanwhile, has plenty of opportunity to align her with the behind-the-scene traditionalists of "the Firm" who manage the palace machinery.

In an age where everyone has opinions, Queen Elizabeth II's epic stoicism has come to signify the unity of a nation. In other words, it is the exact opposite of trying to divide groups of people. This will work against popularity and long-term brand building.

5.6 Selflessness in the service of ego

It was a warm Autumn afternoon at the West Lake in Hangzhou. Lucy had arrived the previous night from Shanghai. She had that problematic meeting in the morning and planned to stay over for the weekend. In her thoughts, she went over the meeting again and again. "It turned out to go quite well, in fact, better than I predicted," she said to herself. "The whole team can be satisfied; it's a great team accomplishment."

She knew that now, she could relax a bit. A well-deserved weekend break was on the cards. Her brisk walk had taken her around this beautiful lake walk while her thoughts vanished slowly. The sight of the lake, the ancient pagodas and the small boats lulled her into a nostalgic mood. Her footsteps started slowing down, and she found herself genuinely enjoying the magnificent views. The blue sky and the warm breeze gave her the space to get the feeling and the pleasure of an enjoyable evening.

Lucy assumed the terrace she could see ahead on her path would be the tea house she had agreed to meet with her friend Roy.

"My dear Roy, it is so nice to see you again after so long! How have you been? You must tell me everything about your experience in Paris for these last eight months!"

"I had the best time ever! No question." He answered. "I learned so much. Not only about my job but much more about the difference in leadership styles. I needed to adapt to a new culture, but I would have thought the gap would be wider."

"What do you mean?" Lucy asked him. "Not sure I understand what you mean."

"Look. To work in such a huge Head Office, with all the legacy of the organisation, long-time employees, a company culture built up for decades . . . I thought I would have such a shock. And in the end, it was not that much of an adjustment, really." mentioned Roy.

"Oh, that's surprising. What is it, then, the disparity between what you expected and what you got there?"

"As next-generation leaders in corporate China, we are aware that change is happening. We come from a corporate culture of building team pride and referring to success as a collective team effort and ambition. In a way, in Chinese companies, leaders often take on a parental role and see their employees as family members, and – as we both know – the boss is much respected."

Roy continued: "Speaking up and challenging the status quo, suggesting new ways of working, coming up with innovative ideas, working in an agile and less hierarchical manner . . . all these subjects are still evolving in most Chinese companies".

"While I got all this during my experience in Paris, and I enjoyed special autonomy and a relatively flat organization, I also have to say that my colleagues shared with me that they longed for more altruistic-based management. Maybe not paternalistic, not in Con-

fucian regard, but striving for harmony, mutual respect and benevolence. Where lead-
ers focus on 'caring for the group' and where trust is central". He ended up looking at
Lucy with his eyes wide open.

"That's interesting", Lucy commented. "Where we were expecting you to breeze through
all of the frustrations you encounter day in and day out, it turns out that your col-
leagues also had some to share. Hmmm, that's unexpected. What are you going to do
about it? What did you learn for yourself, Roy?"

There is a strong paradox in the corporate world today. Organizations sincerely wish
for a sense of community where humility and collective intelligence can thrive. Many
leadership programs within those organizations include topics to drive culture in that
direction. However, the profiles of executives promoted in most companies are often
people who have been able to put themselves and their agenda forward and first,
with little interest in others, occupying the political field and speaking louder than
others. In real life, ego and arrogance still drive things forward. Between discourse
and reality, there is a whole other world.

Nevertheless, listening generously to others, not occupying all the space, taking a
break before speaking, being concerned about the collective well-being and apologiz-
ing, if necessary, are all behaviours deemed more empathetic and are certainly more
beneficial for an organization and its collective intelligence. To achieve an environment of connected people who feel safe and trusted so that ideas and progress can
thrive, leaders need to allow vulnerability to get a space. Walk the talk, as the saying goes.

Simon Sinek concedes this is not easy at all: "The ability to be vulnerable is one of the
greatest and most difficult leadership lessons any of us can learn." And he continues
his explanation by referring to his own experience sharing his struggles during the
COVID pandemic with his team. With the objective of allowing his team to be able to
do the same.

This is what would also be called "servant leadership". These leaders share the ability
not to let ego get in their way and instead opt for selflessness. Selflessness is not thinking less of yourself but thinking of yourself less. This is basically what it is, to be
humble.

As I mentioned earlier in the chapter, some of the best servant leadership examples I
have found that have a high level of popularity and so many people may relate to are
the late Queen Elizabeth II and President Zelensky from Ukraine.

There are eight leadership traits they have in common and continuously reinforce
and action. I have borrowed these key traits from Raj Sisodia – a founding member of
the Conscious Capitalism movement [28].

1. **Strength**
    Servant leaders will exercise their strength as power with, not power over, those they seek to lead. Their firmly embedded set of values will drive them to stand up to those who get in the way of their convictions. This comes from their rare ability to totally master confidence without being arrogant.

2. **Enthusiasm**
    Conscious leaders generate great energy and enthusiasm because of their commitment to moral authority, integrity and a higher purpose.

3. **Love**
    The opposite of love is fear, and when fear permeates an organization, it stifles creativity and innovation. Love is actionable and noble: it creates psychological safety and connects with employees.

4. **Flexibility**
    Servant Leaders are agile, adaptable, open and able to switch modes and make swift changes while considering all the moving parts of the business.

5. **Long-term orientation**
    This is leading with an eye toward the future, beyond your tenure with the company and even beyond your lifetime.

6. **Emotional Intelligence**
    This is a force of blending self-awareness (understanding oneself) and empathy (the ability to feel and understand what others are feeling) in day-to-day interactions and decision-making.

7. **Systems Intelligence**
    Thinking systematically about how each part of the business interrelates within the context of the larger organization. Understand the roots of problems and how they relate to organizational design and culture.

8. **Spiritual Intelligence**
    It is a moral intelligence to access more profound meanings, values, purpose and higher motivations. It helps Servant Leaders discern when things are beginning to go off track from their intended purpose. From this intelligence, they exercise their truth, kindness and compassion.

To practice vulnerability and improve one's humility, it is vital to have acquired the traits of every highly likeable person described in the previous section. This is fundamental as a starting point. I have experienced people throughout my career that are genuinely likeable, and I refer to them and their capacities when having to improve myself in particular situations. Their way of connecting with others is always authentic and feels real under every circumstance. They might not be the most efficient or knowledgeable in the organization. Still, they have a role to play and a refreshing and highly appreciated skill. I recommend observing and learning from people you believe to be exceptional and display qualities you would like to emulate. Look out, especially for those who never or rarely have anyone be critical of them, always polite, always caring for everyone. Be aware that some of these people are not necessarily perfect or entirely genuine. Still, they have the skills to ensure appearances count.

Conversely, I have equally experienced false likeability by work colleagues, which exudes a sense of connection that feels fake – the same end game but with less skill. What may be learned from those people is a kind of "fake it until you make it", and finding yourself being used by those people can be very infuriating. Beware of appearing fake yourself; there is always a risk – master the skill of appearing totally genuine and, even better, master the skill and have the confidence of actually being genuine.

Once likeability is assured, why not take a moment at the end of each day to reflect on all the people who made your day successful? This helps you develop a natural sense of humility by acknowledging that you are not necessarily the master of your success. And end the reflection by actively sending a message of gratitude to those people.

Even if we may be keen to practice vulnerability and adhere to prerogatives stated by Simon Sinek and Adam Grant, I need to warn you that it's not always so straightforward in corporate; there may be relentless impediments to vulnerability being put into practice and mastered.

Let's say you are in a new working environment where you might have taken the risk of deviating significantly from your comfort zone to engage and learn more about your profession. Or, you might have been recruited for a specific expert mission. In both these situations, you probably think you should appear strong, confident and assertive. Well, would you then want to show signs of vulnerability?

Suppose, in contrast, you feel very safe in your working environment, with a relatively longer tenure than your colleagues and a strong network of working connections. In that case, you may exude the courage to make yourself heard and get things done. Is there any need in this situation for vulnerability?

The same goes for confidence. There may be something to retain from Tom Cruise's coach in his latest *Mission: Impossible* movie, *Dead Reckoning Part One*, when he prepares him for a series of base jumps on a motorcycle – he said, "Don't be careful – be confident!" Nevertheless, suppose you are an overconfident leader who lacks connection to others. In that case, everything will be about you, and you'll alienate the people around you.

What can be done then in these situations? Might there be a way to turn a risk into an opportunity?

In the example of the overly competitive working environment, there could be a situation where you have the opportunity to lead a whole department or a larger group of people and may be able to influence change.

Suppose you find yourself out of your comfort zone and amid a circumstance with very high expectations relating to the outcome of your work. Would it not be smarter to appear as a person eager to learn from others and have greater understanding of this new environment? "Evidence shows that when people consider working with you, they care at least as much about whether you're collaborative as whether you're capable," Adam Grant explains. "And I've found that one of the ways to signal that you're collaborative is to talk about some of your shortcomings. It shows you're receptive to input and open to learning."

For the example of the person in a work environment with high tenure, low questioning and no need for courage really, David Bowie's advice for young artists may help: "Always remember that the reason that you initially started working was that there was something inside yourself that you felt that if you can manifest it in some way, you would understand more about yourself and how you co-exist with the rest of society . . . if you feel safe in the area you're working in, you're not working in the right area. Always go a little further into the water than you feel you are capable of being in. When you don't feel that your feet are quite touching the bottom, you're just about in the right place to do something exciting."

To avoid situations where everything seems to be centring on you and your struggle to connect with others, this would be the perfect opportunity to ask for help or advice when needed. It is a sign of strength, not weakness. It's something genuinely confident people are never afraid to do.

What about people with seemingly over-inflated egos? How to handle that?

In my experience, it's first and foremost about controlling your ego, followed by dealing with the ego of the person you are confronting. I have noticed people getting quite a different impression of me after a first short encounter on several occasions. These were people with whom I had a common interest. Why was that? I figured out that it was not gender or hierarchy related. In fact, it was ego related. For the people for whom it's all about them, I sensed that they were not really listening and interested in what I was saying and had their own agenda. Whatever effort I made from my side seemed to fall upon deaf ears. The only way to create a positive outcome from the conversation and avoid losing your time is to lean in. That is, to handle their over-sized egos. Stroking someone's ego with some flattering and praise is the easiest way to turn them around.

This may be easier said than done because often you may not be aware in the moment, but only later when you have deliberated and comprehended. By this time, it is typically too late. But it can be sensed with some practice. Observation and learning

in these situations are crucial and may save you from future potential struggles. Encountering oversized egos may be disconcerting and make you feel less at ease and
even a little nervous. It might also trigger some emotions and reactions you would
prefer to avoid, resulting in a less-than-optimum tone of voice, losing your assertiveness or even the conversation thread.

The best ways to handle huge egos in a conversation are to listen actively to the person, take time to analyse their words, use a calm and thoughtful voice, take a break
before answering, make sure your thoughts are well elucidated and practice how to
roll a transition, a soft one, not a hard transition.

Sometimes, it may also be your own ego that needs to get in check. I have explained
some tactics to practice gratitude, humility and vulnerability, which might be very
useful in these situations. Empathy also works. Empathetic listening will allow you to
not judge others by yourself. Because it's not about you; it's about the generosity of
your presence and time.

You may not be the jealous type, but how about the person in front of you?

You may never have experienced imposter syndrome in yourself – but what about
the person in front of you?

You may not suffer from a lack of confidence – but what about the person in front
of you?

Getting one's ego in check is also a way to manage conflict: being right all the time is
very often not a solution, but being empathetic nearly always will be.

Try to make sure that your mission in your conversation is to make the other person
feel good about your exchange and you as a personality.

"When I talk to a manager, I get the feeling that they are important. When I talk to a
leader, I get the feeling that I am important." This quote summarizes perfectly what it
means to lead with humility.

5.7 Impact is all there is

"Well, the decision finally fell into place today: we are moving forward and will build the first foreign holiday resort in Sanya on Hainan Island!" Lucy mentioned with enthusiasm to her team as the very first announcement in their weekly meeting.

Everyone started clapping and smiling big smiles – a relief was felt in the air.

"How did it go? Tell us all; we really hadn't expected to get the green light so fast".

So true – thought Lucy. She had been non-stop preparing data and arguments for the pro and con sides for the past three weeks. The people at Headquarters in the US had not seemed wholly convinced of the proposal and argument, and there had been continuous back and forth.

The position of the Greater China office was to move forward with this project. Still, Global Leadership was unconvinced and remained hesitant: there was a risk to the brand equity.

How significant was the brand equity risk vs the sales growth potential and a first mover positioning into this key Chinese family staycation setting? The China team had to endure the barrage of questions to ensure the strategy was sound.

By this morning, they felt, all questions had been fully addressed with fact-based reasoning.

Lucy was proud of her colleagues and team. She was reviewing in her head how the presentation went and was impressed by how their female CEO carefully listened to all participants in the meeting. One after the other. She asked some questions, rephrased the answers to make sure she fully understood the implications, asked some related questions to her trusted CFO and came back to the slide with all the numbers . . . .

At some point, everyone in the room knew that there was no more to say. All questions had been addressed, all the unknowns had been dealt with, and implications for each decision were made very clear – it was time for a decision to be made.

There was silence in the room. The CEO stood up. She walked around the table and briefly looked outside the window and then to her leadership team. She returned to her seat, sat down, breathed calmly and only then announced in a slow but confident voice that the company would proceed with the project. She then summarized and underlined the most valuable reasons for the decision.

Lucy could not avoid a slight smile on her face with mixed feelings of relief, pride and gratitude. But she quickly wished it off her face since she knew this would not sit well with many of the other people in the room, who had been campaigning for the contrary decision to be taken.

As we approach the final pages of this book, it is time to connect all the dots to navigate a successful career in a corporate environment.

Some of the key learnings are:

- train and improve your assertive verbal and non-verbal communication from day one;
- build up your resilience levels daily;
- use empathy, play, and sense of humour to build up connection and trust regularly to allow creativity and innovation to flow;
- be conscious about your corporate culture, and adjust your behaviour accordingly as a leader;
- find your own leadership style by being mindful of its impact; experiment with it;
- always remain conscious about the power map you are in;
- develop your range of power;
- do your best to be likeable under all circumstances; and
- practice humility.

Once you have reached the intersection of having built the right measure of power with a good fit within your specific corporate culture, you will start the journey of really having an impact.

And impact is all there is.

Everything that has been touched upon in this book is areas for personal development, thoughts, ideas and tools to help you improve the necessary skills – combined with traits that are prevalent within the organization but not always visible and not always discussed in the open. Be aware of what not only lurks above the surface but also below it – the same as you do in your personal life and with your personal relationships. There are many parallels. Because corporate organizations are people organizations. If you contribute with your leadership style to make the workplace a better place for everyone while still achieving your team's goals, this is true impact, in my view. You should go for both: functional skills for functional impact and human skills for human impact.

To finalize this section, I would like to ensure you have all the ingredients to maximize your chances of a successful career. Use your leadership style and skill to impact corporate culture with appropriate behaviour and good judgement.

Once everything is in place and you feel set and ready, then you should absolutely follow Amanda Gorman's guidance: "Success arrives when preparation meets opportunity".

Amanda Gorman is an American poet and activist who became famous worldwide in 2021, at the age of 22, when she delivered her poem "The Hill We Climb" at the inauguration of U.S. President Joe Biden.

You can either wait for an opportunity to happen or proactively make opportunities happen. Equally important is to know and understand when these opportunities arise and catch them, not letting them pass you by.

Amanda chose to seize the opportunity and not rule herself out due to her age, fear, uncertainty or discomfort. Amanda was not well known on the world stage, but her work portfolio was impressive enough to catch Oprah Winfrey's attention. She was also invited to the Obama White House to perform for Al Gore, Hillary Clinton, Malala Yousafzai and others. Her most significant endorsement came when the first lady, Dr Jill Biden, convinced the inaugural committee that she was the perfect choice for the inaugural ceremony. Give your sponsors, advocates and allies something to work with. Your portfolio is what gives your sponsors a voice to speak on your behalf.

As Dr Richard Osibanjo wrote in his Feb 2021 column in *Forbes* magazine: "Amanda's amazing success is a win for all of us. She is a reminder that success is not a function of your age, race, gender, or your challenges. You are never too young to change the world and never too old to inspire it. Like Amanda, believe and fight for your dreams. Place a bet on yourself, and do not wait for permission to share your gifts with the world. Remember, leadership is not about you. It is about making a difference in other people's lives. It is never too late or too early to embark on your journey of adding value to the world. You are the leader you have been waiting for" [29].

Your professional career is not a destiny; it is a way. There will always be detractors in your life and career who will bet against you. However, remind yourself that you are the owner of your thoughts and actions, and those will ultimately determine what you can achieve. Dare to set your ambitions high: each step, every success and every pitfall is an opportunity to learn, reflect and decide how you wish to live and the imprint you want to leave.

An interesting quote – attributed to multiple people – highlights precisely that: "Watch your thoughts; they become words. Watch your words; they become actions. Watch your actions; they become a habit. Watch your habits; they become a character. Watch your character; it becomes your destiny".

5.8 How to build a fulfilling career

"This is the best example of a truly fulfilled professional career I have been told. It is the story of my mum's best friend. Her name is Francesca".

All eyes were looking at Carla. Her team has always been fascinated by her stories. Tonight they found themselves having some drinks around the fireplace after dinner. The annual communication plan presentation had been a huge success. Everyone was in an exuberant mood.

"Francesca was raised in London and enjoyed that perfectly happy childhood with an enviable balance of urban and country-style upbringing. Later, she went to university in Exeter and studied English Literature and Sociology. How she ended up in a big pharmaceutical company is a mystery to me. But what I have always heard about her is that she was able to apply all her talents, interests and values at any of her jobs. Her background in human sciences allowed her to navigate better than others the emotions and dynamics of different executive groups. She enjoyed good financial autonomy, had the knowledge to be paid equally to her male colleagues and contributed to all needs within the family. I have always felt her serene and calm in any circumstance. Once, she explained to me that the ability to expand her skill sets through mentoring and training had been possible through one single thing: she was trusted for her potential. That's also why she got progressively more challenging and rewarding projects".

"This begs the question: how did she continually gain that trust?" Carlos from the PR team asked.

"Well, she found herself within a very supportive and caring culture at the company where she started out and decided to stay. Why leave when she was happy there? She told me. In fact, that happiness was shining back at her. Everyone liked her in the office, and nobody spoke badly about her. I know for certain that she was adept at employing the 'Pokerface', but I can also assure you that she had a very generous character and gave up loads of her time and energy supporting others. A 'real giver', I would say. She only recently retired, and what sums it up for me is her saying: 'I regret nothing'."

"Can this not be viewed as a fulfilling career and life? When we have no regrets?" Carla questioned.

"Yes, certainly. An amazing statement, but where there no moments of struggle?" someone asked.

"Of course. Francesca did encounter several ups and downs. Sometimes the risks she took made her fall flat on her face. But instead of regretting the decision or choice, she mentioned that these failures generated a sense of courage that otherwise would not have existed to underpin her freedom and wisdom".

The last and final step in this book, and this last section, will be dedicated to how to find ways to build not only a successful career but also a fulfilling one.

A fulfilling career does not endure in the eyes or expectations of others or can be read on a resume. A fulfilling career is felt deep inside you, in your soul.

Our soul becomes apparent to us – in other words, the soul awakens – but only when the ego is put to rest. Or at least it is entirely under our control. In previous sections, we addressed the topic of humility and selflessness. This will be the first step on the road to accomplishment.

Here, I should also mention Viktor Frankl's "Man's Search for Meaning" book [30]. He survived several concentration camps during the Second World War. He discovered that those who somehow managed to find meaning in their terrible experience and suffering had a better chance of surviving. He concluded that life is not a quest for pleasure or power. It is instead a quest for meaning, which ultimately is the path to fulfilment and happiness. According to him, one can find meaning in three places: work, love and courage. As Hubert Joly points out in his book "The Heart of Business", they often converge, doing something significant through work and usually involves caring for others and overcoming adversity.

If Viktor Frankl's experience may seem difficult to comprehend, let me point you to a paper written in November 2022 by Jim Hemerling, managing director and senior partner at BCG. He speaks about leadership in times of uncertainty and crisis. The best way to overcome such adversity is by using the courage of your convictions and empathy to connect accurately and timely with all stakeholder groups. The ethos for purposeful leadership is to leave the world a better place than you found it.

Well, how is it possible to get to our soul and inner purpose? You may have heard about the Ikigai Model. If not, I strongly recommend spending some time to become familiar with the concept or model. It is a valuable framework to help you find your purpose in life and feel more aligned in everything you do and how you should progress with whatever decision you need. I am sure you will find it surprisingly valuable for life's decisions and direction. To help set yourself a framework for a fulfilling life.

If we apply the model to a fulfilling career, I find it helpful to take the lessons given by Pol Polman. He uses a simplified version of the Ikigai model, making it even more powerful.

Pol Polman is the former CEO of Unilever from 2009 to 2019, author of "Net Positive: How Courageous Companies Thrive by Giving More Than They Take", and founder of an organization called "Imagine", helping businesses eradicate poverty and inequality, and stem runaway climate change. In 2018, the *Financial Times* called Polman "a standout CEO of the past decade".

In his words, to become a brilliant leader, it is necessary to build a fulfilling career.

He offered this advice for how to get there:

1. Find out what you are passionate about.
2. Discover what you are good at.
3. Understand what the world needs.
4. Look at the intersection to see what opportunities are available.
5. Decide if you want to do something yourself or work with others already focused on that intersection.
6. If you choose to collaborate with other people or businesses, make sure your values are aligned.

By following these steps, you will be able to unlock a tremendous amount of energy that will lead to success, Pol assures.

In my humble opinion, there is a missing last piece. Let me add a seventh step: it is critical that you embrace that the fulfilment of your loved ones is also aligned. Double-check that your partner, your kids and maybe even some friends are also supportive and fulfilled by your choices. If you don't, you will be missing out on an essential piece of the model, which profoundly impacts your happiness and balance.

See this modelling also as a dynamic exercise. Redo it every now and then, when changes happen in your life, key decisions need to be made or even if external factors (like a pandemic) influence your outlook on life and career.

To conclude, I would like to highlight and even pay tribute to another significant and irreplaceable element to reach a fulfilling career. It is the mentors you need and develop in your life.

I have had several mentors at different career stages, and I owe them enormously for their support, guidance and advice. My way to be thankful and give back from my side is to mentor others, who reach out to me, or whom I have coached before within my teams or through university or business school workshops and lectures.

The mentors you need in your life are several and will support and guide you for different goals and intents [31].

Let's have a look at the first type; it is **"the master of craft"**.

Here you will be looking out to the most iconic figure in your field of expertise. Who is this person?

Define the field of expertise you are in. There could be several, connected or not, more geared to your functional or relational skills. These people may be in your direct reach or not. Equally inspiring can be someone you can persuade to have a real or virtual coffee with. It could be someone you read about in articles or from a book they have written. Don't restrict your mentors to one or two; the more, the better, ones who will help you identify, realize and hone your strengths towards your visualised state of perfection.

The second type is the "**champion of your cause**".

This is someone who will talk you up to others; having at least one of these in your current workplace is important. These are the people who are your advocates and always have your back. They are promoters and connectors who may change your career trajectory. For them to help and support you, it is vital that you align with the values of your organization. Similar to what Paul Polman said in point 6 of the steps to a fulfilling career. Alignment with the corporate culture and connection with its members is a prerequisite for advocates. As mentioned, it is important to anticipate their potential departure from the organization thoughtfully. When you lose an ally, political dynamics can change very quickly.

The third type is "**the copilot**".

Here we are referring to your best work bud. It is that work colleague who can talk you through projects, advise you in navigating the personalities at your company and listen to you vent over coffee. These are peers committed to supporting each other. It is vital to have a couple of buddies of this type. Such a relationship grows as with any relationship in life, with time and by building trust. It takes commitment. This is a precious support you should commit to. One potential risk is that you, in error, team up with the wrong person or be disappointed in the medium term, or that the person leaves the company. This is a dynamic to keep in mind.

The fourth type of mentor one should have in life is "**the anchor**".

This person doesn't need to work in your industry. This person could be a friend or a family member. The anchor is a confidante and a sounding board. Since they know you well, your genuinely authentic self, they will help you see the light through the cracks in challenging times. This person will be particularly helpful in setting priorities, achieving work-life balance and not losing sight of your values. They are, therefore, a pivotal person for sustaining your integrity.

Finally, we should all look out for "**the reverse mentor**".

While you are mentoring people, I suggest paying attention and learning from the people you are mentoring. Or the team members you are coaching. It is a pivotal opportunity to collect feedback on your leadership style, to engage with the younger generation and keep perspectives fresh and relevant.

Hopefully, the concept of these mentor types will prove helpful. Remember that all five mentor types should be nurtured continuously. Like the power map and the dynamic between people in your organization and yourself, the map of your five types of mentors works the same way. We need to take the time to develop genuine connections with those we admire and assist them when we can. Mentorship isn't a one-way street. It's a relationship between humans and not a transaction. Mentors can impact our lives and, at times, change our course. The best mentors help define us, but it is never the result of just one person.

I have summarized the ideas stated by Anthony Tjan, CEO and Managing Partner at the Cue Ball Group, and that he shared in a TED Talk back in 2018.

"We need mentors at all stages of our life. Some mentors come into your life for a short time, and others become lifelong friends. Never stop building relationships."

"The best mentors can help us define and express our inner calling", says Anthony Tjan [32].

Similarly, as Melinda Gates points out: "If you are successful, it is because somewhere, at some time, someone gave you an idea that started you off in the right direction."

This is why the most important quality in a mentor, teacher or coach is not how much they know. It's how much they care. Caring is more than taking pride in your success. It's feeling joy as you progress. The people you want in your corner are the ones who celebrate your growth.

"People don't care how much you know until they know how much you care."

The best coach is one who believes you can do the thing. And then makes you believe you can also.

Bibliography

[1]   Clayton M. "Cultural Web: Johnson & Scholes on Where Culture Originates". 2021.
[2]   Johnson G, Scholes K, Whittington R. "Fundamentals of Strategy": Financial Times Prentice Hall; 2011.
[3]   Clayton M. "Edgar Schein's 3 Levels of Organizational": @ManagementCourses, YouTube; 2021.
[4]   Schein EH, Schein PA. "Organizational Culture and Leadership": Wiley; 2016.
[5]   Barsade S, O'Neill OA. "Manage your emotional culture": Harvard Business Review; 2016.
[6]   Clayton M. "French and Raven: Social Power Bases in Organizations". 2021.
[7]   Daimler M. "Why great employees leave great cultures": Harvard Business Review; 2018.
[8]   Sull D, Sull C, Cipolli W, Brighenti C. "Every leader needs to worry about toxic culture": Sloan Review; 2022.
[9]   McGregor L, Doshi N. "How company culture shapes employee motivation": Harvard Business Review; 2015.
[10]   Knight M. "Simon Sinek Performance vs Trust": @Mikeknight7878, YouTube; 2019.
[11]   Grant A. "Are you a giver or a taker?": TED; 2017.
[12]   Good A, Kander D. "We interviewed 50 'bad bosses' to learn it only takes a few toxic behaviors for everything to go". FastCompany. 2022.
[13]   Zenger J, Folkman J. "The Three Elements of Trust". Harvard Business Review. 2019.

[14] Sinek S. "Leaders Eat Last: Why Some Teams Pull Together and Others Don't": Portfolio Penguin; 2014.

[15] Storoni M. "Smart Leaders Prevent Burnout With 3 Golden Rules": Inc.; 2017.

[16] Sinek S. "What Does It Mean To Be an 'ALPHA'". 2021.

[17] Gruenert S, Whitaker T. "School Culture Rewired": ASCD; 2015.

[18] Joly H. "The Heart of Business: Leadership Principles for the Next Era of Capitalism": Harvard Business Review Press; 2021.

[19] Dewar C. "Leading with authenticity: A conversation with Bill George". McKinsey.com. 2023.

[20] Chesky B. "Airbnb's design for employees to live and work anywhere". 2022.

[21] "Apple's Tim Cook gives commencement speech at Gallaudet University". 2022.

[22] Sharp I. "Four Seasons: The Story of a Business Philosophy": Portfolio; 2012.

[23] Bryant A. "You Need Leaders With Courage And A Willingness To Take Risks". 2022.

[24] Schwartz T. "Create a Growth Culture not a performance-obsessed one". Harvard Business Review. 2018.

[25] Goyder C. "The surprising secret to speaking with confidence". TEDx Talks. 2014.

[26] Sytch M. "How to figure out how much influence you have at work". Seattle Times. 2019.

[27] Galinsky A. "How to speak up for yourself". 2016.

[28] Schwantes M. "8 Signs to Immediately Recognize Someone With the Gift of Leadership". Inc.

[29] Osinbanjo R, D. "The Next Generation Leader: Lessons from Amanda Gorman". Forbes. 2021.

[30] Frankl V. "Man's Search for Meaning": Beacon Press.; 2006.

[31] Fawal J. "The five types of mentors you need in your life": IdeasTed; 2018.

[32] Tjan A. "Here's how to assemble your personal dream team".

Conclusion: A call for action

Awareness is key. From three critical standpoints. Awareness of Self, awareness of the dynamics among people in an organisation and awareness of the organisational culture's impact on people.

Growth is key. Without learning, we stand still, and evolution is impossible. We must remain convinced that we should strive to become a better human and consummate professional.

Collaboration is key. Many changes are coming. Most of them are conceptual, and it seems that only technology will allow us to face them at an affordable cost. And so, we need to be open to innovation and go through that transformation in incremental steps. The only way to succeed is to work as a solid team and avoid creating siloes within the organisation.

I advise developing positive relationships with everyone to navigate a career trajectory and professional transitions in corporate life. The corporate world is an entanglement of people, plenty of them.

Improving one's relational skills to contribute to a healthy workplace is mission critical. This is a prerequisite and undoubtedly the only way to reach a culture of trust amongst members of an organisation.

The last step is to consider and efficiently evaluate the existing and shifting power levels, power dynamics and range of power within the organisation. It may substantially impact your perception and understanding of absolute red lines that always exist – for you to decide your course of action in a defining way.

Assuming we feel aligned with the organisational culture and purpose of the company. In that case, we will be able to find fulfilment in our job and have our integrity honoured.

The ambition of this book is for you to discover the essential tools to accomplish your goals, personally and collectively. This will allow you to confidently step into new territory and transition successfully into a leadership role.

The necessary tools have been described in this book to avoid discovering them by yourself and sometimes too late. I have hopefully guided you with ease along this uncertain path and helped you master the human dynamics of business.

The main areas I have addressed are the following:

- train and improve your assertive verbal and non-verbal communication from day one;
- build up your resilience levels daily;

https://doi.org/10.1515/9783111335339-007

- use empathy, play and a sense of humour and regularly to build up connection and trust, allowing creativity and innovation to flow;
- be conscious of the corporate culture, and adjust your behaviour accordingly as a leader;
- find your own unique leadership style and be mindful of its impact; experiment with it;
- always remain cognizant about the power matrix you are in;
- develop and expand your range of power;
- do your best to be likeable under all circumstances; and
- practice humility.

In Chapter 1, we addressed the importance of assertiveness in group dynamics, active listening, empathy, compassion and forgiveness, positive affect and the non-violent communication process to normalise emotions in business. We also tackled the difference between relational and technical skills and vital workplace communication styles and how to develop a sense of trust and belonging in the office. Also, how to articulate appreciation and recognition. One will have to first learn to lead one's team, and then to lead one's peers and bosses. I would advise always to enjoy and relish the excitement and passion of the journey you are embarked upon.

In Chapter 2, we introduced the notion of lateral thinking, which will allow for entirely new and different ways of reasoning. This could be using a reverse approach or a transitional object. We could also decide to either stop doing something or change the current corporate narrative. We have also seen how a culture of curiosity can be influential in many ways and even drive discussions and help make decisions. We have analysed how staying ahead of expectations has become necessary for companies and how courage and competitiveness often witnessed in sporting spheres may be adapted and implemented in a corporate environment. Five working relationships must be fully understood: conflict, competition, independence, cooperation and collaboration. This will enable us to navigate better the different people interacting in an organisation. For innovation to happen, it is crucial to adopt the perspective of the job to be done, and to develop some specific habits, like exposing yourself to intellectually diverse groups, getting stimulated frequently, doing forest and outdoor walks and continuous learning.

In Chapter 3, we appreciate that the search for perfection may lead us nowhere, that life is the sum of all our choices and that we should avoid judging others by ourselves. Next, we addressed the notion of developing resilience over time: with challenge, commitment and personal control. We have also investigated how to endure difficult situations and, importantly, how to recover and recharge after or during these situations. We have also learned that relationships bolster resilience and comprehensive ways to build a resilient attitude. Five key resilience pillars to recharge have been presented in detail, ways of getting along with anyone at work and tackling incivility –

like gossip and lying. I have shown the three most effective ways of learning: teaching others, developing a habit and failing. We could also call it successful failing since it enables progress. We have also recognised that embracing change needs to be trained regularly. Similar to how we improve dealing with uncertainty.

In Chapter 4, we have learned how important it is to manage our energy and not just our time. Similarly, for others, it is not about getting more out of people but investing more in them. We have highlighted the existence of the three selves: the child self, the defender and the adult self, and how you transition through and into each of them. A differentiation has been made between overcoming ambiguity and overcoming uncertainty. For the first, ambiguity, a successful leader will separate what is clear and accepted from what's up for debate, build cross-disciplinary thinking, use intuition in decision-making, be open to switching to a different action plan and always take responsibility. For the second, uncertainty, we should be inspired to develop a more egalitarian environment for our teams and colleagues, have a solid moral compass and always read the situation holistically. We have also learned about the importance of diversity and inclusion and how to preserve one of the most critical aspects of business: integrity.

Further in the chapter, we have expounded on objectively identifying toxicity risk in an organisation. This will occur when one of these 4 R's is overemphasised within the corporate culture: Relationships, Results, Rules and Risk. Good judgement in leaders can also be objectively gauged by assessing these six components: learning, trust, experience, detachment, options and delivery.

In Chapter 5, we explored the importance of organisational culture, where two types coexist: cognitive and emotional (even if by omission). We have also learned that there are several ways to assess and measure the culture. And that, no matter what, there are always these key elements to consider: behaviours, systems, practices and values. We also have countless ways to create and nurture a great culture and ways to manage toxic leaders. Here, we analysed the lessons provided by the givers and takers matrix. We also identified what kind of predictors of trust we might observe and how to use another matrix of relationship to trustworthiness in the workplace. Hubert Joly speaks about the creation of a purposeful human organisation in five steps:

1. Connecting individual search for meaning with the company's noble purpose.
2. Developing authentic human connections.
3. Fostering autonomy.
4. Growing mastery.
5. Nurturing a growth environment.

What about the handling of power? This is probably the topic where the least research and literature exists, and very few conversations seem to be had. In this chapter, you have come across positional and personal power sources and the power audit elaborated by Maxim Sytch. Remember the importance of continuously expanding your range or reach of power and how to do it. We have learnt about servant leadership, vulnerability and humility and how to handle huge egos. The choice is yours; set your own goals – either power and ego or true impact. Achieving impact, though, has a double positive effect: you contribute with your leadership style to make the workplace a better place for everyone while still achieving your team's goals. And to accomplish that, you should develop functional skills for functional impact and human skills for human impact.

Success arrives when preparation meets opportunity – this is a reminder from poet Amanda Gorman. This book provides the tools you need to prepare yourself for when that opportunity unfolds. Without forgetting that to reach success, you don't walk it alone; others will have helped you pave your way – these are the mentors in your life. And if you wish for fulfilment and success, the Ikigai model may guide you.

> Excellence is never an accident. It is always the result of high intention, sincere effort, and intelligent execution; it represents the wise choice of many alternatives – choice, not chance, determines your destiny. – Aristotle.

In an interview process for a Marketing Leader I would seek the following: an alchemist, an orchestrator and a catalyst. As a Marketing executive, you need to be able to distil the vital, impactful data, information, projects, processes, insights and intuitions, from those that are superfluous. Alchemist is the first stage. As soon as you start to manage teams and projects, you need to become a successful orchestrator to gain achievements and learn from pitfalls. And to become a leader – in Marketing, or any discipline for that matter – you need to become a catalyst for change. You need to sense the right moment with the right support, resources, efficient plan, market and teams. This demands experience and shifting gears, tapping not only into your technical skills but mostly into your relational skills. This is what this book is about, and hopefully, it has helped you find the path you need to take to make this evolution from manager to leader or to have the tools when your time has arrived to transition, and you are ready.

Until then, don't hesitate to lean on the necessary mentors in your life. I have given you an explanation of who they may be. They will be able to challenge you about how well you know about yourself and the types of questions you will need to ask yourself to establish the best possible positioning at any time in your career. They will help you to better decide for yourself and rebound when necessary. And if things do not go as planned, you will have a group of trusted people to contact.

This book exists to fill in a potential gap. A potential gap in knowledge and experience can become apparent when you are suddenly required to step into a leadership position.

- What if you don't get the appropriate mentorship or learning program?
- What if your workplace or boss does not provide you with the necessary support and protection?
- What if you remain too focused on your mission's tasks and not the relationships that will make it work?
- What if you are unaware of the relational human forces manoeuvring around you?

If any of these scenarios were to happen in the future, you had better be prepared. The nuggets I have outlined with this book will alert you to the possible circumstances where you might realise that there's a pebble in your shoe before it is too late. This book can provide you with the necessary insights to spot waves arising on the horizon and steer your career trajectory most appropriately.

Difficulties, doubts and worries will surface many times on this journey. Unexpected and unprepared for events can quickly sabotage your career. I wish to prevent you from failing or not having been adequately prepared on relational skills to succeed in the corporate world.

These so-called soft skills have never been prioritised in the business school curriculum, and my mission is to change that. The development of relational skills for potential leaders needs to be addressed in an efficient and timely manner, and students should be aware of their importance for success. The ambition is to build up those skills and apply those lessons to their leadership path – a step at a time. Commit to continuous training to be prepared when the critical moment arrives, and keep improving.

The most indispensable lessons we learn in life don't come from a 90-minute lecture. They come from layers of interactions and experiences that build one after another. Real learning is not like scrolling through the newsfeed on our mobile devices. Real learning is a slow process. Real learning takes real time.

It's one thing to feel information crash and overwhelm you. It's another thing to coherently internalise information to change a mindset, to change behaviour, to change the trajectory of a life.

As has already been said in the pages of this book: leadership revelations are not taught but observed. This book has provided the necessary insights to reflect, practice and improve as a caring mentor would do for you. If you don't have this person (yet), this book will help guide you.

This book is for disparate audiences. I have encountered genuine interest in this topic from postgraduate students I have spoken to; hopefully, this book meets their expectations. As a leader, you may have learned something new or been reassured by the skills you might already be practising. As an established mentor yourself, you may find valuable tools to nurture the growth path of your mentees. And as a professor, you may find some thought-provoking additions for your learning programs to ensure the necessary pointers for a leadership growth path are included.

The time has arrived when these relational skills become fundamental for next-generation leaders to succeed. The current business context results from several unsolved crises that provide an uncertain outlook for the future. At the same time, four generations – with very different management and leadership expectations – are coinciding in the workplace. This requires plentiful flexibility in employees' attitudes and mindsets.

In a world of continuous technological disruption in the quest for efficiency, mastering human connection will become the new 'hard skill' that cannot be automated.

For all the reasons mentioned, we find ourselves at an interesting crossroads: we can choose to ignore the call for a change in leadership practice or listen to the wisdom of the new and impressive leadership strategies and the benefits they can provide us and our businesses.

My suggestion would be to show up to leadership with a curious mindset. Listen to experienced mentors, learn one topic at a time, experiment thoughtfully and creatively with your team, develop your leadership style and then own it consistently.

The words in this book may inspire you, but only action creates change (Simon Sinek).

Index

https://doi.org/10.1515/9783111335339-008

www.ingramcontent.com/pod-product-compliance
Lightning Source LLC
Chambersburg PA
CBHW071959220326
41599CB00034BA/6936